911 Carrera 6600052 . . .

. . . being tested by Autocar for road test published 24th June 1976 and . . .

. . . now owned by the author

Porsche 911 1974-77 Autobook

By Kenneth Ball

Associate Member, Guild of Motoring Writers
and the Autobooks Team of Technical Writers

Porsche 911, N, S, Targa 1974-77
Porsche 911 Carrera 1974-77

Autobooks Ltd. Golden Lane Brighton BN1 2QJ England

The AUTOBOOK series of Workshop Manuals is the largest in the world and covers the majority of British and Continental motor cars, as well as the majority of Japanese and Australian models.

Whilst every care has been taken to ensure correctness of information it is obviously not possible to guarantee complete freedom from errors or omissions or to accept liability arising from such errors or omissions.

CONTENTS

ISBN 0 85147 652 X

First Edition   1977

© Autobooks Ltd 1977

889

Printed in Brighton England for Autobooks Ltd by G. Beard and Son Ltd
Bound in Hove England for Autobooks Ltd by Jilks Ltd   A

ACKNOWLEDGEMENT

My thanks are due to Porsche for their unstinted co-operation and also for supplying data and illustrations.

Considerable assistance has also been given by owners, who have discussed their cars in detail, and I would like to express my gratitude for this invaluable advice and help.

Kenneth Ball
Associate Member, Guild of Motoring Writers
Ditchling Sussex England.

INTRODUCTION

This do-it-yourself Workshop Manual has been specially written for the owner who wishes to maintain his vehicle in first class condition and to carry out the bulk of his own servicing and repairs. Considerable savings on garage charges can be made, and one can drive in safety and confidence knowing the work has been done properly.

Comprehensive step-by-step instructions and illustrations are given on most dismantling, overhauling and assembling operations. Certain assemblies require the use of expensive special tools, the purchase of which would be unjustified. In these cases information is included but the reader is recommended to hand the unit to the agent for attention.

Throughout the Manual hints and tips are included which will be found invaluable, and there is an easy to follow fault diagnosis at the end of each chapter.

Whilst every care has been taken to ensure correctness of information it is obviously not possible to guarantee complete freedom from errors or omissions or to accept liability arising from such errors or omissions.

Instructions may refer to the righthand or lefthand sides of the vehicle or the components. These are the same as the righthand or lefthand of an observer standing behind the vehicle and looking forward.

CHAPTER 1

THE ENGINE

1:1 Description

The vehicles covered by this manual are fitted with a rear mounted engine of 2.2 litre (2195cc actual), 2.4 litre (2341cc actual), 2.7 litre (2681cc actual), or 3.0 litre (2994cc actual) capacity. The design features of these engines are identical although they are dimensionally different in relevant respects. They are air-cooled, four-stroke, six cylinder engines with the cylinders arranged horizontally in two banks of three. Bore and stroke dimensions, compression ratios and other technical information for all engines are included in the **Technical Data** section of the **Appendix**.

FIGS 1:1 and **1:2** show partial transverse and longitudinal cross-sections through an engine. Note that **FIG 1:1** includes components of the fuel continuous injection system (CIS) and that **FIG 1:2** relates to the fuel injection pump (FIP) model. The third type of fuel system, carburetter models, is included, together with the CIS and FIP, in **Chapter 2**.

The six throw crankshaft runs in seven shell-type plain bearings which are carried in a two-piece vertically split crankcase and a single sleeve-type plain bearing at the

rear. It will be evident that the two banks of cylinders are staggered. Axial movement of the crankshaft is controlled at the forward main bearing. The connecting rod plain big-end bearings are shell-type and are retained by caps which are attached to the rods by bolts and nuts. The small-end bearings are bush-type.

The intermediate shaft is driven at half crankshaft speed by helical gearing at the rear end of the crankshaft. The two coaxial oil pumps are driven from the forward end of the intermediate shaft. A sprocket wheel on each side of the helical gear provides a chain drive for each of the overhead camshafts. Each chain is tensioned by a hydraulically loaded jockey pulley and is controlled by three guide ramps. A skew gear rearwards of the crankshaft helical gear drives the ignition distributor. The flywheel or, in the case of semi-automatic transmission models, the torque converter drive plate is mounted on the forward end of the crankshaft. The clutch, in the case of manual transmission models, operates on the forward face of the flywheel. The transmission bellhousing, final drive and gearbox casing is directly attached to the forward face of the engine crankcase and the combined

FIG 1:1 Transverse cross-section through engine (CIS model)

Key to Fig 1:1 1 Air duct 2 Control pressure regulator 3 Throttle valve 4 Starting enrichment valve 5 Control pressure regulator (warm running compensation) 6 Heat exchanger 7 Crankshaft 8 Oil pumps 9 Oil strainer 10 Connecting rod 11 Piston 12 Cylinder 13 Exhaust valve 14 Valve guide 15 Tank to pump hose connection 16 Valve spring 17 Rocker arm shaft 18 Camshaft 19 Rocker arm 20 Inlet valve 21 Injection valve 22 Intake pipe 23 Intake housing 24 Air sensor plate 25 Mixture control unit

engine and transmission must be removed as a unit from the vehicle and subsequently separated when either the engine, clutch or transmission is to be overhauled.

The individual cylinder barrels may be of cast iron or of composite structure with a bore sleeve of cast iron and aluminium cooling fins. Each barrel carries a separate cylinder head but the camshaft/rocker gear housings each span a bank of cylinders. Cooling air from the belt driven blower at the rear of the engine is ducted over the cylinder barrels and heads and, after passing through heat exchangers associated with the exhaust system, is available to warm the interior of the vehicle. Pistons are of aluminium alloy. The gudgeon pins are retained by circlips and have a slight interference fit in their piston bores. Pistons are fitted with two compression rings and one oil control ring.

Exhaust and inlet valves of each bank of cylinders are operated via rockers by a camshaft and provision is made for the adjustment of the clearance between the valve stem tips and their rockers. Valve seats and valve guides are inserts in the aluminium heads. Each valve is provided with two valve springs. Inlet valves are solid; exhaust valves have hollow stems which are filled with sodium to improve cooling. The camshafts are handed to each bank of cylinders and differ between engine types. In the case of fuel injection pump models, the injection pump is driven by a toothed belt from the lefthand camshaft.

The engine has a 'dry' sump and the lubrication oil is contained in a separate tank. The forward of the two coaxial pumps draws oil from the tank and feeds it under pressure to the crankshaft, intermediate shaft and camshafts. Drain oil is scavenged from the bottom of the crankcase by the second larger capacity pump via a gauze strainer and intake tube and returned to the tank. Pressure oil when hot is passed through a cooler which is bypassed when the oil is cold. The main cooler is closely associated with the engine. A secondary cooler is located at the forward end of the vehicle. The lubrication system is fully covered in **Section 1:16**.

With engines of four capacities, variations which are related both to performance and to year by year modification standards, it is most important that, when new parts are required, **they are identical with those originally fitted or that alternative parts are only those nominated by the spares supplier as** being suitable for the specific engine to which they are to be fitted.

Emission control systems and features are included in **Chapter 4**.

1:2 Maintenance

General:

At least every 6000 miles (10,000km) on all models, visually check over the engine and its lubrication system

FIG 1:2 Longitudinal cross-section through engine (FIP model)

Key to Fig 1:2 1 Air filter housing 2 Air intake pipe 3 Fuel injection lines 4 Oil pressure transmitter 5 Crankcase 6 Oil pump casing 7 Pressure oil pump 8 Scavenge oil pump 9 Connecting shaft 10 Oil strainer 11 Drain plug 12 Crankshaft 13 Connecting rod 14 Sprocket wheel 15 Intermediate shaft 16 Heat exchanger 17 Silencer 18 Distributor drive gear 19 V-belt pulley 20 V-belt 21 Alternator 22 Upper air duct 23 Coverplate 24 Helical gear (crankshaft) 25 Helical gear (intermediate shaft)

for oil leaks. Do not omit to check the ancillary oil cooler at the front righthand wing. Ensure that it is firmly mounted and that the feed and return pipes are secure.

Engine oil:

Maintain the level in the oil tank within the specified range at all times.

Every 6000 miles (10,000km) on 2.2 litre and 2.4 litre models and every 12,000 miles (20,000km) on 2.7 litre and 3.0 litre models, renew the engine oil. Drain off and discard the old oil from the tank and from the bottom of the crankcase. Do this after a run while the oil is hot. The procedures are included in **Section 1:16**. Refill the system with SAE 30 oil of a reputable brand (approximately 8 to 9 litre (14 to $15\frac{3}{4}$ pints) will be required) and, after running the engine, check the level in the tank and top up if necessary.

Oil filter and gauze strainer:

At the same time as the engine oil is being renewed, renew the disposable oil filter canister and clean the gauze strainer in the bottom of the crankcase. These procedures are included in **Section 1:16**.

Valve clearances:

Every 12,000 miles (20,000km) on all models, check and, if necessary, adjust the valve clearances with the engine cold.

Remove the rocker gear covers and turn the engine until the piston of No 1 cylinder (rearmost lefthand) is at TDC of its firing stroke. Both valves will be closed and the Z1 TDC mark will be aligned with the crankcase mark as shown in the upper part of **FIG 1:3**.

Using a 0.1mm (0.004in) feeler gauge, a screwdriver and a ring spanner as shown in the lower part of **FIG 1:3**, adjust both the inlet and the exhaust valve clearances ensuring that the feeler gauge is located immediately above the valve stem tip. Hold the adjuster with the screwdriver when retightening the locknut and recheck the clearance before proceeding.

Turn the crankshaft through 120° to the next TDC mark and deal with the clearances of the valves of No 6 cylinder.

FIG 1 : 3 Adjusting valve clearances. Distributor rotor pointing to notch on body and pulley mark Z1 in line with crankcase joint with both valves closed, gives TDC on No 1 cylinder (top view). Using feeler gauge to set valve clearance (bottom view)

FIG 1 : 4 Righthand and lefthand engine mountings at rear (top view). Transmission support from below (lower view)

Continue, following the firing order, to cylinder Nos 2, 4, 3 and 5.

Rocker arm shafts:

At the same time as the valve clearances are being adjusted as described earlier, check the tightness of the rocker arm shafts as described in **Section 1 : 4**.

Compression pressures:

Every 12,000 miles (20,000km), have the compression pressure of each cylinder measured as a check on the condition of the piston rings and the valves with their seats. The difference in the compression pressure between the six cylinders should not exceed 1.5kg/sq cm (21lb/sq in).

1 : 3 Removing and refitting the engine

The engine and transmission are removed as a complete unit by lowering it out from beneath the vehicle. Using a trolley jack beneath the unit is the officially recommended removal method. If a trolley jack is not available, overhead lifting gear may be used but this method will require the lid of the engine compartment to be removed as described in **Chapter 13, Section 13 : 2**. With the engine/transmission unit removed, the transmission may be separated from the engine and work may proceed on either or both.

Removal:

1 Disconnect the battery earth lead(s). Drain the oil tank as described in **Section 1 : 16**. Chock the front wheels. Raise the rear of the vehicle and position it on stands at a height which will allow removal of the engine/transmission unit downwards and rearwards.

2 Disconnect the hoses from the oil tank. Disconnect the hoses from the air cleaner. Remove the air cleaner assembly.

3 Uncouple the cables from the starter motor and from the alternator. Identify and disconnect all electrical wiring which bridges the body and engine (ignition, instrument transmitters, CIS wiring on relevant models, etc). Similarly deal with those which bridge the body and transmission (reversing light, Sportomatic transmission cables on relevant models, etc).

4 Uncouple the throttle linkage and, if relevant, the choke control. Disconnect the fuel feed pipe(s) as relevant to the type of fuel system fitted.

5 In the case of manual transmission models, uncouple the clutch cable at the release lever, and in transmission types 915/40/45 remove the release lever to clear the new exhaust pipe system. Mark the lever so that it can be installed in exactly the same position. In the case of Sportomatic transmission models, disconnect the pipelines.

6 Uncouple the hot air ducts from the heat exchangers. Uncouple the drive shafts from the transmission as described in **Chapter 8, Section 8 : 4**. Uncouple the gearchange linkage from the transmission as described in **Chapter 6, Section 6 : 11**.

7 Using either a trolley jack or overhead lifting gear. just take the weight of the engine/transmission unit. Refer to **FIG 1 : 4** and release the engine rear supports and the transmission support from the body mountings.

8 Check that all pipes, wiring and controls which bridged the engine/transmission unit and the body have been removed or disconnected before lowering the unit and withdrawing it from beneath the vehicle.

FIG 1:5   Positions of camshaft drive chain guide ramps

Key to Fig 1:5   A, B See text

9 Separate the transmission from the engine as described in **Chapter 6, Section 6:3** or **Chapter 7, Section 7:4**.
10 Refer to **Chapter 2** and remove the fuel system components. Refer to **Chapter 4** and remove the cooling fan, cooling deflectors and covers, the exhaust system, heater ducts and, from relevant models, the emission control air injection equipment. Refer to **Chapter 12** and dismount the alternator and starter motor.

Refitment:

Reverse the removal sequence when refitting the engine/transmission unit.

1:4 The rocker gear and camshafts

Each camshaft is driven by a separate duplex chain from separate sprocket wheels on the intermediate shaft. Each chain is provided with three guide ramps and is tensioned by a hydraulically loaded jockey pulley. The arrangement is shown on **FIG 1:5**. The camshaft sprocket wheels are dowelled to camshaft flanges and vernier dowel holes in these components allow precise adjustment of the valve timing. Camshafts are specific to an engine type and are handed to lefthand and righthand cylinder banks. If a replacement camshaft is required, **ensure that the correct component is obtained**.

Camshaft and camshaft housing removal:

1 Remove all sparking plugs. Remove the rocker covers from the relevant bank of cylinders. Mark the rockers so that they may be refitted to their original positions.
2 Refer to **FIG 1:6**. From each rocker shaft remove the socket-headed screw 4, push out the shaft 2, collect cones 1 and 3 and lift out the rocker. Rocker removal should be carried out with the relevant valves closed.
3 Remove the hose from between the crankcase and the chain housing cover. Remove the chain housing cover. In the case of fuel injection pump models, engines fitted with emission control air injection equipment

FIG 1:6   Components of rocker shaft. Cones expand ends to secure shaft in housing

Key to Fig 1:6   1 Nut cone   2 Rocker shaft   3 Bush cone   4 Allen screw

FIG 1:7   Withdrawing dowel which aligns vernier hole in camshaft sprocket with that in flange

FIG 1:8 Sealing ring 3 and thrust washer 4 determine the end float of camshaft

Key to Fig 1:8 1 Paper gasket   2 'O' ring   3 Sealing ring   4 Thrust washer   5 Spacer   6 Camshaft sprocket flange

and Sportomatic transmission models, refer to **Chapter 2, Section 2:8, Chapter 4, Section 4:3** and **Chapter 7, Section 7:10** when the lefthand camshaft is being dealt with.

4 Refer to **Section 1:5** and remove the chain tensioner and jockey pulley. Remove the nut securing the camshaft sprocket wheel (the official tools are P202 and P203). Withdraw the dowel pin from the sprocket wheel as shown in **FIG 1:7**. The official extractor is P212.

5 Remove the outer guide ramp **A** in **FIG 1:5** by lifting the spring retainers with a screwdriver or wire hook. Refer to **FIG 1:8**. Withdraw the sprocket flange 6. Remove the drive key. Withdraw the thrust washer 4 and the spacer 5.

6 Remove the three retaining screws and push out the sealing ring 3, the 'O' ring 2 and the gasket 1. Withdraw the camshaft rearwards.

7 Remove the housing retaining nuts (hexagon) and three socket-headed nuts. Dismount the camshaft housing. Clean off all components and check them as described later.

Camshaft and camshaft housing refitment:

This is the reverse of the removal sequence except that, additionally, the camshaft timing procedure which is described in **Section 1:6** must be carried out. Use a new 'O' ring and gasket. Apply Tereson Atmosit or an equivalent jointing compound on relevant faces. Torque tighten the camshaft sprocket retaining nut to 10kgm (72 lb ft). Ensure that the rocker shafts are centrally disposed in their carrier bores by proceeding as follows. Insert a very thin feeler between the rocker and the housing and locate the rocker shaft so that the feeler drops into the groove in the shaft. Push the shaft until the feeler is trapped between the groove and the housing. Withdraw the feeler and push the shaft along by approximately 1.5mm (0.06in). Each groove will now be recessed into the housing bores by the same amount. Torque tighten screws 4 in **FIG 1:6** to 1.8kgm (13lb ft). Set the valve clearances as described in **Section 1:2**.

Chain housing removal and fitment:

Dismount the engine rear mounting bracket after removing four nuts. Carry out operations 1 to 6 of the camshaft and camshaft housing removal procedure described earlier. Detach the chain housing after removing the nuts which retain it to the crankcase. Chain guide ramps **B** in **FIG 1:5** are removed by lifting the spring retainers as shown in **FIG 1:9** and removing the stud bolts. The procedure for renewing the chains is included in **Section 1:13**.

Refitment is the reverse of the removal sequence. Use Tereson Atmosit or an equivalent jointing compound on the housing to crankcase face.

Component inspection:

Discard 'O' rings and gaskets 1 and 2 in **FIG 1:8**. Clean off old jointing compound. Check that the camshaft and the camshaft housing oilways are clear by blowing through with compressed air and oil. Slight scuffing of

FIG 1:9 Lifting spring on chain guide ramp out of groove in mounting stud

camshaft cams may be judiciously cleaned up by stoning but more severe wear will dictate the fitment of a new shaft. Rocker contact areas may be similarly treated. Check the adjusters for wear. Worn guide ramps should be renewed.

1 : 5 The chain tensioner

Removal:

Remove the relevant chain housing cover as described in **Section 1 : 4**. In the case of a lefthand tensioner, use a block of hardwood between the crankcase and the jockey sprocket wheel to jam the wheel against the chain. In the case of a righthand tensioner, use wire round the sprocket arm and a cover stud to take the load off the tensioner plunger pin. Remove the retaining nut and withdraw the tensioner noting that the plunger is under spring load. The jockey pulley assembly (note that they are handed) may now be removed if necessary.

Fitment:

Fit the jockey pulley assembly if it was removed and constrain it against the chain. If the **original tensioner** is being refitted, bleed the unit as described later and compress the assembly slowly in a vice fitted with soft jaws (a quick compression may damage the 'O' rings). Constrain the plunger in this depressed condition (the official tool is P214). Fit the tensioner and its retaining nut. Remove both constraints. If a **new tensioner** is being installed, leave the clamp 18 in **FIG 1 : 10** in position, slide the unit onto the sprocket wheel carrier shaft to a point where half the plunger pin is engaged with the arm of the tensioner. At this point turn lockring 17 until the temporary clamp 18 can be removed. Push the tensioner fully into position and fit the retaining nut.

Dismantling a tensioner:

1 Remove the tensioner as described earlier. Hold the assembly in a vice fitted with soft jaws. Refer to **FIG 1 : 10**. Hold the spring retainer down and, using a small screwdriver, extract the locking ring 17. Remove retainer 16 and spring 15.

2 Use pliers to withdraw piston 12 and, while holding plunger 10, extract lockring 11 with a small screwdriver. Discard 'O' rings 13 and 14.

3 Slowly release the plunger and withdraw it. If the intermediate piece 8 sticks inside the plunger, free it by tapping the plunger on a piece of wood.

4 Withdraw the intermediate piece and 'O' ring if it did not come away with the plunger. Discard the 'O' ring. Remove ball 7, ball retainer 6, spring 5 and guide 4. Remove bleed screw 3 and washer 2.

5 Clean and oil the bore of the housing and all internal parts. Check the action of piston 12 in the housing bore by positioning it on plunger 10 and sliding the assembly into the housing. It should move freely without drag. High spots may be eased by careful stoning.

6 At mid-1970 a modified intermediate piece and 'O' ring 9 was introduced and, if these new parts are available from the spares supplier, they may be fitted.

FIG 1 : 10   Components of chain tensioner

Key to Fig 1 : 10   1 Cylinder housing   2 Copper washer
3 Bleed screw   4 Spring guide   5 Plunger spring   6 Ball
retainer   7 Ball   8 Intermediate piece   9 'O' ring
10 Plunger   11 Lockring   12 Oil retainer piston   13 'O'
ring   14 'O' ring   15 Oil retainer spring   16 Spring retainer
17 Lockring   18 Clamp (supplied only with new tensioner
to assist in installation)

FIG 1:11 Secure the assembly in a vice as shown, preparatory to bleeding

Reassembling a tensioner:

Assemble with all internal parts wetted with SAE 30 oil. Proceed as follows:

1 Fit a new 'O' ring to the intermediate piece and insert the assembly into the plunger with the ball and ball retainer. Fit the bleed screw and its washer.
2 Fill the housing with SAE 30 oil. Insert the spring into the plunger, position the guide 4, insert this assembly into the oil filled housing and secure it by fitting lockring 11.
3 Bleed the tensioner as follows. Depress ball 7 with bent wire inserted through the hole in the plunger which is arrowed in **FIG 1:10**. Press the plunger up and down keeping the unit filled with oil. Continue until air bubbles cease to emerge.
4 Hold the unit in a vice as shown in **FIG 1:11**. Fill the upper part of the housing with SAE 30 oil, fit 'O' rings 13 and 14 to piston 12 and position it over the plunger. Do not depress the piston at this stage.
5 Place the special gauge ring P214V over the plunger pin so that it rests on top of the piston. Simultaneously, open the bleed screw and depress the gauge ring until it firmly contacts the top of the housing. As soon as contact is made, tighten the bleed screw.
6 Fit the spring 15, the retainer 16 and secure with lockring 17. Check the operation of the tensioner by holding it vertically in a vice and resting a weight of 5.5kg (12lb) squarely on the plunger pin. The plunger should not yield by more than 10mm (0.40in) during a period of 5 to 10 minutes.

1:6 Valve timing

Timing of the camshafts in relation to the crankshaft is carried out in two stages. Stage 1, preliminary, timing may be carried out before the rockers have been assembled to the camshaft housing. If, however, the rockers have been installed, **it is imperative to note that all operations of turning the crankshaft and camshafts with the drive disconnected are undertaken with great care.** Unless the pistons and valves are correctly timed there is a possibility that they will make contact when the top of each stroke is reached. If the slightest resistance to turning is noticed, stop at once, back off a little and reset the relative positions of camshafts and crankshaft.

State 1 valve timing:

1 Refer to **FIG 1:12** and turn crankshaft so that pulley mark Z1 lines up with crankcase joint.
2 Camshafts are marked on the end with a punch. Turn these marks until they are vertically above camshaft centres (see outer arrows in illustration), taking the precautions mentioned at the start of this section.
3 One hole in each camshaft sprocket will line up with one in the sprocket flange. Insert the dowel (see **FIG 1:7**). Fit spring washer and tighten nut to 10kgm (72lb ft).

Stage 2 valve timing:

The accuracy of the preliminary timing is checked and, if necessary, adjusted as follows. The inlet valve rockers of at least Nos 1 and 4 (the rearmost cylinders of each bank) cylinders must be fitted before carrying out this procedure.

1 Set the valve clearances of Nos 1 and 4 inlet valves to 0.10mm (0.004in) as described in **Section 1:2**.
2 Set up a dial gauge as shown top left in **FIG 1:13**. The plunger must rest on the valve spring collar and be in line with the valve stem. Arrange for the plunger to extend a further 10mm (0.40in) as the valve opens. Zero the gauge.
3 Use a screwdriver to press the tensioner sprocket firmly against the chain, as shown, and block the tensioner in that position. Turn crankshaft through a complete turn so that No 1 cylinder is now at TDC on the inlet stroke and the inlet valve should have started to open. Read the dial gauge. This will be the amount of inlet valve lift at TDC and figures for the different engine types are listed in the **Technical Data** section of the **Appendix**.
4 If the lift shown by the dial gauge differs from the figure quoted for the relevant engine type, adjust the timing as follows. Remove the camshaft sprocket nut and spring washer, withdraw the dowel and check that the crankshaft pulley mark is aligned with the crankcase joint.
5 Turn the camshaft with special tool P202 as shown in **FIG 1:13**. Do this until the dial gauge shows the desired adjustment value specified.
6 Find the holes in sprocket and flange which line up and insert dowel. Fit washer and nut and tighten to correct torque.
7 Turn crankshaft two complete turns and check gauge reading. Readjust if necessary.

Repeat the procedure on cylinder No 4 to set the timing of the other camshaft, making sure the tensioner sprocket is firmly pressed into the chain. When adjustment is completed, remove blocks used to maintain position of tensioners. Note in **FIG 1:13** that a screwdriver is being used to press the tensioner into the chain to take up all backlash.

1:7 Removing and refitting the cylinder heads

With the engine/transmission unit removed from the car as described in **Section 1:3** (the transmission need not be separated from the engine unless it also is to be worked on), a bank of three heads complete with their camshaft housing may be removed as an assembly or,

FIG 1:12 Checking valve timing. Outer arrows point to camshaft markings, central arrow to pulley mark Z1 aligned with crankcase joint

after removing the camshaft housing, an individual cylinder head may be removed. The procedures are as follows.

Removing a bank of cylinder heads:

Refer to **Section 1:4** and carry out operations 1 to 6 of the camshaft housing removal procedure. Remove the socket-headed nuts which retain the cylinder heads and lift off the camshaft housing and the cylinder heads as a unit.

Removing an individual cylinder head:

Remove the camshaft housing as described in **Section 1:4**. Remove the socket-headed nuts which retain the relevant cylinder head. Lift off the cylinder head.

Refitment:

Refitment is the reverse of the removal sequence in each case. Use new cylinder head gaskets and torque tighten the socket-headed retaining nuts to 3.0 to 3.3 kgm (21 to 24lb ft). Set the valve timing as described in **Section 1:6**.

1:8 Servicing the cylinder heads

Remove the cylinder heads as described in **Section 1:7** and separate them from the camshaft housings if they were removed in banks of three. Keep each head identified to the cylinder from which it was removed.

Decarbonising:

Decarbonise the combustion chambers and valve heads before removing the valves. Decarbonising at this stage protects the valve seats. Use a scraper and wire brush and avoid the use of sharply pointed tools which could damage the surfaces. Be careful not to damage the joint faces. Use a tap to clear carbon from the sparking plug threads.

Valve removal:

Use a block of hardwood profiled to an approximate shape of the combustion chamber and a suitable spring compressing tool to remove the valve springs. Remove any burrs from the cotter grooves in the valve stems before pushing the valves out. Identify the valves, springs and seats to their locations and also any shims **B** in **FIG 1:14** which may be fitted under the valve spring seats.

Heads:

Clean the joint faces and, using a straightedge and a feeler gauge, check the head/cylinder faces and the head/camshaft housing faces for distortion. Distortion must not exceed 0.15 mm (0.006in). Excessively distorted heads cannot be salvaged and must be replaced by new components.

FIG 1:13 Valve timing check. Dial gauge records inlet valve lift while camshaft is turned with tool P202

FIG 1:14 Installed length of outer valve spring at A, adjustment shims at B (lefthand view). Check X for length of valve stem projecting above spring seat (righthand view)

Check the tightness and the condition of valve seats and guides. The desired diametrical clearance between an inlet valve stem and its guide is 0.03 to 0.05mm (0.001 to 0.002in) with a wear limit of 0.15mm (0.006in) and that between an exhaust valve stem and its guide is 0.05 to 0.075mm (0.002 to 0.003in) with a wear limit of 0.20mm (0.008in). If the wear limit is exceeded and if the fitment of new valves alone will not result in acceptable clearances, new valve guides or new heads will be required. Similarly, if the valve seats are excessively worn, pitted or burned and will not clean up, new seats or renewal of the heads will be dictated.

Removal of unserviceable valve guides and seats and fitment and machining of new parts requires experience and facilities which will not normally be within the scope of an owner. If, however, skills and facilities are available, the procedures are as follows.

FIG 1:15 Correct position of valve guide with respect to valve spring seat in head. Width of valve seat is indicated at A

Valve guide replacement:

Drill through the old guide with an 11mm (0.433in) twist drill. Heat the head to 200°C (390°F) and, using a shouldered drift, drive out the shell of the old guide in the direction of the camshaft housing face. Spare guides are oversize and must be machined to give an interference fit with the head location of 0.03 to 0.06mm (0.0012 to 0.0024in). Cool the prepared guide in a deep freezer. Heat the head as before. Apply tallow to the guide as a lubricant and drive it in from the camshaft housing face side to the position shown in FIG 1:15. Ream the bore of the guide to 9.000 + 0.015mm (0.3543 + 0.006in).

Valve seat replacement:

Machine away the old seat until it is loose and can be knocked out without damaging the seat location. Measure the location bore very accurately. Machine the spare seat insert to give an interference fit of 0.14 to 0.18mm (0.0055 to 0.0071in) in the case of an inlet valve or 0.16 to 0.20mm (0.0063 to 0.0079in) in the case of an exhaust valve. Heat the head to 200°C (390°F). Cool the seats in a deep freezer and drive them in with a shouldered drift. Allow the head to cool slowly. Stabilise by reheating the head to the same temperature. Hold this temperature for two hours and again allow it to cool slowly. Machine the new seats ready for the valves to be lapped-in. The valve seat width A in FIG 1:15 should be 1.25 ± 0.10mm (0.050 ± 0.004in) for an inlet valve and 1.55 ± 0.10 mm (0.060 ± 0.004in) for an exhaust valve.

Valves:

Exhaust valves have hollow stems which, to assist cooling, are filled with sodium.

Valves with excessively worn or bent stems must be rejected. Valves with seats which are excessively worn, pitted or burned cannot be salvaged although some judicious machining of the seat faces is permissible. The valve seat angle is 45°.

Lap valves to their head seats with grinding paste. Lap until the valve and the valve seats have a smooth continuous matt grey appearance over the full width of the seat areas. Wash off all traces of lapping paste, dry thoroughly, hold the valve in position and, using petrol, check for leakage into the cylinder head port. Refer to FIG 1:14 and check dimension X. This should be 47.50 ± 0.60mm (1.870 ± 0.024in) with a wear limit of 0.5mm (0.020in). If this limit is exceeded new valve seats should be fitted.

Valve springs:

If one spring of a pair is defective, renew both. With both spring seats fitted to a pair of springs and a load of 20kg (44lb) applied, the overall length should be 42.0 to 42.5mm (1.653 to 1.673in) but, on used springs, a variation of 5% is acceptable. Obtain new springs if the loaded dimension is less than this limit.

Reassembly:

Apply a smear of oil to the valve stems. Use new stem seals. The close-coiled ends of the outer springs must be fitted towards the cylinder head spring seats. Ensure that the collets are correctly seated. Refer to FIG 1:14 and measure dimension A. Using shims at B, adjust A in each case to bring it within the dimension quoted in the following tabulation for the inlet or exhaust valve of the relevant engine capacity and type.

Engine type	Inlet valve	Exhaust valve
2.2 litre TC ..	36.0 ± 0.3mm 1.417 ± 0.012in	As inlet
2.2 litre EC ..	36.0 ± 0.3mm 1.417 ± 0.012in	35.0 ± 0.3mm 1.378 ± 0.012in
2.2 litre SC ..	35.5 ± 0.3mm 1.398 ± 0.012in	34.5 ± 0.3mm 1.358 ± 0.012in
2.4 litre TV ..	35.0 ± 0.3mm 1.378 ± 0.012in	As inlet
2.4 litre T-USA ..	35.0 ± 0.3mm 1.378 ± 0.012in	As inlet
2.4 litre E ..	34.0 ± 0.3mm 1.339 ± 0.012in	As inlet
2.4 litre S ..	35.0 ± 0.3mm 1.378 ± 0.012in	As inlet
2.7 litre	35.0 ± 0.3mm 1.378 ± 0.012in	35.5 ± 0.3mm 1.398 ± 0.012in
2.7 litre Carrera ..	35.5 ± 0.3mm 1.398 ± 0.012in	34.5 ± 0.3mm 1.358 ± 0.012in
3.0 litre	34.5 ± 0.3mm 1.358 ± 0.012in	As inlet

FIG 1:16 How flywheel is secured. Bush 4 supports rear end of gearbox input shaft

Key to Fig 1:16   1 Flywheel   2 Socket head screws   3 Crankshaft   4 Bush and seal   5 Spacing washer

1:9 The flywheel

Removal and refitment:

Remove the clutch as described in **Chapter 5, Section 5:4**. Block the flywheel from turning, refer to **FIG 1:16** and, using a long-handled wrench, remove the socket-headed bolts 2. Collect the spacing washer 5 and dismount the flywheel.

Refitment is the reverse of this sequence. Torque tighten bolts 2 to 15kgm (108lb ft) and apply about 2cc of graphite or molybdenum-disulphide grease into the pilot bearing 4. Refitment of the clutch assembly is covered in **Chapter 5, Section 5:4.**

Servicing the flywheel:

Slight damage to the starter ring gear teeth or to the forward face on which the clutch operates may be corrected by salvage machining. This work should be entrusted to a Porsche agent who can not only carry out the salvage work but can also rebalance the flywheel.

Renew a flywheel which is seriously damaged, worn or defective. Note that since flywheels and crankshafts are balanced as separate items during manufacture, no problem arises if a new flywheel has to be matched to an existing crankshaft.

The pilot bearing may be renewed by pressing it out and fitting a new one.

1:10 The cylinders and pistons

Cylinder removal:

Identify the cylinders and detach the air deflector plates before pulling them gently off their pistons. Ensure that neither the pistons nor the connecting rods are allowed to drop against the crankcase. Discard the joint gaskets. To preclude entry into the crankcase of dirt, etc. use lint-free rag round the connecting rods and pistons to blank off the crankcase apertures.

Cylinder fitment:

Using clean engine oil, lightly oil the pistons, rings and cylinder bores. Stagger the ring gaps evenly. Clean the crankcase and cylinder faces and fit a new gasket to the base of each. Compress the piston rings with a suitable clamp and slide the cylinders into place. Check that the holding-down studs are not fouling the cooling fins. Refit the air deflector plates.

Piston removal:

Identify each piston to its cylinder and mark which way round each is fitted in relation to the front (flywheel) end of the engine. To preclude entry of circlips, dirt, etc. into the crankcase, ensure that the lint-free rag fitted earlier is blanking off the crankcase apertures. Using a thin screwdriver at the slots provided, prise off the gudgeon pin circlips.

Gugeon pins have an interference fit in the piston bores and a piston must be heated before its gudgeon pin can be pushed out. The official tool is an electric piston heater P1a. If access to this piece of equipment cannot be arranged, hot water must be used to raise the temperature of the pistons to a minimum of 80°C (176°F). With a piston heated, the gudgeon pin can be pushed out and the piston separated from the connecting rod.

Piston fitment:

Piston fitment requires the reverse of the removal procedure and each piston must be heated to allow fitment of its gudgeon pin. Use new gudgeon pin circlips and ensure that they are correctly seated in their grooves.

FIG 1:17 Checking points of cylinders and pistons

Key to Fig 1:17   **D1** To determine cylinder wear   **D2** To determine cylinder ovality and wear

Cylinder inspection:

Refer to **FIG 1:17**. Measure the cylinder bores up to 1974 models 2 to 3mm (0.08 to 0.12in) below the point reached by the top piston ring **D1** and at the crankcase face level **D2**. Measure round the bore at several positions so that a picture of wear and ovality can be built up. The wear limit at **D1** is 0.10mm (0.004in) and ovality should not exceed 0.04mm (0.0016in).

On 1975 and subsequent models the measuring point **D1** for wear and ovality is 30mm (1.2in) below the top edge of the cylinder and maximum wear is 0.08mm (0.0032in) more than the new size specifications. Ovality must not exceed 0.04mm (0.0016in).

Oversize pistons are available for 2.2 litre and 2.4 litre engines but not for 2.7 litre and 3.0 litre engines. This means that standard size 2.2 litre and 2.4 litre engine cylinders which are scored, scuffed worn or over the acceptable ovality can be considered for possible reworking but such cylinders from 2.7 litre and 3.0 litre engines cannot.

Piston inspection:

Refer to **FIG 1:17**. Measure piston diameters up to 1974 models at **h**. This position differs for different makes of piston and for different pistons and is given in the following tabulation. The wear limit is 0.10mm (0.004in).

Engine capacity and type	h and make of piston Mahle	Schmidt
2.2 litre TC ..	11.5mm (0.45in)	15mm (0.59in)
2.2 litre EC and SC ..	2.5mm (0.10in)	—
2.4 litre S and T	8mm (0.32in)	12.5mm (0.49in)
2.4 litre E ..	2.5mm (0.10in)	—
2.7 litre Carrera and S ..	6mm (0.24in)	—
2.7 litre S ..	6mm (0.24in) *	18mm (0.71in) *

* 'LS' type pistons

On 1975 and subsequent models the measuring point **h** is raised to a point level with the lower edge of the gudgeon pin bore, and renewal depends on the piston and cylinder clearance.

Cylinder/piston clearance:

The desired diametrical clearance between the pistons and cylinder bores differs for different engines and for gudgeon pin bore, and renewal depends on the piston and cylinder clearance.

Engine capacity and type	Cylinder/piston clearance Mahle	Schmidt
2.2 litre TC	0.025 to 0.045mm (0.0010/0.0018in)	0.023 to 0.048mm (0.0009/0.0019in)
2.2 litre SC	0.045 to 0.065mm (0.0018/0.0026in)	—
2.2 litre EC	0.025 to 0.045mm (0.0010/0.0018in)	—
2.4 litre S	0.045 to 0.065mm (0.0018/0.0026in)	—
2.4 litre T	0.025 to 0.045mm (0.0010/0.0018in)	0.023 to 0.048mm (0.0009/0.0019in)
2.4 litre E	0.025 to 0.045mm (0.0010/0.0018in)	—
2.7 litre Carrera and S	0.025 to 0.045mm (0.0010/0.0018in)	—
2.7 litre S	0.028 to 0.052mm * (0.0011/0.0020in)	0.035 to 0.060mm * (0.0014/0.0024in)
3.0 litre from Engine No 6660446 or 6669091 ..	0.043 to 0.067mm 0.023 to 0.044mm	(0.0017 to 0.0026in) (0.0009 to 0.0017in)

* 'LS' type pistons

Serviceability of cylinders and pistons:

From the measurements of the cylinder bores and piston diameters, the ovalities and actual cylinder/piston clearances can be calculated and related to the limits and desired clearances quoted earlier and their serviceability assessed. Renew pistons and cylinders if clearance exceeds 0.15mm (0.006in).

Standard cylinders and pistons are available in three grades but only in complete matched engine sets. One size of oversize cylinders and pistons (in three grades) are available for 2.2 litre engines and two sizes (each in three grades) for 2.4 litre engines and, as stated earlier, only standard sizes (in three grades) are available for 2.7 and early 3.0 litre engines. Later 3.0 litre engines in four grades.

Where relevant, the possibility of exchange replacing or reconditioning cylinders to suit oversize pistons should be considered. Consultation with the Porsche spares supplier will be essential as the diameter to which unserviceable cylinders should be reworked will not only depend upon the minimum degree of salvage required or exchanged replacements available but may also be dependent upon the oversize pistons to suit the specific engine being in stock. The new pistons must be of **exactly the same type** and make as those being replaced and the engine set must be within a weight variation of 6 to 8gr (0.21 to 0.28oz). If spare pistons of the original make are not available, it will be necessary (where relevant) to fit a **complete engine set** of the alternative make.

There are two cylinder height tolerances for new cylinders and two height tolerances for reconditioned cylinders. The cylinders fitted to one bank must be of the same height tolerance. The height tolerance code is marked on the skirt of each cylinder and the spares supplier will advise on this point.

Gudgeon pins:

Gudgeon pins at low temperatures must have an interference fit in the piston bores. Two tolerances (colour coded white and black) are available. The desired clearance of the gudgeon pin with the connecting rod small-end bush is 0.020 to 0.039mm (0.0008 to 0.0015in) with a wear limit of 0.050mm (0.0020in).

Piston rings:

Each piston is fitted with two compression rings and one oil control ring. They must be fitted with 'TOP' towards the piston crown. Certain types of oil control rings are unmarked and, being symmetrical, may be fitted either way up.

Ring gaps, measured by feeler gauge with the rings squarely in the bores of their cylinders, should be up to 1974 models generally 0.30 to 0.45mm (0.012 to 0.018in) with a wear limit of 1.0mm (0.04in). Note, however, that the rings for 'LS' type pistons should have gaps of 0.20 to 0.40mm (0.008 to 0.016in) for the top ring, 0.15 to 0.35mm (0.006 to 0.014in) for the second ring and 0.40 to 1.40mm (0.016 to 0.055in) for the oil control ring. The recommended wear limit for the compression rings is 1.0mm (0.04in) and 2.0mm (0.08in) for the oil control ring.

The gaps on 1975 and subsequent models are 0.1 to 0.2mm (0.004 to 0.008in) for compression rings with a

FIG 1:18 Oil pumps and intermediate drive shaft. Arrows point to pump fixings

wear limit of 0.8mm (0.032in) measured at position **D2** (see **FIG 1:17**), and 0.15 to 0.30mm (0.006 to 0.012in) for oil control rings with a wear limit of 1.0mm (0.039in). Where the 3-piece 'LS' ring is fitted the limits are as noted previously.

Groove side clearances up to 1974 models should be 0.075 to 0.11mm (0.003 to 0.004in) for a top ring, 0.06 to 0.072mm (0.0023 to 0.0028in) for a second ring and 0.025 to 0.052mm (0.001 to 0.002in) for an oil control ring. The wear limit in each case is 0.20mm (0.008in).

The side clearance on 1975 and subsequent models is 0.070 to 0.102mm (0.0028 to 0.0040in) for the top ring, 0.040 to 0.072mm (0.0016 to 0.0028in) for the second ring and 0.020 to 0.052mm (0.0008 to 0.002in) for the oil control ring with a wear limit on compression rings of 0.2mm (0.008in) and 0.1mm (0.004in) for oil control rings.

Ensure that, when new rings are being obtained, they are the correct type and size for the specific standard or oversize pistons to which they are to be fitted. The spares supplier will advise on this point.

1:11 The crankcase and crankshaft

Separating the crankcase halves:

With the cylinders, pistons, flywheel, distributor drive, V-belt pulley, etc. removed, refer to **Section 1:16** and remove the oil strainer, relief and safety valves, oil and breather pipe connections, thermostat and oil pressure transmitter. Remove the cover at the rear of the intermediate shaft. Remove the camshaft drive chain ramps as described in **Section 1:4**.

Remove the nuts securing the crankcase halves including two cap nuts which are located inside the oil cooler mounting flange. Remove the through bolts. Remove the single nut inside the lefthand chain housing aperture. Position the assembly with the righthand side downwards and lift off the lefthand half crankcase.

Crankshaft, oil pump and intermediate shaft removal:

With the lefthand half crankcase removed as described earlier, the crankshaft assembly can be lifted out. Identify all shell bearings if they are to be refitted. Remove the three nuts arrowed in **FIG 1:18** and lift out the oil pump and intermediate shaft. Remove the camshaft drive chains by disengaging them from the intermediate shaft sprocket wheels.

FIG 1:19 Removing 'O' ring from No 8 bearing (left). Marking position of dowel hole on face of bearing housing to ensure correct location (right)

Cleaning and inspection:

Clean old compound from the joint faces and check he faces for flatness, freedom from burrs, etc. Check that all oil passages are clear and clean by blowing through with compressed air and oil. Check that, on engines produced from December, 1970, the oil spray jets for piston cooling are operative. The jets open at 3 to 4kg/sq cm (42 to 56lb/sq in).

The work necessary to renew the crankcase bearings will be dictated by whether the original crankshaft is serviceable, whether the original crankshaft main bearing journals have had to be reground or whether an exchange replacement crankshaft is being fitted. Whichever course is adopted, the crankcase must match and it may be that an exchange replacement will be required. Note that the crankcase halves must be bolted together for measurement of the main bearing bores. The standard bore for the bearings is 62.000 to 62.019mm (2.4409 to 2.4417in). To allow oversize bearing shells to be accommodated bores may be opened out to 62.269 to 62.250mm (2.4515 to 2.4508in). The forward intermediate shaft bearing bore should be 29.800 to 29.821mm (1.173 to 1.174in) and the rear bore 24.000 to 24.021mm (0.945 to 0.946in).

Reassembly:

With the crankshaft assembly and intermediate shaft serviced as described in **Sections 1:12** and **1:13**, follow the dismantling sequence in reverse. Assemble with all internal parts adequately wetted with clean engine oil. Ensure that all bearing shell and oil feed holes coincide. Use new sealing rings on all oil passages. Use new 'O' rings and crankshaft oil seals. Apply jointing compound sparingly to the faces but keep it away from the bearings, annular grooves, etc. Torque tighten through bolts and studs evenly and gradually to 3.5kgm (25lb ft) and all nuts to 2.2 to 2.5kgm (16 to 18lb ft).

Renewing rear bearing 'O' rings:

Refer to **FIG 1:19**. To renew the 'O' ring without dismantling the engine, remove the V-belt pulley, push a small screwdriver carefully under the lip of the seal and lever out the ring. Take care not to mark the surface of the crankshaft. Coat the new 'O' ring with oil and fit it using tool P216.

Renewing front end oil seal:

This may be carried out without splitting the crankcase. Remove the flywheel as described in **Section 1:9**. Displace the seal from its recess with a chisel and prise it out taking care not to damage the sealing surface of the crankshaft. Lightly radius the outer corner of the recess. Remove all swarf. Lightly coat the outer surface of the new seal with jointing compound and press it into place using tool P215. It must finish flush with the crankcase. Apply oil to the sealing lip.

1:12 Servicing the crankshaft and connecting rods

Connecting rod removal:

Remove the crankshaft assembly as described in **Section 1:11**. Check that the rods and caps are identified to each other. Remove and **discard** the cap retaining bolts. Dismount the connecting rods. Inspect the rods as described later.

Connecting rod fitment:

Inject oil through the crankshaft oilways before fitting the connecting rods with the bearing shells thoroughly wetted with oil. Ensure that the shells are correctly located and that the caps are fitted the right way round and to their correct rods. Use new bolts and torque tighten the nuts to 5kgm (36lb ft). When correctly fitted the rods should swing down under their own weight.

Removing the drive gears:

Remove the circlip and, using a suitable puller, draw off the distributor drive gear, the spacer and the helical gear in one operation. Remove the spring washer and the drive key.

Fitting the drive gears:

Fit the spring washer and drive key. Heat the helical gear to 150°C (300°F) in an oil bath and, with the shoulder forwards, fit it fully onto the shaft. Fit the spacer. Heat the distributor drive gear to 100°C (212°F) and fit it onto the shaft. When cool, check that the gears are tight. Fit a new circlip.

Crankshaft inspection:

If a bearing failure has occurred, the oilways in the crankshaft, crankcase, etc must be very thoroughly cleaned and flushed. After cleaning, have the shaft magnaflux tested for cracks. A crankshaft which is cracked cannot be salvaged.

Bearings are numbered 1 to 8 from the front (the axial control bearing is No 1). After cleaning, support the shaft in V-blocks at bearings 1 and 7 and check that the eccentricity at bearings 4 and 8 does not exceed 0.04mm (0.0022in) total DTI reading. Main bearing journals 1 to 7 and all crankpin bearing clearances are best checked by using Plastigage (see **Hints on Maintenance and Overhaul** in the **Appendix**). No 8 bearing clearance must be checked by measurement of the diameters. The desired clearance at journals 1 to 7 and also at the crankpins is 0.030 to 0.088mm (0.0010 to 0.0034in) and, at No 8 journal, 0.048 to 0.104mm (0.002 to 0.004in). Crankshaft axial clearance controlled at No 1 main bearing should be 0.100 to 0.200mm (0.004 to 0.008in).

A crankshaft with excessive wear of the journal or crankpins may be salvaged by regrinding followed by surface rehardening. This work is outside the scope of an owner and must be undertaken by a Porsche agent. Alternatively, an exchange replacement crankshaft may be fitted. Bearing shells are available to suit three stages of regrinding.

Connecting rod inspection:

A dismantled connecting rod is shown in **FIG 1:20**. The desired big-end clearance has been quoted earlier. If the small-end bore to gudgeon pin clearance (see **Section 1:10**) exceeds the wear limit of 0.05mm (0.002in), a new small-end bush may be shrunk into the rod. An interference of 0.020 to 0.055mm (0.0008 to 0.0022in) on diameter is required. The bore should be finished reamed to 22.033 to 22.020mm (0.8674 to 0.8669in).

A bent or twisted connecting rod cannot be salvaged. The weight of a replacement rod up to 1970 models must be within 5gr (0.18oz) of the other rods in the engine set. From 1970 models weight variation in a set must not exceed 9gr (0.32oz). Used cap retaining bolts must be discarded and new bolts fitted on reassembly.

1:13 The intermediate shaft

Removal and fitment:

The procedure for the removal of the intermediate shaft requires the crankcase to be split and is included in **Section 1:11**. Following the lifting out of the intermediate shaft, the camshaft drive chains may be removed.

With the intermediate shaft inspected and serviced as described later, refer to **Section 1:11** for the refitment procedure. The camshaft drive chains must be fitted to both sprocket wheels before positioning the intermediate shaft into the righthand half crankcase. If the freedom of rotation of the shaft and oil pumps seems restricted, reposition the connecting shaft splines in relation to the pumps and intermediate shaft and finally mark the optimum relative position.

Gear backlash:

Backlash between the crankshaft and intermediate shaft helical gears should desirably be 0.018 to 0.050mm (0.0005 to 0.0020in). Backlash cannot be adjusted and, if excessive, can only be corrected by the fitment of a new

FIG 1:20 Connecting rod dismantled, showing bearing shells

crankshaft gear and/or a new intermediate shaft assembly. Note that the intermediate shaft gear is finally machined during manufacture after fitment to the shaft and cannot be renewed separately. **Do not attempt to separate the gear from the shaft.**

Bearing clearances:

The desired bearing clearance at both bearings is 0.020 to 0.054mm (0.0008 to 0.0020in) with a recommended wear limit of 0.100mm (0.0040in). Bearing clearances are best checked by using Plastigage (see **Hints on Maintenance and Overhaul** in the **Appendix**) and it will be found convenient to measure these clearances at the same time as the crankshaft main bearing clearances are being checked.

Shaft bore cleaning:

A shaft which has been in service for any considerable mileage should have its bore cleaned of sludge, etc. Remove the blanking plug from the rear end of the shaft by drilling, tapping and fitting a suitable bolt to allow the plug to be pulled out. Clean the bore of the shaft and press in a new blanking plug. Check that the oilways are clear.

Axial clearance:

The desired axial float of the intermediate shaft is 0.08 to 0.12mm (0.003 to 0.005in). This is controlled by the flanged rear bearing shells and should it be excessive will require the fitment of new shells.

Sprocket wheel alignment:

Alignment of the intermediate shaft sprocket wheels with the camshaft sprocket wheels is checked and adjusted if necessary during engine reassembly. The procedure is included in **Section 1:14**.

FIG 1:21 Checking camshaft drive sprockets for correct alignment, using a straightedge and depth gauge

FIG 1 : 22   Layout of lubricating system. Inset (top right) is a section through oil filter

Key to Fig 1 : 22   1 Strainer in crankcase   2 Scavenge pump   3 Pressure pump   4 Safety valve   5 Thermostat   6 Oil gauge transmitter   7 Pressure relief valve   8 Oil cooler   9 Oil tank   10 Anti-foaming plate   11 Bypass valve   12 Fullflow oil filter   13 Filler   14 Temperature gauge transmitter   15 Crankcase breather connection   16 Tank breather connection   17 Oil pressure and temperature gauges

1 : 14 Engine reassembly :

Assembly instructions are given in the text of each relevant section. These are largely the dismantling procedures in reverse but, as this may not always be so, the point should be checked against the text. It is then simply a matter of tackling the work in the correct sequence, of applying normal automobile engineering practice, fitting only Porsche replacement parts, using new seals, 'O' rings and gaskets and ensuring that joints are well made as it may not easily be possible to rectify an oil leak which is not discovered until the assembly and installation of the engine has been completed.

If the engine has been completely dismantled, the assembly sequence will commence with the fitment of the crankshaft and connecting rod assembly and the intermediate shaft to the crankcase halves and the assembly sequence will be the reverse of that taken during dismantling. If the engine was only partially dismantled, reverse the sequence which was then followed. Assemble working parts wetted with clean engine oil and use jointing compound where applicable. Refer to sectional texts for torque tightening figures. At each stage of assembly check, where relevant, the free rotation of the component or assembly.

To avoid the possibility of valves and pistons fouling each other, do not fit the rockers until the stage 1 valve timing procedure (see **Section 1 : 6**) has been carried out.

At this point check and, if necessary, adjust the alignment of the camshaft sprocket wheels with the intermediate shaft sprocket wheels. The procedure is as follows:

1 Refer to **FIG 1 : 21** and, using a straightedge across the crankcase face and a depth gauge, measure **A** at the intermediate shaft forward sprocket wheel and at the righthand camshaft sprocket wheel. Any difference must not exceed 0.25mm (0.010in).
2 Check the corresponding dimensions for the intermediate shaft inner sprocket wheel and the lefthand camshaft sprocket wheel noting that the offset is 54.8mm (2.1575in).
3 Adjustment is made by adding or removing spacers 5 in **FIG 1 : 8** at each camshaft sprocket wheel. Stage 2 of the valve timing procedure may now be carried out.

To preclude oil draining from the old type chain tensioners, it is preferable not to invert the engine once the tensioners have been installed and it will consequently be appropriate to mount the heat exchangers, etc. before fitting the tensioners. Tensioners with self-contained oil reservoirs are not affected.

Fit the distributor and time the ignition as described in **Chapter 3, Sections 3 : 4** and **3 : 6** noting that final adjustment to the timing must be made stroboscopically after installation of the engine. Fuel system adjustments are also made on recommissioning the installed engine.

FIG 1:23   Lubrication system (1969 to 1971 models)

Key to Fig 1:23   1 Auxiliary oil cooler   2 Main oil cooler   3 Oil pumps   a Scavenge pump   b Pressure pump   4 Oil tank   5 Mounting   6 Oil filter   7 Auxiliary thermostat   8 Breather pipe   9 Oil strainer   10 Main thermostat   11 Air cleaner   12 Filter bypass to engine   13 Oil tank vent to air cleaner

1:15 Recommissioning an overhauled engine

On completion of the installation of the overhauled engine and transmission into the vehicle, fill the oil tank and the transmission with the correct approved oils. Tension the cooling fan drive belt and also, if relevant, the emission control air pump drive belt. Check over to ensure that all pipes, leads and controls are reconnected and that no tools or other items have been left behind.

So that the engine may be turned without starting it, unclip the distributor cap and tape it to one side. Use the starter motor to turn the engine for some revolutions to prime the pressure oil pump. Refit the distributor cap and start the engine. Repeat the priming process if there is not an immediate rise in oil pressure. Once oil pressure has been established, check that the charging circuit is operative and that the 'no-charge' warning light goes out when a fast idling speed is reached.

Run the engine at about 2000rev/min until the oil temperature rises to about 60°C. Check that all joints and oil and fuel pipe connections are free of leaks. At idling speed, check the level in the oil tank and top up as necessary. Run the engine up to normal operating temperature and check that the oil pressure is within the range of 78 to 100lb/sq in at 5000rev/min at 80°C. Check the ignition timing stroboscopically, adjust the fuel system as described in the relevant section of **Chapter 2**. Check, where relevant, the operation of the emission control as described in the appropriate section of **Chapter 4**.

After operating the vehicle for about 100 miles (160km), recheck for oil leaks, re-tension the drive belt(s), re-tighten the rocker shaft bolts and adjust the valve clearances. If the overhaul was extensive (new bearings, pistons, cylinders, etc.), treat the engine as if it was new and, after careful running-in, clean the oil strainer and renew the oil filter and the engine oil after 600 miles (1000km) from overhaul.

1:16 The lubrication system

The lubrication system is shown diagrammatically in **FIG 1:22**. Oil is drawn from the tank 9 by the pressure pump 3. Pressure oil is delivered via the main thermostat 5 either direct to the engine lubrication system when the oil is cold or through the main cooler 8 when the oil is

FIG 1:24   Lubrication system (1972 models)

Key to Fig 1:24   1 Auxiliary oil cooler   2 Main oil cooler   3 Oil pumps   a Scavenge pump   b Pressure pump   4 Oil tank   5 Mounting and auxiliary thermostat   6 Oil filter   7 Breather to oil tank   8 Oil strainer   9 Main thermostat   10 Air cleaner   11 Oil tank vent to air cleaner

hot. The bearings of the crankshaft, intermediate shaft and camshaft are pressure fed and, on later models, jets in the crankcase spray oil onto the undersides of the pistons.

The scavenge pump 2 draws drain oil (aerated) through the strainer 1 and returns it to the oil tank via a fullflow filter 12 and an auxiliary thermostat if the oil is relatively cold or via an auxiliary cooler if the oil is hot. Neither the auxiliary thermostat nor the auxiliary cooler are shown in **FIG 1:22**, but will be found in **FIGS 1:23** and **1:24**.

The main cooler is a matrix type. The auxiliary cooler is a matrix type on earlier models and a coiled pipe unit on later models (see **FIG 1:25**).

Gauze strainer removal and fitment:

Refer to **FIG 1:2**. Remove the magnetic plug 11 and drain off the residual oil from the base of the crankcase.

Remove the nuts and washers which retain the coverplate 23 and strainer 10 to the crankcase halves and withdraw the assembly. Separate the two gaskets from the strainer and coverplate. Clean the strainer in petrol. Clean metallic particles from the drain plug.

Fitment is the reverse of this sequence. Use new gaskets. Do not distort the coverplate by overtightening the retaining nuts.

Renewing the oil filter:

The canister type disposable filter is screwed to a housing on the oil tank. The filter cannot be cleaned. To renew, unscrew and discard the old canister and fit a new one. Ensure that the faces of both the canister and the housing are clean and that the sealing ring is in good condition and correctly positioned.

FIG 1:25 Lubrication system (1974 models)

Key to Fig 1:25 1 Oil tank 2 Auxiliary thermostat 3 Scavenge pump to auxiliary thermostat line 4 Auxiliary thermostat return line 5 Auxiliary cooler (coiled pipe type) 6 From scavenge pump

Draining the oil tank:

With the engine oil hot after a run, jack up and remove the righthand rear road wheel. To preclude the possibility of oil contaminating the brake pads or linings, protect the wheel hub assembly with plastic or equivalent sheeting. Position a container of adequate capacity before removing the drain plug from the bottom of the tank. Allow the old oil to drain off completely before refitting the drain plug.

Initially pour 8 litres (14 pints) of approved oil into the tank, run the engine and top up as necessary.

Oil pumps:

The gear type pressure and scavenge oil pumps are a single assembly and are shown in cross-section in **FIG 1:2**. To accommodate the considerable degree of aeration of the scavenged drain oil, the scavenge pump is approximately twice the capacity of the pressure pump. The pumps are driven at half crankshaft speed by the intermediate shaft through a splined connecting shaft. No procedures are prescribed for the overhaul or repair of the oil pumps by an owner and, if either becomes unserviceable, the unit must be removed and a new or exchange replacement assembly installed.

Access to the pump assembly requires the crankcase to be split. The procedure for the removal and fitment of the

FIG 1:26 Locations of relief and safety valves

Key to Fig 1:26 R Relief valve S Safety valve

pumps is included in **Section 1 :11**. When refitting the pumps, use new joint seals and ensure that they are correctly seated.

Relief and safety valves:

These valves are located in the crankcase and are shown arrowed **R** and **S** in **FIG 1 :26**. The relief valve opens at approximately 5.5kg/sq cm (78lb/sq in) and allows excess pressure oil to pass to the crankcase. Should the oil pressure be excessive with the relief valve fully open or should the relief valve become inoperative, the safety valve opens and prevents excessive pressure being applied to the main cooler, oil pipes, etc.

Access to each valve and valve spring requires removal of the relevant plug **R** or **S**. Do not get the valves or springs mixed. The valve bores and the surface of the piston valves must be unscuffed and unscored.

Oil pressure transmitter:

The transmitter is located adjacent to the main thermostat and may be removed by unscrewing after disconnecting the electrical lead. A defective transmitter must be replaced by a new unit.

Main thermostat:

The main thermostat is in the pressure feed circuit. It opens at 83°C (182°F) to allow hot oil to flow through the main cooler before delivery to the engine. A defective thermostat must be replaced by a new unit.

To remove the thermostat, disconnect the lead to the oil pressure transmitter, disconnect the hose from the breather outlet, remove two retaining nuts and withdraw the thermostat.

On refitment use new 'O' rings. The offset holes in the flange preclude incorrect fitment.

Auxiliary thermostat:

The function of the auxiliary thermostat is to open the scavenge oil return line to the auxiliary cooler when the return oil temperature rises above 83°C (182°F). Incorrect operation of the thermostat will be indicated by excessively high tank oil temperature and 'coldness' of the auxiliary cooler. If the thermostat becomes defective, fit a new replacement unit.

The position of the auxiliary thermostat differs with different models but may be located by tracing the relevant scavenge oil lines.

Main oil cooler:

The main oil cooler 8 in **FIG 1 :22** is mounted on the crankcase and may be dismounted with the engine installed in the vehicle. Access requires removal of the upper, the front and the righthand coverplates. Hold the pipe connection hexagon when releasing the inlet pipe. Remove the upper and lower retaining nuts and lift out the cooler. Discard the seals fitted between the cooler and the crankcase.

Fitment is the reverse of this sequence. Use new seals and ensure that they are correctly seated. Hold the connection hexagon when reconnecting the inlet pipe.

Auxiliary oil cooler:

The auxiliary oil cooler is located at the front righthand wing of the vehicle as indicated in **FIGS 1 : 23, 1 : 24** and **1 : 25**. The cooler may be either of matrix or, on later models, of coiled pipe construction. Should it be necessary to dismount the cooler, hold the connection hexagons when releasing the feed and return pipes. On refitment, ensure that the connections are correctly tightened.

1 :17 Fault diagnosis

(a) Engine will not start

1 Ignition system defective electrically
2 Ignition system defective mechanically
3 Dirty, pitted or incorrectly set contact breaker points
4 Ignition wires loose, insulation faulty
5 Water on sparking plug leads
6 Battery discharged, corrosion of terminals
7 Faulty or jammed starter
8 Sparking plug leads wrongly connected
9 Vapour lock in fuel pipes
10 Defective fuel pump
11 Starting fuel enrichment excessive or insufficient
12 Fuel system filter, injectors or carburetter jet(s) blocked
13 Leaking valves
14 Sticking valves
15 Valve timing incorrect
16 Ignition timing incorrect
17 Engine flooded with fuel

(b) Engine stalls after starting

1 Check 1, 2, 3, 4, 5, 10, 11, 12, 13 and 14 in (a)
2 Sparking plugs defective or gaps incorrect
3 Retarded ignition
4 Mixture too weak
5 Water in fuel system
6 Fuel tank vent blocked
7 Incorrect valve clearances

(c) Engine idles badly

1 Check 2 and 7 in (b)
2 Air leaks at manifold joints
3 Idling adjustment wrongly set
4 Over-rich mixture
5 Worn piston rings
6 Worn valve stems or guides
7 Weak exhaust valve springs

(d) Engine misfires

1 Check 1, 2, 3, 4, 5, 8, 10, 12, 13, 14, 15 and 16 in (a) ; 2, 3, 4 and 7 in (b)
2 Weak or broken valve springs

(e) Engine overheats

1 Weak mixture, ignition over-advanced
2 Fan belt slipping
3 Defective oil thermostat
4 Oil cooler internally blocked or externally choked with dirt
5 Loss of cooling air through badly fitted covers

(f) Low compression

1 Check 13 and 14 in (a); 6 and 7 in (c); and 2 in (d)
2 Worn piston ring grooves
3 Scored or worn cylinder bores

(g) Engine lacks power

1 Check 3, 10, 12, 13, 14, 15 and 16 in (a); 2, 3, 4 and 7 in (b); 6 and 7 in (c); and 2 in (d). Also check (e) and (f)
2 Leaking joints and gaskets
3 Fouled sparking plugs
4 Automatic ignition advance not working
5 Exhaust system blocked

(h) Burnt valves or seats

1 Check 13 and 14 in (a); 7 in (b); and 2 in (d). Check (e)
2 Excessive carbon in head

(j) Sticking valves

1 Check 2 in (d)
2 Bent or scored valve stems, defective guides
3 Defective stem seals
4 Incorrect valve clearance

(k) Excessive cylinder wear

1 Check 11 in (a); and check (e)
2 Dirty or insufficient oil. Wrong grade
3 Piston rings wrongly gapped, gummed or broken
4 Bent connecting rods
5 Dirt under cylinder mounting flanges

(l) Excessive oil consumption

1 Check 6 and 7 in (c); check (k); and 3 in (j)
2 Ring gaps too wide
3 Oil control rings ineffective
4 Scored cylinders
5 Defective scavenge oil pump
6 External oil leaks
7 Incorrect grade of oil

(m) Crankshaft or connecting rod bearing failure

1 Check 2 and 4 in (k)
2 Blocked oilways
3 Bent or worn crankshaft
4 Bearing shells wrongly fitted
5 Worn pressure oil pump, defective lubricating system
6 Loose bearings or connecting rod caps

(n) High fuel consumption

1 Car in poor mechanical condition
2 Bad driving habits, excessive acceleration in low gears
3 Incorrect ignition or fuel system adjustments
4 Flooding float chamber (carburetter models, fuel leakage)
5 Incorrect jet sizes (carburetter models)
6 Carburetter accelerating pump wrongly adjusted

(o) Engine vibration

1 Mounting failures
2 Loose alternator mounting
3 Fan out of balance
4 Clutch and flywheel unbalanced
5 Misfiring due to mixture, ignition or mechanical faults

NOTES

CHAPTER 2

THE FUEL SYSTEM

2:1 Description

The fuel tank is installed at the front of the vehicle below the luggage compartment floor. It is provided with a drain plug. The electrically actuated tank contents gauge is operated from a transmitter unit fitted to the fuel tank. Fuel is transferred from the tank to the engine fuel system by an electrically operated pump. The tank to engine fuel line arrangement is not identical on all models and, on relevant vehicle types, incorporates emission control equipment which is covered in **Chapter 4, Section 4:4**.

The vehicles covered by this manual are fitted with one of the three following quite distinctly different fuel systems.

Carburetter models:

The engines of carburetter models are provided with twin three-choke Solex-Zenith downdraught type 40TIN carburetters each of which serves one bank of cylinders. Emission control standards, where mandatory, are met by the incorporation of a mixture enrichment device for overrun conditions. Carburetters fitted to engines of differing capacities are of the same type but are fitted with jets of different calibration sizes. These variations are listed in the **Technical Data** section of the **Appendix**.

Carburetter adjustments and servicing procedures are included in **Section 2:7**.

Fuel injection pump (FIP) models:

In this system a Bosch mechanical fuel injection pump delivers an individually metered quantity of fuel to each cylinder as each inlet valve is due to open. The injection pump receives fuel under pressure from the electrically operated supply pump. The injection pump itself is driven by a toothed flexible belt from the lefthand camshaft and is timed to the engine. The inlet port of each cylinder is provided with a fuel injector and cold starting enrichment is provided separately.

Adjustment and servicing procedures are included in **Section 2:8**.

Continuous fuel injection (CIS) models:

In this system fuel is continuously sprayed into the inlet ports at a metered rate of flow. The engine shown in **Chapter 1, FIG 1:1** is fitted with this continuous fuel injection system and this illustration identifies the location of certain of the regulators, control units and injection valves which comprise this system. Cold starting enrichment is actuated electrically. Adjustments and servicing procedures are included in **Section 2:9**.

FIG 2:1   Cross-section through air pre-heater

Key to Fig 2:1   1 Fresh air flap   2 Hot air flap
3 Thermostat   A Hot air   B Fresh air

FIG 2:2   Pump and mounting bracket

FIG 2:3   Hand controls

Key to Fig 2:3   A Hand throttle control adjuster
B Friction adjustment nut (hand throttle)   C Friction
adjustment nut (heater controls)

Intake air:

On all models, intake air is filtered. On certain models the intake air is preheated within a thermostatically controlled range of temperature.

2:2 Maintenance
General:

At least every 12,000 miles (20,000km), check over the fuel system pipelines to ensure that all pipes and joints are tight and sound. Lightly lubricate the control pivots and ball joints and, if necessary, adjust the hand throttle control as described in **Section 2:6**.

Air cleaner:

Every 6000 to 12,000 miles (10,000 to 20,000km) depending upon how dusty the terrain in which the vehicle is operating may be, clean or renew the air filter element as described in **Section 2:3**.

Fuel filter:

If fitted, renew the in-line fuel filter every 12,000 miles (20,000km). Refer, if necessary, to **Section 2:4**.

Carburetter models:

Refer to **Section 2:7** for idling speed and CO content adjustments and other procedures.

FIP models:

Refer to **Section 2:8** for idling speed, CO content adjustments, drive belt tensioning and other procedures.

CIS models:

Refer to **Section 2:9** for idling speed, CO content adjustments and other procedures.

2:3 Air cleaner and preheater
Air cleaner element:

Access to the element is achieved by releasing the spring clips or the flexible straps and removing the cover from the canister. In the case of a dry type element, lift out the element and dislodge the accumulated dust by tapping lightly and blowing off with compressed air. Renew the element after two or three cleanings or if it is torn or damaged in any way. In the case of an oil wetted type element, wash off the contaminated oil film in petrol, dry thoroughly and re-wet the element with clean engine oil. Allow excess oil to drain off. In both cases, clean the interior of the canister before refitting the element and the canister cover.

Air preheater:

The preheater unit which controls the temperature of the intake air thermostatically is not fitted to all models. A cross-section through the unit is shown in **FIG 2:1**. Air flap 1 is controlled by the throttle linkage. Air flap 2 is controlled by the thermostat 3 which begins to close the hot air flap at 45°C (112°F) and opens the air bypass duct which it closes in the hot air position. At 50°C (122°F) the hot air flap should be fully closed. The throttle control linked air flap 1 starts to open at a throttle valve position of approximately 20° and is fully open at full throttle.

FIG 2:4   Components of Solex-Zenith carburetter type 40 TIN

Key to Fig 2:4   1 Self-locking nut   2 Velocity stack   2a Gasket   3 Clamp pan   4 Gasket   5 Threaded plug   6 Ring gasket   7 Float needle valve   8 Gasket   9 Hollow bolt   10 Gasket   11 Filtering screen   12 Connector   13 Gasket   14 Fillister head screw   15 Lockwasher   16 Carburetter cover   17 Gasket   18 Roundhead screw   19 Float, complete   20 Pre-atomiser   21 Retaining clip   22 Venturi   23 Air correction jet   24 Emulsion tube   25 Pump inlet valve   26 Injection tube   27 Plug   28 Fuel jet for enrichment valve   29 Enrichment solenoid   30 Gasket   31 Fillister head screw   32 Lockwasher   33 Pump shaft   34 Roundhead screw   35 Pump cover   36 Diaphragm   37 Pump spring   38 Hollow bolt   39 Gasket   40 Fuel line, complete   41 Gasket   42 Fillister head screw   43 Lockwasher   54 Fillister head screw   45 Lockwasher   46 Enrichment valve top   47 'O' ring   48 Diaphragm   49 Diaphragm plunger   50 Spring   51 Enrichment valve bottom   52 Idle jet   53 Air bypass control screw   54 Threaded plug   55 Auxiliary mixture control screw   56 Jet housing   57 Gasket   58 Main jet   59 Idle mixture control screw   60 Spring   61 Idle speed adjusting screw   62 Spring   63 Nut   64 Lockplate   65 Cam track   66 Spring washer   67 Housing   68 Plug

Adjustment of air flap 1, if necessary, is carried out with the throttle valve in the idling speed position. Release the locknut, adjust the lever actuating roller tappet so that the roller just touches the cam on the throttle valve lever and retighten the locknut.

No procedures are prescribed for the repair or renewal of the thermostat by an owner and, should the unit be defective, a complete new or exchange replacement preheater assembly should be fitted.

2:4 Fuel filter

Carburetter models:

Gauze thimble filters are fitted in the fuel inlet banjo connections. Access requires the banjo retaining bolt to be removed. Clean the gauzes by agitating in clean petrol and, if necessary using a brush. Do not use rag or cotton waste.

FIP and CIS models:

If necessary, refer to **Section 2:8** or **2:9** for the location of the in-line filter. A disposable-type filter cannot be cleaned and must be replaced by a new unit. Ensure that the new filter is fitted the correct way round. In the case of filters which have renewable elements, ensure that the correct new element is obtained.

2:5 Fuel pump

In 1970 models the fuel pump is located at the front of the vehicle adjacent to the rear of the fuel tank. In 1971 and later models the pump is repositioned into the engine compartment. In carburetter and FIP models, two fuel lines connect between the tank and the pump. These are the fuel supply (suction, marked **S**) and the pressure relief (marked **R**) line. The third pump connection is the fuel delivery line to the engine fuel system. Pumps fitted to CIS models have two connections only, the suction and the delivery.

No procedures are prescribed for the repair or overhaul of a fuel pump by an owner and, if a pump should be defective, it must be removed and a new or an exchange replacement pump fitted. Since pumps are not identical on all models, ensure that the replacement pump obtained is the same type as that removed.

Removal and fitment:

Disconnect the battery earth leads. Identify and disconnect the leads from the pump. Remove the mounting retaining nuts up to 1975 models and withdraw the pump and its mounting bracket (see **FIG 2:2**). Loosen the clamp which retains the pump to the bracket and remove the bracket. Uncouple the pipes from the pump and blank off the pipes and pump connections to preclude loss of fuel and/or ingress of dirt.

On 1976 models, remove the guard, unscrew the retaining clip and pull the pump downwards. Pinch the intake hose with a clamp to prevent flow when disconnected. Disconnect the electrical leads. Remove the hollow bolt from the delivery hose and collect draining fluid. Loosen the intake hose clip and remove the hose and pump.

Fitment is the reverse of this sequence. Coat the pump electrical terminals with lithium grease to suppress corrosion. Ensure that the rubber boot is correctly fitted.

On 1976 models note the following points:

The hollow bolt must be fitted with new sealing washers, the thicker washer between the banjo coupling and the pump body, and the thinner washer under the head of the bolt. Torque tighten the hollow bolt to 1.6 to 2.3kgm (11.5 to 16.5lb ft).

Position the pump with the top terminal inclined backwards about 35° and secure with the clip.

Finally, check that the pipe connections are tight and free from leaks.

2:6 Controls

Hand throttle control:

When the hand throttle control is fully 'open', the engine speed should be between 3500 and 3800rev/min with the engine at full operational temperature. Adjustment, if required, is made at the nipple arrowed **A** in **FIG 2:3**. Access requires the cover to be lifted. Ensure that in the 'off' position the hand throttle does not affect the idling speed.

The procedure for dismantling the control is included in **Chapter 11, Section 11:8**. On reassembly, reset the pivotal friction of the lever by tightening nut **B** until a load of 6kg (13lb) applied at the clevis pin hole and at right angles to the below-floor lever is required to move the lever in its pivot.

Foot control:

Keep the pivots lightly lubricated and ensure that in the released position the control does not influence the idling speed. An adjustable stop is provided to limit the fully depressed position of the foot pedal.

2:7 Solex-Zenith carburetters

Each bank of cylinders is served by a single three-choke Solex-Zenith type 40TIN carburetter. These are down-draught carburetters in which three chokes are fuelled by two float chambers in each carburetter. Accelerator pump injection is provided and, where emission control is mandatory, the carburetters incorporate an overrun mixture enrichment arrangement. The components of a carburetter are as shown in **FIG 2:4**. The calibration sizes of jets incorporated into carburetters fitted to different engine capacities are quoted in the **Technical Data** section of the **Appendix**.

Filter gauzes:

The fuel feed to each float chamber incorporates a gauze filter 11 in **FIG 2:4**.

Adjustments:

Maintain the idling speed at 850 to 950rev/min. Note that when setting the idling speed, carburetter synchronisation and mixture adjustments must be carried out concurrently. Note also that the engine must be at normal operating temperature and that the following procedure assumes that the ignition system and sparking plugs are in good order and that the stroboscopically checked ignition timing is correctly set.

1 Close the hand throttle. Remove the air cleaner. Uncouple the throttle actuating linkage from the cross-shaft. Refer to **FIG 2:5**. Set the datum by screwing in the mixture control screws **b** until they gently

bottom. Back off each by $2\frac{1}{2}$ turns. Close the bypass screws **c**.

2 Start the engine and connect the P227 (or equivalent) synchrotester. Make initial adjustments to the carburetter sections serving Nos 1 and 4 cylinders by adjusting screws **a** until an idling speed of 1000rev/min is obtained.

3 Synchronise the lefthand and righthand banks of cylinders. If, with the air bypass screws **c** closed, there is one throat with a higher rate of air flow than the other two, the bypass screw on that throat should be left closed whilst the other two throats are adjusted by opening their bypass screws as little as possible.

4 Equally adjust the screws **b** inwards until the engine begins to run unevenly. Gradually unscrew until the engine runs evenly. Concurrently adjust screws **a** to achieve equal air flows in both banks of cylinders and a stable idling speed of 850 to 950rev/min. If necessary repeat the procedure.

5 Adjust the CO content to within 3 to 4% at screws **b**. Repeat operations 3 and 4 if necessary. Reconnect the linkage ensuring that the connections engage without bias and that the cross-shaft is free and does not bind.

Overrun mixture enrichment:

Unless corrected, excessive CO emission in the exhaust gases can result from lean conditions during

FIG 2:5 Adjustment screws

Key to Fig 2:5 a Idle speed b Idle mixture control c Air bypass control

FIG 2:6 Schematic illustration of overrun system

Key to Fig 2:6 1 Velocity stack 2 Injection tube 3 Accelerator pump 4 Adjusting screw 5 Threaded plug 6 Fuel inlet 7 Float needle valve 8 Accelerator pump inlet valve 9 Double float 10 Enrichment solenoid 11 Vacuum line 12 Throttle valve 13 Air control screw 14 Connecting hose 15 Hollow bolt for vacuum line 16 Mixing valve 17 Flow rate adjusting screw 18 Diaphragm 19 Auxiliary mixture control screw 20 Nut 21 Stud

FIG 2:7   Accelerating jet adjustment screws

Key to Fig 2:7   a Actuating lever adjustment
                      b Actuating finger adjustment

overrun at higher engine speeds. Correction is by enrichment over the relevant range. This enrichment system is only incorporated into models which are exported to countries in which emission control is mandatory. Refer to **FIG 2:6**. The system comprises an auxiliary mixture valve 16, a solenoid valve 10 and an engine speed transducer.

During overrun (throttle closed) at engine speeds in excess of 1350rev/min, the transducer activates the solenoid valve and admits high vacuum from below the throttle

valve 12 to the diaphragm 18 of the mixing valve 16. This results in the valve opening and releasing a flow of correctly proportioned air/fuel mixture into the induction manifolds. At overrun below 1300rev/min, the mixing valve is closed and the normal idle mixture circuit operates. When, on acceleration, the throttle valves are opened, a microswitch on the throttle control linkage cuts out this overrun enrichment arrangement.

One enrichment valve assembly is incorporated in each of the two carburetters and is located in the sections which serve Nos 2 and 5 cylinders. Adjustment should not be attempted by an owner and, if malfunctioning is suspected, a Porsche agent should be consulted.

Acceleration pump:

The desired injection quantity is nominally 0.4 to 0.6cc per stroke per pump and is measured by operating the throttle rapidly and collecting the fuel delivered from each injection tube 2 in **FIG 2:6** using measuring tube P25a. Carry out these checks with the engine **cold** and with the fuel pump switched on.

If adjustment is needed, proceed as follows. Set the datum by turning screws **a** in **FIG 2:7** to bring the three actuating levers exactly vertical. Loosen locknuts **b**, turn the adjuster screws until they just touch the plungers and retighten the locknuts. Measure the injection quantities and adjust as necessary at the **b** screws.

Float chamber fuel level:

Check the fuel levels by removing plugs 68 in **FIG 2:4** one at a time and fitting gauge P226A. With the engine running at idling speed the level should be between the two **lower** marks on the gauge glass.

Adjust by reducing (lowering the level) or increasing (raising the level) the thickness of gasket 8 in **FIG 2:4**,

FIG 2:8   Diagrammatic layout of mechanical fuel injection pump (FIP) system

Key to Fig 2:8   1 Fuel pump (supply)   2 Fuel tank   3 Fuel filter   4 Cold start enrichment solenoid   5 Injection valve
6 Injection line   7 Injection pump   8 Cold start enrichment hose

FIG 2:9 Control units on the FIP system. These govern fuel injection quantity through the control rack

Key to Fig 2:9 1 Sensor on contoured cam 2 Control rack head 3 Enrichment solenoid 4 Thermostat 5 Barometric cell 6 Check valve 7 Plunger unit 8 Toothed segment 9 Control rack 10 Roller tappet 11 Camshaft 12 Governor control lever 13 Contoured cam 14 Centrifugal governor 15 Idle adjusting screw 16 Shut-off solenoid

noting that 0.5mm (0.02in) change in gasket thickness will alter the float chamber fuel level by approximately 2.0mm (0.08in).

Carburetter removal and fitment:

Remove the air cleaner. Disconnect both battery earth straps. Uncouple the fuel feed and the throttle connection. Disconnect the solenoid valve wiring (if fitted). Disconnect the vacuum pipes. Remove the carburetter retaining nuts, collect the washers, lift off the carburetter, discard the joint gasket and, to preclude entry of dirt, etc. cover the intake openings.

Fitment is the reverse of this sequence. Ensure that the joint faces are clean. Fit a new joint gasket. Adjust the idling speed, etc. as described earlier.

Dismantling and reassembling a carburetter:

If dismantling is necessary, follow the numerical sequence of the components given in **FIG 2:4**. Do not dismantle further than may be necessary to give access to the relevant jet or component. On reassembly, follow the reverse of the dismantling sequence and use new gaskets, joint washers, etc. if the condition of those removed is in any way doubtful.

Jets:

Use only petrol and compressed air to clean jets. Do not attempt to clean them by probing the orifices as this will ruin their calibration.

Refer to the **Technical Data** section of the **Appendix** for jet sizes.

2:8 Bosch fuel injection (FIP)

The layout of the mechanical fuel injection pump system is shown diagrammatically in **FIG 2:8**. An electrically operated pump draws fuel from the tank and delivers it to a filter. Filtered fuel passes to the engine driven injection pump. Excess fuel from the electric pump and from the injection pump is returned to the tank. A metered quantity of fuel is delivered every other engine revolution to an injection nozzle at each inlet port.

FIG 2:10 One of the six adjustable air screws is arrowed

FIG 2:11 Fuel injection pump mixture adjustment points

Key to Fig 2:11 1 8mm bolt 2 Allen screw (access to control rack head) 3 Idle speed mixture adjuster

FIG 2:12 Adjusting the idle speed mixture (later models)

Since no procedures are prescribed for the repair or overhaul of the injector pump by an owner, details of its components and construction are not applicable to this manual but it is relevant to refer to **FIG 2:9** and note that the datum of the fuel control rack is barometrically corrected for atmospheric pressure. Injector pump delivery pressure is of the order of 17kg/sq cm (240lb/sq in). The injector nozzles have check valves but do not have any metering function. The injector pump is driven at half engine speed from the forward end of the lefthand camshaft by a toothed belt. It is timed to the crankshaft so that each fuel injection is delivered just as the inlet valve is about to open. The timing datum of the control rack is set to suit the length of the delivery pipes (they are all of the same length) and corrected for engine speed by the governor shown in **FIG 2:9**. The shut-off solenoid is controlled by a throttle valve actuated microswitch and an engine speed transducer and cuts off injection during overrun. The injector pump is lubricated from the engine lubrication system with which it is connected by an oil feed and a return pipeline.

Cold starting enrichment is automatic and is provided via a solenoid valve which is controlled by time-limit and temperature-limit switches so that cold starting enrichment through separate nozzles is provided over a two-second period or for longer at lower temperatures. The cold starting thermostat responds to engine cooling air temperature.

Idling speed adjustment:

The following procedure assumes that the valve clearances are correctly set (see **Chapter 1, Section 1:2**), that the ignition system and sparking plugs are in good order, that the ignition timing is correct and has been stroboscopically checked and that the engine has been run up to normal operating temperature.

1 Close the hand throttle. Refer to **FIG 2:10** which shows one of the six adjustable air screws. Adjust these screws by small and equal amounts (clockwise to reduce idling speed and vice versa) until the engine is running at 850 to 950rev/min.

2 Run the engine at 1600 to 2000rev/min and, using synchrometer P235 (or equivalent), readjust the air screws as necessary to give substantially equal air flow to each cylinder. Recheck the idling speed.

3 Check and adjust, if necessary, the idling fuel mixture as described later. This may affect the idling speed; if it does, repeat operation 2.

4 Repeat operations 2 and 3 until the idling speed and the CO content of the exhaust gases are simultaneously within the stated limits.

Idling mixture adjustment:

Exhaust gas content measurement equipment is required. The adjustment procedure differs slightly between earlier and later models which have an access hole in the cooling air upper shroud. The spring loaded adjuster is shown in **FIG 2:11**. In the case of models produced prior to 1972 use screwdriver P230b. In the case of later models, use tool P230c as shown in **FIG 2:12**. Adjustment is carried out with the engine stationary.

Earlier models:

With the idling speed set as described earlier, check the exhaust gas CO content. This should be within the range of 2.5 to 5.5% over an air intake temperature range of 15°C (60°F) to 40°C (104°F) proportionately. If outside this range, fit tool P230b to the adjuster, push the adjuster inwards until it engages and, turning clockwise to enrich the mixture or vice versa, make the relevant adjustment. Do not adjust by more than one notch before restarting the engine and rechecking the CO content at idling speed. If adjustment by three notches in either direction does not bring the CO content within limits, have the basic range of the injector pump reset by a Porsche agent.

Later models:

Check that the CO content at idling speed is within the following limits:

Operation in the USA ..	..	2.0 to 3.0%
Operation in Europe ..	..	2.5 to 3.5%
Carrera 2.7 litre models	..	2.0 to 3.0%

Turn the adjuster clockwise to enrich the mixture and vice versa. Do not adjust by more than one notch before rechecking the CO content at idling speed. If adjustment by three notches in either direction does not bring the CO content within limits, have the basic range of the injector pump reset by a Porsche agent.

Microswitch adjustment:

Adjustment is necessary if the throttle valve linkage or the injector pump linkage has been disturbed.

1 Refer to **FIG 2 : 13** and loosen locknut A. Back off the adjuster screw B until there is a small gap between the microswitch plunger and the adjuster screw.
2 Slowly turn the adjuster screw clockwise from this position until the microswitch just closes (listen for the click sound).
3 On **1972 and later models**, turn the adjuster screw clockwise by a further $\frac{1}{4}$ turn. On models **prior to 1972**, turn the adjuster screw by a further $\frac{1}{2}$ to $\frac{3}{4}$ turn. Retighten the locknut.

Removing the injector pump:

1 Disconnect the earth straps from both batteries. Remove the air cleaner. Turn the crankshaft to bring the piston of No 1 cylinder (lefthand rear) to the TDC of its exhaust stroke. Continue turning in the direction of engine rotation to bring the crankshaft pulley F-E mark into alignment with the notch on the cooling fan casing as shown in **FIG 2 : 14**.
2 Identify and disconnect the wiring from the microswitch, the enrichment and the cut-off solenoids. Uncouple the thermostat warm air hose.
3 Disconnect the six injection pipelines, the fuel inlet and return lines, the oil feed and return lines and the linkage between the guide shaft and the governor. Using special tool P120b, remove the pump retaining nuts.
4 Push the toothed belt off the pump wheel and, unless the engine is being dismantled, secure it so that it does not disengage from the camshaft wheel. Taking care not to handle the pump by the barometric cell, lift out the pump.

FIG 2 : 13 Microswitch adjustment

Key to Fig 2 : 13   A Locknut   B Adjuster screw

FIG 2 : 14   The F-E mark on the crankshaft pulley

FIG 2 : 15   The F-E mark on the injection pump pulley (viewed by using a mirror)

FIG 2:16 Diagrammatic layout of continuous injection system (CIS)

Key to Fig 2:16 1 Fuel tank   2 Fuel pump   3 Accumulator   4 Filter   5 Mixture control/distributor   6 Cold start enrichment valve   7 Throttle valve control pressure regulator   8 Warm running compensation control pressure regulator   9 Injection valves   10 Auxiliary air device   11 Fuel return connection

Refitting the injector pump:

1 Lay the pump on its side and pour 300cc ($\frac{1}{2}$ pint) of clean engine oil into the oil return pipe orifice (top hole).

2 Set the pump to its F-E mark (when the pump is in position this may be checked by mirror as shown in **FIG 2:15**). Set the crankshaft as described in operation 1 of the pump removal sequence and as shown in **FIG 2:14**.

3 Install the pump and fit the retaining nuts loosely. Fit the toothed belt. Push the pump sideways using tool P234b until the belt is tensioned correctly (6 to 8mm (0.25 to 0.33in) deflection at the centre of the belt under thumb pressure). Tighten the retaining nuts fully.

4 Refit the fuel and oil lines. Reconnect the wiring to the solenoids and the microswitch. Refit the warm air hose to the thermostat housing.

2:9 Bosch fuel injection (CIS)

The layout of the continuous injection system is shown in **Chapter 1, FIG 1:1** and in **FIG 2:16**. An electrically driven pump draws fuel from the tank and delivers it via an accumulator and filter to the fuel mixture control/distributor unit from which metered fuel (depending upon the control pressure) is piped to the injection valves. An injection valve is positioned adjacent to the inlet valve of each cylinder. Excess fuel is returned to the tank. Cold starting enrichment is provided by a supplementary injection of fuel into the intake manifold.

The accelerator pedal is coupled to the throttle valve and the continuous injection fuel supply is controlled by the throttled rate of air flow which lifts the sensor plate accordingly. The sensor plate lever is pivoted and counterbalanced and in contact with the control plunger of the mixture control/distributor unit. It finds a position in which the forces from the air flow, the controlled fuel pressure acting on the plunger and the counterweight are in balance. At this position the fuel flow is correct for the throttled rate of air and the engine load condition.

During initial running after starting, enrichment is provided for a limited period. This is controlled by the warm running compensation pressure regulator in which either the gradual warming up (electrically) of a bi-metal control gradually reduces the control pressure and cuts out the enrichment, or by an intake manifold depression controlled valve which operates similarly. Excess fuel is then returned to the tank. The throttle actuated pressure regulator operates similarly but controls the pressure of the fuel in relation to the throttle opening. Excess fuel is returned to the tank. The auxiliary air device opens at high manifold depression (overrun conditions) and, by admitting additional air, maintains a combustible mixture and prevents excessively high levels of CO content in the exhaust gases.

The function of the fuel accumulator is to accommodate the initial pressure surge when the pump starts up and so prevents the mixture control/distributor unit control plunger from being loaded before control pressure has built up. It also serves as a reservoir to maintain adequate pressure for a short time when the engine is switched off and so prevents vapour locks in a warm engine.

Since specialised experience and equipment are needed for diagnostic investigation of malfunctioning, the procedures prescribed for action by owners are limited. No procedures are prescribed for the repair or overhaul of defective CIS units by an owner and units which have been diagnosed as defective by a Porsche agent should be removed and replaced by new or exchange replacement units. Where relevant, removal and fitment procedures are described later.

Adjusting idling speed and fuel mixture:

1 Run the engine up to normal operating temperature. Close the hand throttle fully and switch off the engine. Remove the filter element from the air cleaner. Connect in the exhaust gas CO content tester.

2 If an emission control air injection system is fitted, uncouple the air delivery hose at the air pump and blank off the open end of the hose.

3 Start up the engine and refer to **FIG 2:17**. By turning the air bypass screw as shown in the illustration, adjust the idling speed to between 850 and 950 rev/min in the case of manual transmission models or to between 900 and 1000rev/min the case of Sportomatic transmission models. If difficulty is experienced in setting the idling speed, check for a defective auxiliary air device as described later.

4 Refer to **FIG 2:18** and, after withdrawing the blanking off plug, insert fuel mixture adjusting tool P377 as shown. Turning the tool clockwise will enrichen the mixture and vice versa.

5 Without exerting downwards pressure upon the adjusting tool (this will cause the engine to stall), turn the tool in the relevant direction by extremely small amounts until the exhaust gas CO content is within the limits quoted in operation 6.

6 If more than $\frac{1}{2}$ turn of the adjuster in either direction is required, consult a Porsche agent as a malfunction should be suspected. The adjusted CO content of the exhaust gases should be within the following limits for the relevant model:

1973 (2.4 litre models)	1.5 to 2.0%
1974 (2.7 litre models)	1.5 to 2.0%
1975 USA models	1.7 to 2.2%
California	1.5 to 2.0%
European models	2.0 to 2.5%
1976 USA models (air pump	
disconnected)	2.0 to 4.0%
European models ..	1.0 to 1.5%
1977 European models	1.0 to 1.5%
USA models, California and high altitude States with air pump disconnected ..	1.5 to 3.0%

FIG 2:17 Adjusting the air bypass screw

FIG 2:18 Adjusting the idling speed fuel mixture

FIG 2:19 Full power throttle position

FIG 2:20   Microswitch adjustment

FIG 2:21   The auxiliary air device

FIG 2:22   Bleeding the system and checking the sensor lever movement

Key to Fig 2:22   **A** Fuel feed to mixture control/ distributor unit   **B** Wire bow

7 Repeat operations 3 and 5 until the idling speed and exhaust gas CO content are both within the ranges specified. Disconnect the CO tester, reassemble the air cleaner and, if relevant, refit the hose to the air pump.

Adjustment of full power throttle position:

When the accelerator pedal is fully depressed, the throttle linkage must be so adjusted that there is a minimum clearance of 1.0mm (0.04in) at the position which is indicated in **FIG 2:19**.

Microswitch adjustment:

On relevant models refer to **FIG 2:20**. Identify and disconnect both wires from the microswitch. Connect a battery and buzzer or battery and test light to the micro-switch connections so that when the switch is closed the buzzer will sound or the test light will come on. Position a 2mm (0.08in) feeler gauge between the idle stop and the throttle valve lever as shown in the illustration.

Turn the adjuster screw as shown until the buzzer or the test light is off. Turn the adjuster back just to the on position of the switch. Remove the feeler gauge and close the throttle valve. Check that there is still at least 0.5mm (0.02in) clearance in this position. Check that with the hand throttle fully open, the microswitch is in the on position. Disconnect the test wiring and reconnect the operational wiring.

Auxiliary air device:

With the engine at normal operating temperature, note the idling rev/min. Stop the engine and remove the air cleaner element. Refer to **FIG 2:21** and disconnect the hose (see arrow) leading to the auxiliary air device at the throttle valve. Tightly seal off both the connection and the hose. Refit the air cleaner element and cover. Recheck the idling speed. If the idling speed has changed, the auxiliary air device is leaking and a new unit should be fitted.

Bleeding the fuel lines:

The system must be bled (prior to attempting to start the engine) whenever a fuel line or a component of the fuel system has been reconnected. Proceed as follows.

Remove the air cleaner element. Switch on the ignition so that the fuel pump runs. Refer to **FIG 2:22**. Press the air sensor lever upwards briefly so that the fuel lines are filled and the injection valves are heard to spray fuel.

Refit the air cleaner element and cover.

Sensor lever free movement:

If sluggish movement of the sensor lever is suspected, carry out the following check. Remove the air cleaner element and, with the ignition switched **off**, raise the lever by hand as indicated in **FIG 2:22**. An even resistance should be felt through the full range of movement and, on removing the pressure, the lever should drop without resistance (leaving the correctly sluggish control plunger to follow).

Sensor plate/venturi position:

Depressurise the system by spilling fuel from the pressure lines at the accumulator and at the connection arrowed A in **FIG 2:22**. The upper edge of the sensor plate should now be flush with the bottom of the venturi upper taper or, at most, 0.5mm (0.020in) below this point. The flexible stop may be adjusted by carefully bending the wire bow arrowed B in **FIG 2:22**. From April 1976 production this wire bow has been replaced by an adjusting screw.

Mixture control removal and fitment:

The mixture control/distributor unit is 25 in **FIG 1:1** and 5 in **FIG 2:16**. Disconnect the fuel lines from the unit. Remove the six Allen type retaining bolts and lift off the unit and its gasket. Take care that the control plunger does not slide out.

When refitting, use a new gasket and finally bleed the system.

Throttle control pressure regulator removal and fitment:

This regulator is 2 in **FIG 1:1** and 7 in **FIG 2:16**. Disconnect the fuel lines. Remove the Allen type bolts and withdraw the throttle valve housing and regulator. Remove the two Allen-type bolts and separate the regulator from the throttle housing.

Refitting is the reverse of this sequence. Ensure that the housing 'O' ring is correctly positioned. Bleed the system and have the control pressure checked and adjusted by a Porsche agent.

Warm running compensating pressure regulator removal and fitment:

Electrically controlled unit:

This regulator is 5 in **FIG 1:1** and 8 in **FIG 2:16**. Disconnect the earth strap from both batteries. Identify and disconnect the wiring from the regulator. Uncouple the fuel lines. Remove the Allen-type retaining bolts. Dismount the unit.

Vacuum controlled unit:

Disconnect the battery and the warm air intake connection. Release fuel pressure by loosening the central connection at the mixture control unit, soak up escaping fuel with rag, and retighten the connection. Remove the air pump and filter. Remove left and right heater hoses, undo the heater blower clip and swing the blower upwards. Disconnect all connections to the regulator, unscrew the Allen screws and lift off the regulator.

Ensure the bottom of the regulator and holding plate are clean on refitment to ensure proper ventilation and torque tighten the hollow banjo bolt to 1.1kgm (8lb ft).

On completion of refitment, bleed the system.

Cold start enrichment valve removal and fitment:

This valve is 4 in **FIG 1:1** and 6 in **FIG 2:16**. Disconnect the earth strap from both batteries. Dismount the auxiliary air device (10 in **FIG 2:16**). Before disconnecting, identify the disposition of the connector. Remove the Allen-type retaining bolts, withdraw the valve and uncouple the fuel line.

On refitment ensure that the 'O' ring is correctly seated and that the electrical connector is the correct way round. Bleed the system.

FIG 2:23   Fuel tank filter (CIS models)

Key to Fig 2:23   1 Fuel tank   2 Gasket   3 Filter plug

Fuel filter removal and fitment:

The filter is retained by an encircling clamp which, on refitment, must not be overtightened or the filter body may be deformed.

Fuel tank filter plug:

This unit is shown in **FIG 2:23**. The frequency of cleaning this filter will depend upon the standards of cleanliness of the fuel supplies in the country in which the vehicle is operating. On refitment of the filter plug use a new gasket 2 and torque tighten the plug to 0.8 to 0.9kgm (5.8 to 6.5lb ft).

Pressure accumulator removal and fitment:

This unit is shown in **FIG 2:24**. It is retained by an encircling clamp and is fitted between the pump and the in-line filter. To dismount, loosen the mounting clamp, withdraw the unit and uncouple the fuel pipes.

On completion of refitment, bleed the system.

FIG 2:24   Fuel accumulator. The connections are arrowed

Injection valve removal and fitment:

Uncouple the line from the injection valve and fit tool P384. Pull out the valve. Check that the rubber bushing is in good order.

To refit, push in the valve and make sure that the rubber bushing is seated below the bulge in the support sleeve. Refit the pipeline and bleed the system.

Plastic fuel lines:

To remove an unserviceable plastic fuel line, use a soldering iron, heat the fuel line in the connector area and pull off the hose.

Use tool P385 to fit new plastic hose to a connector allowing the push-on section to protrude from the tool. Push the **dry and unlubricated** hose onto the connector.

2:10 Fault diagnosis

It is assumed that the sparking plugs are in good order and that the valve clearances, ignition system and timing, idling speed, etc. are all correctly adjusted and that electrical power is available to all relevant units. Check these basic requirements before consulting the fault diagnosis lists.

Lists (a) to (e) apply to **all models**; lists (f) to (h) relate to **carburetter models** only; lists (j) to (n) are only relevant to **FIP models** and lists (p) to (t) are applicable to **CIS models** only.

All models:

(a) Insufficient fuel delivered

1 Tank air vent restricted
2 Fuel feed pipe blocked
3 Air leak in feed to fuel pump
4 Fuel filter(s) dirty
5 Fuel pump defective
6 Fuel vapourising in pipeline due to heat

(b) No fuel delivery

1 Check all items in (a)
2 Fuel feed pipe ruptured or disconnected
3 Defective fuel gauge or transmitter (tank empty)
4 Punctured fuel tank (tank empty)

(c) Excessive fuel consumption

1 Leaks at fuel line connections
2 Dirty air cleaner element
3 Excessively high engine temperature
4 Idling speed too high
5 Cold start enrichment not cutting out
6 Brakes binding
7 Tyres under-inflated
8 Vehicle overloaded

(d) Idling speed too high

1 Incorrect adjustment
2 Throttle control sticking
3 Hand throttle incorrectly set
4 Incorrect mixture adjustment
5 Worn throttle valve(s)
6 Worn throttle valve spindle bush(es)
7 Air leaks at manifold joints

(e) Difficult starting

1 Incorrect starting procedure

Carburetter models:

(f) Excessive fuel consumption

1 Check all items in (c)
2 High fuel pump pressure
3 High fuel level in float chamber(s)
4 Air bleed(s) blocked
5 Excessive discharge from accelerator pump(s)

(g) Carburetter flooding

1 Check 2 and 3 in (f)
2 Dirt in needle valve(s)
3 Worn needle valve(s)
4 Defective float(s)

(h) Fuel delivery restricted or nil

1 Check (a) and (b)
2 Needle valve(s) stuck in closed position

FIP models:

(j) Difficult starting

1 Check 1 in (e)
2 Enrichment solenoid defective
3 Defective relay
4 Thermoswitch defective
5 Control rod setting incorrect

(k) Rough idling

1 Check 1, 4, 5, 6 and 7 in (d)
2 Restricted warm air flow to thermostat
3 Thermostat defective
4 Injection valve(s) defective
5 Compression varies between cylinders

(l) Excessive fuel consumption

1 Check (c); 2 and 3 in (k)
2 Injection pump basic setting incorrect
3 Defective injection pump
4 Linkage incorrectly set

(m) Poor acceleration transition, backfiring

1 Check 2, 3 and 4 in (l)
2 Check synchronisation of throttles

(n) Backfiring on overrun

1 Check 2 in (m)
2 Microswitch requires adjustment
3 Engine speed transducer defective

CIS models:

(p) Difficult starting

1 Check 1 in (e)
2 Incorrect control pressure
3 Defective cold start enrichment valve
4 Microswitch inoperative
5 Sensor plate datum setting incorrect
6 System requires bleeding

(q) Rough idling

1 Check 1, 4, 5, 6 and 7 in (d) ; 2 and 3 in (p)
2 Auxiliary air device defective
3 Warm running compensation pressure regulator defective
4 Injection valve(s) defective
5 Excessive difference in injection valve opening pressures
6 Compression varies between cylinders

(r) Excessive fuel consumption

1 Check (c) ; 2 and 3 in (p) ; 3 in (q)
2 Mixture control/distributor unit plunger tight

3 Sensor plate lever pivot tight or seized
4 Defective throttle valve control pressure regulator
5 Basic adjustment too rich

(s) Poor performance, backfiring

1 Check 2, 3 and 4 in (r)
2 Check for air leaks after sensor plate venturi position
3 Basic adjustment too weak

(t) Engine 'diesels'

1 Check 3 in (p) ; 2 and 3 in (r)

NOTES

CHAPTER 3

THE IGNITION SYSTEM

3:1 Description

The distributor is driven by 2:1 skew gearing from the rear of the crankshaft (see **Chapter 1, FIG 1:2**, item 18). HT to the distributor is provided by a capacitive discharge system (CDS) which replaces the ignition coil of the conventional earlier system. CDS provides higher voltage for starting with negligible voltage drop at high speeds and greatly reduced wear of the distributor contact breaker points.

The components of the system are shown in **FIG 3:1** and a schematic wiring diagram in **FIG 3:2**. The housing of the CDS unit is made from light alloy, cast with cooling fins to help dissipate heat generated by the system. The voltage transformer looks very similar to a conventional coil, but the resistance, voltage gain ratio and inductivity differ completely and the transformer is designed and constructed to match the electrical characteristics of the CDS unit.

Refer to **FIG 3:2**. When the ignition is switched on the DC converter 5 increases the battery voltage from 12 volts to 450 volts and charges the storage capacitor 7 through periodic impulses at a frequency of approximately 3000 Hz, which produces a high pitched whistle in the DC converter. When the contact breaker points

3 open the igniter trigger unit 8 releases an impulse to the thyristor base 9 which becomes conductive. The storage capacitor then discharges through the thyristor and the voltage transformer 10, causing a high voltage surge on the secondary side that is carried through to the distributor and thence to the sparking plugs. With this system the voltage rise at the sparking plug occurs much faster and current losses, that occur with most conventional systems, are virtually eliminated.

Distributors are not identical for all models and may be of either Marelli or Bosch manufacture. A centrifugally actuated switch is built into all distributors and this automatically limits the maximum engine rev/min which can be attained. All distributors incorporate centrifugal automatic advance/retard of the ignition timing while later models also incorporate automatic vacuum advance/retard in addition.

The firing order on all models is 1, 6, 2, 4, 3, 5.

3:2 Maintenance

Distributor contact breaker points:

Every 12,000 miles (20,000km), remove the rotor arm, apply a smear of grease to the surface of the cams, check and adjust, if necessary, the contact breaker points to a

FIG 3:1 Components of Capacitive Discharge System

Key to Fig 3:1   1 CDS unit   2 Voltage transformer
3 Rev/min sensor

FIG 3:2 Schematic wiring diagram of CD system

Key to Fig 3:2   1 Ignition switch   2 Battery   3 Breaker
points   4 CDS unit   5 DC converter (amplifier)   6 Rectifier
7 Storage capacitor   8 Ignition trigger unit   9 Thyristor
(load sensitive switch)   10 Voltage transformer

FIG 3:3 Earlier type Marelli distributor. Removing the
rotor arm

gap of 0.37 to 0.43mm (0.015 to 0.017in). Check the
ignition timing stroboscopically as described in Section
3:6. Adjust if necessary.

The rotor arm on earlier Marelli distributors (not
provided with vacuum advance/retard) is retained by two
screws (see FIG 3:3) and, on later units (with vacuum
advance/retard), by the single screw arrowed in FIG
3:4. Adjustment of the contact breaker points using a
screwdriver and feeler gauges is shown in FIG 3:5 for
the Marelli distributor and in FIG 3:6 for the Bosch
distributor.

Distributor cap and contact breaker:

At regular intervals, remove the cap and clean it
thoroughly. The inside surfaces must be clean and dry.
Check central brush by pressing it in. It should spring out
again. Slight erosion of the brass terminals is normal.

If dirty, clean the contact points with fuel on a cloth.
Slight corrosion may be rectified with a fine file, but the
mating surfaces must be quite flat and must meet
squarely. The best cure for contact breaker troubles is to
fit a new set, as described in Section 3:4.

Sparking plugs and HT leads:

Clean the plugs and reset the gaps every 6000 miles
(10,000km). The procedure is described in Section 3:7.
Depending upon the type of sparking plug in use and
upon how hard the vehicle is driven, the fitment of a new
set of plugs every 12,000 miles (20,000km) may be
desirable.

Keep the HT leads clean and dry at all times and, if
new leads are required, ensure that the instructions in
Section 3:7 regarding their lengths are followed.

3:3 Ignition faults

If the engine runs unevenly, set the hand throttle to
give an engine speed of about 1000rev/min and disconnect and reconnect each HT cable from its sparking
plug in turn. Doing this to a plug which is firing properly
will accentuate the uneven running but it will make no
difference if the plug is not firing. Locate the faulty plug
and, taking care not to touch any metal part of the lead
while the engine is running, remove the insulator. With
the engine running, hold this lead so that the conductor is
about 3mm (0.12in) away from the cylinder head. A
strong, regular spark will confirm that the fault lies with
the sparking plug which should be cleaned or renewed.
If, on the other hand, there is no spark, suspect the cable
or its connection at the distributor cap.

If the spark is weak and irregular, check the condition of
the HT cable and, if it is perished or cracked, renew it.
If no improvement results, check the distributor cap. It
must be clean and dry. Check that good contact is being
made between the centre carbon brush and the rotor
arm and that there is no 'tracking' which will show as a
thin black line between the electrodes or to a metal part in
contact with the cap. 'Tracking' cannot be rectified
except by fitting a new cap.

If the contact breaker points are serviceable and the
gap is correctly set but there is no spark, use a 0 to 20
range voltmeter and check that there is voltage throughout
the LT circuit with the ignition switched on. Trace and

correct any faulty cable, loose connection or defective ignition switch.

If the LT circuit is in order but the trouble persists, refer to **Section 3:5**.

3:4 Distributor

A Marelli or a Bosch distributor may be fitted. All distributors have centrifugal automatic advance/retard and a centrifugally actuated maximum engine speed limiting switch. Distributors fitted to later models also incorporate vacuum automatic advance/retard. The advance/retard characteristics and the maximum engine cut-off speed are not identical for all models and a new or exchange replacement distributor must be of the same type as that originally fitted.

Fitting new points:

FIGS 3:3 and **3:5** show the earlier Marelli (without vacuum advance/retard) distributor. To fit a new set of points, it is necessary to remove the distributor as described later. Remove the rotor. Remove the points complete with the stationary plate.

FIG 3:6 relates to the earlier Bosch (without vacuum advance/retard) distributor. To renew the points, remove the cap and rotor, loosen the terminal assembly nut, remove the moving arm pivot lockring and lift off the arm. Remove the retaining screw and lift out the fixed contact plate.

Fit the new points and set the gap. Refit a Marelli unit as described later. In both cases, check and adjust the timing stroboscopically as described in **Section 3:6**.

FIGS 3:7 and **3:8** relate to later (with vacuum advance/retard) Marelli and Bosch distributors respectively. Remove the cap, rotor and dust cover. Disconnect the wire from the contact breaker, remove the arrowed screws and lift out the points assembly.

Fit the new points, set the gap and check and adjust the timing stroboscopically as described in **Section 3:6**.

Distributor removal and fitment:

Refer to **FIG 3:9**. To provide a datum, set the crankshaft pulley Z1 mark as shown at arrow **A** with No 1 piston at TDC of its compression stroke (both valves closed). Remove the cap, wiring and vacuum pipe (if fitted) from the distributor.

Remove the retaining nut arrowed in **FIG 3:5** from earlier units but **do not disturb the long clamp bolt**. Mark the position of the slotted bracket in relation to the crankcase on later units before removing the retaining nut arrowed in **FIG 3:7**. In all cases, note the orientation of the rotor arm before withdrawing the distributor from its location.

Refitment of the original distributor is the reverse of the removal sequence. Use a new seal. Set the rotor to the noted position. Align a later type unit to the mark made before removal. Fit the retaining nut and check and adjust the timing stroboscopically as described in **Section 3:6**.

If a new distributor is being fitted, set the pulley to the datum as described earlier. On earlier units (without vacuum advance/retard), set the rotor arm so that it points in the direction of the rear edge of the blower while inserting the neck of the distributor into the crankcase.

FIG 3:4 Later type Marelli distributor with the rotor arm retaining screw arrowed

FIG 3:5 Adjusting earlier type Marelli distributor points gap. The distributor retaining nut is arrowed

FIG 3:6 Adjusting earlier type Bosch distributor points gap

FIG 3:7   Later type Marelli distributor

Key to Fig 3:7   P Points assembly retaining screws
R Distributor retaining nut

FIG 3:8   Later type Bosch distributor

FIG 3:9   Crankshaft pulley timing marks

Key to Fig 3:9   A TDC mark   B 5° ATDC mark

The arm will move as the gears engage. Slacken the long bolt on the split clamp plate and turn the distributor to the left until the contact breaker just opens. The tip of the rotor arm should then be vertically over a notch on the rim of the distributor body. This position is shown in **FIG 3:10**. Check the timing stroboscopically as described in **Section 3:6**.

In the case of later type distributors (with vacuum advance/retard), proceed similarly but leave the retaining nut (see **FIG 3:7**) loosen and rotate the body in the elongated slot until the points just open. Tighten the retaining nut. Check and adjust the timing stroboscopically as described in **Section 3:6**.

Distributor repair or overhaul:

No procedures are prescribed for the repair or overhaul of a distributor by an owner. A suspect distributor should be passed to a Porsche agent for investigation.

3:5 Capacitive discharge system (CDS)

Precautions:

To ensure personal safety and to prevent damage to the CDS unit, the following rules should be observed when performing tests.

(a) Do not attach instruments or components such as a suppressor, test light or stroboscopic timing light to terminal 15, it carries 460 volts.

(b) The ignition voltage transformer cannot be replaced with a conventional induction coil and neither can it be wired or tested as a coil.

(c) Do not stop the engine by placing a jump wire or any other conductor between terminal 15 and earth.

(d) Disconnect the battery earth straps when working on a CDS unit.

(e) Ensure the ignition is switched off before connecting or disconnecting wires and always make sure the dust cover is properly installed on terminal 15.

(f) If a battery is being recharged in situ, the supply and earth straps must be disconnected.

(g) Do not use a battery boost quick charger to start the engine.

(h) Ensure the battery is properly connected, i.e. positive to positive and negative to negative.

(i) Do not touch the leads of the voltage transformer shortly after its removal, there still may be a charge between terminal 'A' and earth which cannot be released by grounding. Do not touch the leads when operating the CDS unit on a test bench or in the car without the transformer; in such cases where the storage capacitor is defective due to an inter-terminal short.

Checking the system in the vehicle:

1 First check the breaker points and all electrical connections.

2 Switch on the ignition. The CDS unit should make a whistling sound; if not, remove the connection from the CDS unit and connect a voltmeter between terminal 'B' (centre terminal of connector) and earth. With the ignition switched on it should read at least 11 volts. It is possible for this reading to be recorded and there is still no whistling sound when the connector is re-plugged in. In these instances and where there is no reading, the CDS unit must be renewed.

3 If the whistle is audible, check terminal 4 for high voltage by disconnecting the HT lead from the voltage transformer and connecting a spark monitor, adjusted to a 10mm (0.40in) spark gap. Crank the engine with the starter and if there is no spark, or if it occurs only infrequently, complete checks 4 and 5.

4 Remove all connections from the transformer. With an ohmmeter measure the resistance in the primary coil between terminals 1 and 15. It should be between 0.4 and 0.6 ohms. Measure the resistance in the secondary coil between terminals 1 and 4; the value should be between 650 and 790 ohms.

5 Check the CDS unit current draw. Connect an ammeter into wire 15, at the coupling from the ignition switch. Disconnect the distributor terminal 1 wire to prevent an incorrect reading. The current draw should be between 1.0 and 1.9amps. If not, renew the CDS unit. Voltage at the unit between terminal 'B' and earth must be at least 11 volts, this can be measured by connecting an additional voltmeter between the ammeter input (+ terminal) and earth. After completing the test, reconnect the distributor terminal 1 wire.

6 The rev/min sensor can be checked only with an ohmmeter. The measured resistance between terminals 'A' and 'B' must be within a range of 170 to 210 ohms and between terminals 'A' and 'C' 200 to 300 ohms.

3:6 Ignition timing

Static timing with a test lamp:

If, on refitting the distributor as described in **Section 3:4**, the engine will not start because the ignition timing has been 'lost'; retime the ignition as follows:

1 Set the crankshaft pulley to the datum described in **Section 3:4**. Remove the distributor cap and the wiring from the distributor body. Check that the points gap is correctly set.

2 Connect a separate battery/test lamp across the contact breaker points so that the light is on when the points are closed and off when the points are open. In the case of earlier distributors, loosen the long bolt on the split clamp. On later units, loosen the retaining nut arrowed **R** in **FIG 3:7**.

3 With the rotor arm pointing towards the position which is occupied by the No 1 cylinder cap segment when the cap is fitted, turn the distributor body clockwise until the test lamp comes on.

4 Slowly turn the distributor body anticlockwise and stop immediately the test light goes out. Tighten the split clamp bolt or, on later units, the retaining nut.

5 Disconnect the test lamp, reconnect the distributor wiring and fit the cap. Check the timing under a stroboscopic light and adjust as necessary.

Dynamic timing with a stroboscopic light:

Follow the manufacturer's instructions and connect up a stroboscopic light triggered to No 1 cylinder so that it illuminates the crankshaft pulley (the area shown in **FIG 3:9**). Run the engine up to normal operating temperature and switch on the stroboscopic light.

With the vacuum line connected (later models), run the engine at 850 to 950rev/min and, after slightly loosening the clamp bolt or, on later models, the nut arrowed in **FIG 3:7**, turn the distributor body until the

FIG 3:10 Distributor timing marks

arrow (**A** or **B**) specified in **Technical Data** for the relevant model appears to align with the stationary datum mark. Tighten the clamp bolt or the retaining nut.

Disconnect the vacuum line (later models) and run the engine up to 6000rev/min. If necessary, readjust the distributor to within the timing range quoted in **Technical Data** for the relevant model. If the adjustment required is more than two or three degrees, some slight malfunctioning of the advance/retard mechanism(s) is indicated and it may be considered desirable to have the distributor investigated by a Porsche agent.

3:7 Sparking plugs and HT leads

Recommended types:

A selection of officially recommended plugs is listed in the **Technical Data** section of the **Appendix**. If the types quoted are not available, consult the manufacturer's lists for equivalent alternatives.

Cleaning, testing, and refitting:

Every 6000 miles (10,000km), have the sparking plugs cleaned on an abrasive-blasting machine and tested under pressure with the gaps correctly set at 0.55mm (0.022in). The gaps must always be adjusted by bending the earth electrode. **Do not attempt to bend the centre electrode or the insulation will be damaged.**

When refitting sparking plugs coat the plug threads with a molybdenum paste (MOLYKOTE HTP-White or similar) and torque tighten to 2.5 to 3.0kgm (18 to 22lb ft).

Plugs as a tuning guide:

Inspection of the deposits on electrodes can be helpful as a tuning guide. Normally, from mixed periods of high and low speed driving, the deposits should be powdery and range in colour from brown to greyish tan. There will also be some slight wear of the electrodes. Long periods of fairly constant speed driving or low speed city driving will produce white or yellowish deposits. Dry, black fluffy deposits are due to incomplete combustion and indicate running with a rich mixture, excessive idling and, possibly, defective ignition. Overheated plugs have a white or light grey look round the centre electrode and the electrodes themselves will appear bluish and burnt. This may be due to weak mixture, poor cooling, incorrect ignition timing or sustained high speed running with a heavily loaded vehicle. Black, wet deposits result from oil in the combustion chambers from worn pistons, rings, valve stems or guides or from worn and scored cylinder bores. Sparking plugs which run hotter may alleviate this problem temporarily but the cure is in an engine overhaul.

HT leads:

When renewing HT leads, use only the best quality of cable. Cut the cable to the **same length as the original lead** and ensure that the different lengths are connected to the relevant distributor cap positions. Check that the connections are well made at both the cap and at the plug connector.

3:8 Fault diagnosis

(a) Engine will not fire

1 Battery discharged
2 Distributor points dirty, pitted or out of adjustment
3 Distributor cap dirty, cracked or 'tracking'
4 Centre contact not touching rotor arm
5 Faulty wire or loose connection in LT circuit
6 Rotor arm defective
7 Defective CDS component
8 Broken contact breaker spring
9 Contact breaker points stuck open
10 Defective ignition switch

(b) Engine misfires

1 Check 2, 3, 5 and 7 in (a)
2 Weak contact breaker spring
3 HT cable cracked or perished
4 Sparking plug(s) loose
5 Sparking plug insulation defective
6 Sparking plug gaps incorrectly set
7 Ignition timing too far advanced
8 Fouled sparking plug(s)
9 HT cables incorrectly connected

CHAPTER 4

COOLING, HEATING AND EMISSION CONTROL SYSTEMS

4 : 1 The cooling system

The engine cooling air is produced by the rear entry, belt-driven, ducted fan blower as shown in **Chapter 1, FIG 1 : 2**. The air is blown forwards into a shroud which extends across the engine and carries it to the two banks of cylinders and cylinder heads. The profiled outline of the shroud is shown immediately above the crankcase and cylinders in **Chapter 1, FIG 1 : 1**. After passing across the fins of the cylinders and heads, a proportion of the air is deflected upwards by deflector pieces.

It will be noted that the hub of the fan is keyed to the alternator drive shaft and that the belt drives both the fan and the alternator.

Maintenance:

This is confined to adjustment of the driving belt for the blower and alternator. The method is shown in **FIG 4 : 1**.

Check the tension by pressing the belt inwards about midway between the pulleys. Light thumb pressure should deflect it 15 to 20mm (0.60 to 0.80in). A belt which is too tight puts a greater strain on the alternator bearings and is more liable to break. A slack belt may slip, causing overheating problems and lowering the output from the alternator.

To adjust the tension, remove the nut from the blower pulley shaft. A steel bar with pegs, similar to tool No P208, can be used to engage the holes in the pulley flange to hold it still. Remove the washer and any spacers which may be fitted. Remove the belt flange.

Removal of spacers from between the pulley flanges will tighten the belt and vice versa. Spacers from between the flanges must be added to those outside so that the total number of washers remains unaltered. A belt which is so stretched or worn that only one spacer remains between the flanges must be renewed. A belt must not run on the bottom of the pulley groove.

Tighten the pulley nut to 4kgm (29lb ft) torque. Check the belt tension. If a new belt is fitted, check the tension after 50 miles of running, as the belt will stretch slightly.

Never remove a belt by levering it over the pulley with a screwdriver. Belts contaminated with oil may be cleaned in a detergent solution and rinsed in water. Any signs of cracking or of frayed edges call for renewal of the belt.

Removing and refitting blower:

The blower is mounted on the alternator shaft and the assembly must be removed complete (engine in or out of car). Details of the mounting can be seen in **FIG 1 : 2**.

FIG 4:1 The tension of the blower belt is adjusted by altering the number of washers between the pulley flanges

Proceed as follows:

1 Remove screws securing upper air channel. Remove the belt as described earlier.

2 Slacken the clip surrounding the blower housing. Pull the housing and alternator to the rear. Identify the cables for correct position before detaching them from alternator.

3 Refit in the reverse order, making sure that the dowel for the blower housing is correctly located.

Removal and fitment of shrouds, deflectors, etc:

Remove the air cleaner canister. Depending upon the fuel system, remove the carburetters, the intake housing or the intake down pipes together with the fuel pipes, vacuum pipes, controls and relevant wiring. Remove the rear coverplate and any fuel pipes which pass over the blower housing. Remove the air hoses to the heat exchangers and the hot air ducts on both sides of the engine. Remove the front coverplates. Remove the side coverplates.

The deflector plates or shrouds between the cylinders cannot be withdrawn until the camshaft housings are removed (see **Chapter 1, Section 1:4**). These plates are held in place with spring clips.

When refitting the shrouds, ensure that the spring clips hold them securely. Secure the coverplates so that there are no gaps where air can leak out and reduce the cooling efficiency.

4:2 The heating system

The layout of the heating system is shown in **FIG 4:2**. Fresh air is drawn in by the engine cooling blower 2. A proportion of this air is diverted by offtake pipes 3 to the heat exchangers 4. Engine exhaust gases traverse the heat exchangers before passing to the exhaust silencers 6. Connecting hoses duct heated air to spill-valve control boxes 8 from which, depending upon the setting(s) of the hand control(s), the warmed air passes via ducts and air silencers to the various distribution points in the interior of the vehicle. The silencers, heat exchangers and ductings as fitted to later type models are shown in **FIG 4:3**.

Air passes through the heat exchangers whenever the engine is running. Control of its distribution to the interior of the vehicle is by manually opening or closing the control valves and allowing less or more warmed air to be spilled overboard. A single hand lever control for the spill valves is fitted to earlier models while, on later models, twin hand levers as shown in **Chapter 2, FIG 2:3**, are provided. Automatic control may be fitted in some models.

The auxiliary self-powered heater 16 in **FIG 4:2** may, when required, be switched in to supplement the primary heater system.

FIG 4:2 How heated air is supplied to the car interior. The heavier arrows indicate hot air after it has left the heat exchangers

Key to Fig 4:2 1 Slots in rear engine hood   2 Cooling air blower   3 Offtake pipes   4 Heat exchangers   5 Exhaust pipes   6 Silencer   7 Connecting hoses   8 Heat control box   9 Heater pipe   10 Air silencer   11 Windshield defroster nozzle   12 Rear window defroster nozzle   13 Sliding valves   14 Fresh air unit   15 Pivoted lever   16 Self-powered heater   17 Air intake for self-powered heater

FIG 4:3 Components of the exhaust and heater systems

Key to Fig 4:3   1 Clamp   2 Hose   3 Clamp   4 Hose   5 Clamp   6 Adaptor   7 Screw   8 Clamp   9 Blower
10 Screw   11 Washer   12 Bolt   13 Washer   14 Adaptor   15 Clamp   16 Hose   17 Bolt   18 Lockwasher   18a Washer
19 Bracket   20 Nut   21 Bolt   22 Gasket   23 Screw   24 Clamp   25 Silencer   26 Nut   27 Bolt   28 Primary
silencer   29 Gasket   30 Gasket   31 Nut   32 Bolt   33 Clamp   34 Flange   35 Seal   36 Disc   37 Nut   38 Bolt   39 Pipe
40 Gasket   41 Clamp   42 Hose   43 Screw   44 Washer   45 Clamp   46 Adaptor   47 Heat exchanger   48 Strap

FIG 4:4 Control cable equaliser. The spring clip is arrowed

FIG 4:5 Heater system spill valve

FIG 4:6 Diagrammatic layout of the air injection system (earlier models)

Key to Fig 4:6   1 Air filter   2 Air pump   3 Regulator (pressure relief and check valves)   4 Exhaust port   5 Cylinder head
6 Silencer   7 Inlet manifold   8 Intake stacks   9 Throttle valve   10 Compensator dashpot   11 Distributor

Silencers and heat exchangers:

The relative position of the silencer(s) and heat exchangers is shown in **FIG 4 : 3**. Reference may also be made to **Chapter 1, FIG 1 : 2**.

Note that the main silencer is supported by retaining clips. To dismount the silencer, remove the flange bolts and the bolts from the support clips. Check the unit for cracks, corrosion and deterioration. Do not attempt to salvage a defective silencer but obtain a replacement of the appropriate type. On refitment, use new gaskets and ensure that the flange joints are well made. Tighten the flange bolts gradually and alternately and, after running the engine up to full operating temperature, recheck the joints.

To remove the heat exchangers, detach their air intake pipes and the hoses which connect between the exchangers and the heater control boxes. Withdraw the exhaust flange bolts. Remove the mounting bolts and lift out the units. Inspect carefully for cracks, corrosion and damage. This inspection is particularly important to preclude the possibility of contaminated heated air being distributed to the interior of the vehicle. On refitment, use new gaskets and follow the procedure described earlier for the silencer(s).

Heating system control(s):

FIG 4 : 4 shows the arrangement on earlier models in which the single hand lever operates the cables which control the position of the spill valves. One of the spill valves is shown in **FIG 4 : 5**. On later models, each of the two hand levers operates a cable and the equaliser arrangement is eliminated.

Adjustment, if required to compensate for control cable stretch, is carried out at the spill valves by loosening the cable clamp nut, repositioning the cable and re-tightening the clamp nut. Adjustment is best carried out with the valve in the position shown in the illustration (open). Operate the hand lever and check that the valves close fully on the 'on' position(s).

The procedure for dismantling the hand control(s) is included in **Chapter 11, Section 11 : 8**. On reassembly, reset the pivotal friction of the lever(s) by tightening nut **C** in **Chapter 2, FIG 2 : 3** until a load of 10kg (22lb) applied at the clevis pin hole and at right angles to the below-floor lever(s) is required to move the hand lever in its pivot.

4 : 3 Exhaust emission control

By injecting air into the incandescent exhaust gases immediately after they leave the engine cylinders, combustion of unburned hydrocarbons is encouraged and the final exhaust gases when they leave the exhaust pipe contain less carbon monoxide (but more of the less noxious carbon dioxide) than would be the case with untreated exhaust gases.

The layout of the system as applied to earlier carburetter fuel system models is shown diagrammatically in **FIG 4 : 6**. The components of the system as fitted to later models are shown in **FIG 4 : 7**.

Refer to **FIG 4 : 6**. An engine driven pump 2 provides pressure air to a regulating control valve assembly 3. This assembly incorporates a relief pressure valve and, for each bank of cylinders, a non-return valve. The relief

valve releases excess air back to atmosphere. The non-return valves prevent exhaust gases passing into the air system should air pressure fail due to a broken pump driving belt or to a defective pump. On relevant models, a throttle compensator dashpot is fitted. This limits the rate of closing of the throttles irrespective of the rate at which the accelerator pedal is released. This precludes excessively rich mixture being fed to the engine under overrun conditions and provides a more readily combustible mixture.

On earlier models the emission control air pump is driven from a pulley on the rear end of the lefthand camshaft. On later models (see **FIG 4 : 7**), the air pump is driven from a pulley attached to the alternator/cooling fan pulley.

On 1975 models with California equipment where the nitrogen oxide (NOx) content of the exhaust gases has to be reduced an exhaust gas recirculation system (EGR) is installed to dilute the fuel/air mixture during partial throttle positions.

An EGR valve under control of depression in the intake manifold directs exhaust gas from the silencer through a line filter into the intake housing as required.

An elapsed mileage odometer is installed beneath the blower housing to indicate the inspection intervals. The EGR lamp will light up after 30,000 miles have been driven to indicate inspection or replacement is required.

All 1976 models for the USA are fitted with a modified switch. The indicator lamp lights when the ignition is switched on and goes out when the engine starts to indicate serviceability of the bulb.

Maintenance:

Adjust the belt tension if, under thumb pressure at the midway point between the pulleys, the belt can be made to yield by more than 10mm (0.4in) in the case of earlier models, or by more than 15mm (0.6in) in the case of later models. **Do not overtighten the belt**, however, as doing so will stress the pump and alternator bearings. Adjustment is made by loosening the bolt which engages the elongated slot (see **FIG 4 : 8** for earlier models and **FIG 4 : 9** for later models), swinging the pump away from the driving pulley and retightening the adjuster bolt.

Every 6000 to 12,000 miles (10,000 to 20,000km) depending upon how dusty the terrain may be in which the vehicle is operating. Follow the procedure for cleaning the filter as described in **Chapter 2, Section 2 : 3**.

Air pump removal and fitment:

No procedures are prescribed for the repair or overhaul of an air pump by an owner and an unserviceable pump should be removed and a new or an exchange replacement unit fitted.

Loosen the belt adjuster bolt and swing the pump towards the drive pulley. Remove the belt. Remove the pipe(s) from the pump. Withdraw the mounting bolt and lift out the pump. Refitment is the reverse of this sequence. Refit the belt if it is serviceable and tension it as described earlier.

Valves, earlier models:

A defective valve should be replaced by a new or an exchange replacement component. Renewal of minor parts is possible.

FIG 4:7   Components of the air injection system (later models)

Key to Fig 4:7   1 Bolt   2 Washer   3 Washer   4 Drive belt   5 Nut   6 Washer   7 Bracket   8 Rubber mounting
9 Adjuster strap   10 Clamp   11 Hose   12 Nut   13 Washer   14 Washer   15 Bolt   16 Washer   17 Washer
18 Rubber bush   19 Spacer   20 Air pump   21 Nut   22 Filter cover   23 Filter element   24 Filter housing   25 Nut
26 Washer   27 Pulley   28 Drive key   29 Bracket   30 Mounting grommet   31 Non-return valve   32 'O' ring   33 Manifold   34 Jet   35 'O' ring   36 Pulley

Refer to **FIG 4 : 6**, disconnect the hoses, remove the flange bolts and lift the assembly 3 away from the engine rear shield. Remove the two long through bolts and separate the three valve parts.

Check the condition of the flowback and pressure relief valves. Renew worn parts. Renew the rubber diaphragm in the flowback check valve if the edges are torn or frayed. Use new gaskets when reassembling, fitting the valve housings so that their arrows point outwards, with the pressure relief valves pointing downwards.

When refitting the valve assembly, fit new gaskets under the flanges, and new 'O' rings on the relief valve nozzles.

Valves, later models:

A single non-return valve 31 in **FIG 4 : 7** covers the air supply pipe to both banks of cylinders. This valve may be unscrewed from the air manifold after removing hose 11. It is a push fit in the mounting grommet 30. On refitment, use a new 'O' ring 32.

The excess pressure valve is incorporated in the pump and cannot be separately removed or renewed.

Air jets, removal and fitment:

Access to the jets requires removal of the heat exchangers as described earlier and, on earlier models, removal of the valve assembly 3 in **FIG 4 : 6**. Use new 'O' rings on refitment.

Drive pulley removal and fitment, earlier models:

1 Remove the engine transverse support and the silencer. Remove the regulation valve from the rear shield as described earlier.
2 Remove the rear shield and the pump drive belt. Do not lever the belt over the pulley flanges but slacken the pump off the camshaft extension.

When refitting the parts in the reverse order, make sure that the belt is correctly tensioned as described earlier.

Camshaft pulley bearing removal and fitment, earlier models:

This bearing is mounted in the lefthand camshaft chain cover. Remove the pulley as just explained, remove the retaining nuts and withdraw the bearing cover. Use a puller to draw the bearing off the camshaft, after removing the chain cover.

Clean the parts and check condition of bearing when unlubricated. Check the oil seal in the cover and renew if leaking. Lubricate the sealing lip after fitting. Refit the bearing on the camshaft after lubricating.

Fit the chain cover on a new gasket. Fit the bearing cover on a good gasket. Refit the pulley and tension the belt as described earlier.

Servicing the throttle valve compensator and vacuum pipes:

Remove the hose from the compensator (10 in **FIG 4 : 6**). Detach the connecting rod ball joint socket, release the compensator from the mounting bracket and lift away.

The vacuum lines are a push fit on the connections. The pipe from the compensator goes to a T-piece with

FIG 4 : 8 Adjusting the drive belt tension (earlier models)

FIG 4 : 9 Adjusting the drive belt tension (later models)

FIG 4 : 10 Throttle valve compensator

Key to Fig 4 : 10 Upper arrow, adjuster Lower arrow, clearance

FIG 4:11   Fuel tank vapour venting (earlier models)

Key to Fig 4:11   1 Expansion chamber   2 Vent chamber   3 Activated charcoal filter   4 Engine cooling air duct   5 Pressure air pipe   6 Filter to air cleaner pipe

branches to intake ports of cylinders 1 and 3. Branches from cylinders 1 and 4 go to a T-piece which is connected to the distributor vacuum control unit. Check that the pipes are in sound condition.

Adjusting the compensator and its linkage:

Before embarking on any adjustments, check that the ignition timing and idling speed are correctly set. Run the engine up to operating temperature and then check the compensator adjustment as follows.

Shut the throttle quickly from an engine speed of 3000rev/min. Engine speed should then fall to around 1000rev/min within 4 to 6 seconds. If this is not so, loosen the side screw which locks the adjusting screw indicated by the top arrow in **FIG 4:10**. Turn the adjusting screw right in.

Accelerate the engine quickly and shut off to draw the compensator rod up into the device and check the engine speed at once. It should be 2000 to 2200rev/min. If the speed is greater, lengthen the rod; if it is lower, shorten

the rod, but make sure there is always slight clearance between the levers as indicated by the lower arrow when the engine is idling again.

Now adjust the time lag taken for the engine speed to drop. It must lie between 4 and 6 seconds, so turn the adjusting screw to the left to reduce the lag and to the right to increase it. In case of difficulty, check that the compensator is not sticking when the engine oil temperature is at least 90°C (200°F), or the indicator needle is in the green sector. Keeping the time lag to the upper limit will reduce exhaust backfiring to a minimum.

Checking:

Run the engine at a fast-idle until the pipe between the EGR filter and the valve feels hot. Increase engine speed to about 4000rev/min, the pipe between the valve and the intake housing should also heat up. If the pipe does not heat up either the valve is defective in which case it will have to be renewed, there is a blockage in the system or a leak in the vacuum hoses.

FIG 4:12   Fuel tank vapour venting (later models)

Key to Fig 4:12   1 Fuel tank   2 Expansion chamber   3 Activated charcoal filter   4 Engine cooling air duct   5 Pressure air pipe   6 Filter to air cleaner pipe   7 Air cleaner canister   8 Fuel vapour pipe

Removing:

Disconnect the vacuum hoses. Unscrew the outlet pipe union at the valve. Remove the mounting bolts.

Refitting:

Proceed in the reverse order of removal connecting the upper chamber vacuum hose to the lefthand connection on the throttle housing looking from the rear and the lower chamber hose to the other.

Odometer:
Resetting to zero:

Disconnect the battery and remove the tachometer. Using a small tommy bar or similar, press the pin on the housing into the stop.

4:4 Vapour emission control
Engine breathing:

On all models the crankcase is vented to the oil tank and the oil tank is vented to the air cleaner canister (see **Chapter 1, FIGS 1:23, 1:24** and **1:25**). Oil fumes and blow-by gases are consequently consumed in the engine. A flame trap is provided at the crankcase breather outlet. The system ensures that noxious vapour is not discharged to atmosphere.

The flame trap should be cleaned in petrol at intervals of 12,000 miles (20,000km). The breather pipes should be blown through at the same time.

Fuel tank breathing (see FIGS 4:11 and 4:12):

A vented fuel tank filler cap will allow air to enter the tank as fuel is consumed but will not allow fuel vapour to leak to atmosphere. The vapour is vented via a vapour pipe to an activated carbon filter which is connected to the air cleaner canister. Accumulated vapour in the filter is drawn into the air cleaner and consumed in the engine so precluding its discharge to atmosphere. Pressure air from the cooling blower is fed to the filter to assist this flow of vapour.

Every 12,000 miles (20,000km), check that all hoses are securely connected. Every 60,000 miles (100,000km), remove and discard the activated carbon filter and fit a new replacement.

4:5 Fault diagnosis
(a) Engine overheats

1 Blower fan belt requires tensioning
2 Cooling air spilling from joints
3 Deflectors and/or shrouds wrongly fitted
4 Cooling fins (crankcase, oil cooler, cylinder) caked with dirt
5 Exhaust system blocked
6 Fuel system out of tune
7 Ignition timing incorrect

(b) Heating system ineffective

1 Check 1 in (a)
2 Control cables broken or out of adjustment
3 Spill valves stuck open
4 Hoses disconnected or leaking
5 Auxiliary heater defective or inoperative

(c) Vapour emission system ineffective

1 Breather pipe disconnected
2 Breather pipe blocked
3 Flame trap blocked
4 Fuel vapour pipe disconnected or blocked
5 Carbon filter requires renewal

NOTES

CHAPTER 5

THE CLUTCH

5 : 1 Description

5 : 2 Maintenance

5 : 3 The control cable

5 : 4 Removing and refitting the clutch

5 : 5 Servicing the clutch components

5 : 6 Fault diagnosis

5 : 1 Description

The clutch fitted to manual transmission models is of the single dry-plate variety incorporating a diaphragm spring (see **FIG 5 : 1**). The cover 1 is bolted to the front face of the flywheel 10 and carries diaphragm spring 4 on pins and fulcrum rings. The spring bears on pressure plate 2 and spring pressure at points 14 traps driven plate 3 between the faces of the flywheel and the pressure plate. The driven plate is splined to the gearbox input shaft 7 and thus transmits drive from the flywheel to the gearbox. When the clutch pedal is depressed, release bearing 5 presses on the fingers of the diaphragm of the diaphragm spring. As spring pressure on the pressure plate is relieved, the driven plate is no longer trapped, and there is no drive from the flywheel to the input shaft and gearbox. The hub 15 of the driven plate incorporates shock-absorbing springs to eliminate clutch engagement snatch. Clutches fitted to earlier models are not identical to those fitted to later models.

The clutch is operated by a Bowden-type cable arrangement in which, on earlier models, the outer cable pushes the throwout fork lever but, on later models, the inner cable pulls the fork lever. Referring to **FIG 5 : 2** the forward end of the earlier clutch cable is attached to the pedal by an adjustable fork end, and at the rear end to an integrally cast lug on the transmission housing. The outer cable housing is adjustable and is supported at the centre tunnel rear panel and the clutch throwout fork. It is routed in an upward arc through a guide bracket that prevents the cable moving sideways but allows it to move vertically and towards the throwout fork.

When the pedal is depressed the cable is tensioned and because it is fixed firmly to the transmission housing the pressure is then exerted on the cable housing. The housing reacts against the rear wall of the centre tunnel and is forced to move in the direction of the throwout fork. As it approaches its fully extended condition it reacts also against the throwout fork pushing the end away from the centre tunnel rear panel. When the gap between the end of the fork and the tunnel rear panel has increased by about 15mm (0.60in) the clutch is fully disengaged.

In later models the throwout fork and clutch lever are mounted on a shaft which is splined on both ends and located within the transmission tunnel. The fork is located on the shaft by a roll pin and the lever is secured to the shaft by a lockring and the lever is now pulled by the inner cable instead of being pushed by the cable housing as on earlier models.

1977 models have a servo arrangement where the adjusting lever is splined to the shaft and the release lever is located by a roll pin, an adjusting screw and locknut are located in the release lever.

5:2 Maintenance

Every 6000 miles (10,000km) in the case of earlier models and every 12,000 miles (20,000km) in the case of later models, check and adjust the clutch pedal free play if necessary. The free play at the pedal pad should be

FIG 5:1   Cross-section through clutch assembly

Key to Fig 5:1   1 Cover   2 Pressure plate   3 Driven plate   4 Diaphragm spring   5 Release bearing   6 Crankcase   7 Input shaft to gearbox   8 Release lever   9 Ring gear   10 Flywheel   11 Release lever pivot stud   12 Starter motor pinion   13 Retaining bolt   14 Spring loading points   15 Driven plate hub

within the range of 20 to 25mm (0.80 to 1.00in) on all models. The adjustment procedures are described in **Section 5:3**.

When the limit of adjustment is reached, a new release bearing and/or a new driven clutch plate should be fitted.

5:3 The control cable

Earlier type cable assembly:

The layout of this type of cable is shown in **FIG 5:2**. The cable assembly must be correctly arced so that, when the inner cable is tensioned by operation of the clutch pedal, the outer cable 'straightens' and pushes the clutch release lever. When operated, a correctly set cable assembly will move up and down in the guide bracket between positions indicated at **A** and **B**. The procedure for resetting the arc of the cable assembly is included in the following pedal free play adjustment sequence.

Free play adjustment, earlier type cables:

1 Loosen the cable housing locknut (see **FIG 5:3**) and turn the adjusting nut to obtain a free play in the clutch pedal of 20 to 25mm (0.80 to 1.00in). To check, measure the travel of the pedal as it is pulled upwards. Tighten the locknut without turning the cable housing.

2 When the clutch pedal is fully depressed the throwout fork should move approximately 15mm (0.60in) to disengage the clutch fully. If it does not move this distance the clutch pedal stop must be adjusted.

3 Refer to **FIG 5:2**. If the cable rests at D (the bottom of the guide bracket) when the pedal is fully depressed, adjust the inner cable at the fork end. To check the location of the cable in the fork end, use slide calipers and measure from the end of the cable to the outer face of the locknut as shown in **FIG 5:4**. The correct measurement should be between 17 and 22mm (0.70 and 0.90in).

4 If, after adjusting, the cable still rests on the bottom of the guide bracket, lengthen the inner cable at the fork end.

5 If the arc of the cable is too large with the cable coming out of the top of the guide bracket (C in **FIG 5:2**) in the pedal released position, the inner cable must be shortened at the fork end.

Later type cable assembly:

As indicated in **Section 5:1**, the inner cable is operated by the clutch pedal and actuates clutch release by pulling on the release lever. This arrangement is that usually designed for Bowden-type cables and is not illustrated.

Free play adjustment, later type cables:

Refer to **FIG 5:5**. Using two spanners, hold the cable end while turning the self-locking nut in the appropriate direction to obtain a free travel at the clutch pedal of 20 to 25mm (0.80 to 1.00in) when it is pulled upwards. Operate the clutch pedal a number of times and recheck the pedal free play. No adjustment is required at the pedal end of the cable. If a new cable is fitted, the cable end should be screwed fully into the clevis so that it is flush but does not protrude.

FIG 5:2   Clutch cable assembly (earlier models)

Key to Fig 5:2   A, B, C, D See text

FIG 5:3   Adjusting earlier type cable

Servo type clutch:

Clutch play cannot be measured at the pedal, but is measured at the adjusting and release levers. Check that the clutch cable is tight. Release the locknut on the adjusting screw at the release lever and set the adjusting screw so that there is a clearance of $1.0 + 0.1$mm ($0.040 + 0.004$in) between the screw and the adjusting lever. Tighten the locknut.

5:4 Removing and refitting the clutch

Removal:

Remove the engine and transmission assembly, as described in **Chapter 1, Section 1:3**. On models with the type of fork lever shown in **FIGS 5:2** and **5:3** it is necessary before separating the engine and transmission to release the tension on the throwout bearing and disengage the fork lever as follows:

1 Remove the starter and turn the flywheel to bring one of three equally spaced threaded rivet heads into sight through the starter mounting aperture.
2 Install a spacer sleeve on each of the three rivet heads secured with a M6 × 12 Allen screw. By tightening the three screws evenly, as shown in **FIG 5:6**, the diaphragm spring will be lifted to release the tension on the throwout bearing.

FIG 5:4   Measuring end of cable to outer face of locknut dimension

FIG 5:5   Adjusting later type cable

FIG 5:6 Relieving tension on release bearing. One of the spacers is arrowed

3 Refer now to **FIG 5:7** and with a screwdriver inserted through the opening in the transmission housing, turn the throwout bearing 90° until the throwout fork lever can be slid past the bearing. Remove the three Allen screws and spacers. If the clutch cable is loose detach the cable and adjust play between the adjusting lever and the adjusting screw to 1.2mm (0.047in). Attach the cable and tighten until play is 1.0 + 0.1mm (0.040 + 0.004in).

Support the engine and transmission assembly and remove the nuts, bolts and washers holding the two units together. Taking care not to strain the gearbox input shaft in any direction, separate the transmission from the engine and clutch. Loosen the bolts which attach the clutch assembly to the flywheel by a turn at a time. Work diagonally and evenly and gradually release the spring load. Dismount the pressure plate assembly and the clutch driven plate from the flywheel.

Fitment:

Position the pressure plate assembly and the clutch driven plate on the flywheel. Fit the attachment bolts and their washers but do not tighten them. Align the clutch plate using a stub shaft or a mandrel inserted through the plate hub and into the pilot bearing. Working diagonally and evenly tighten the retaining bolts and finally torque them to 3.5kgm (25lb ft). Remove the centring mandrel and press about 2cc of molybdenum disulphide grease into the bore of the pilot bearing.

On models with the earlier pattern fork lever, refit the three Allen screws and spacers used during removal (stage 2 of removal procedure).

Refit the transmission to the engine as described in **Chapter 6, Section 6:3**.

Where applicable, refer to **FIG 5:8** and use a screwdriver, as shown, to turn and guide the throwout bearing into engagement with the fork lever. Loosen the three Allen screws evenly and remove them and the spacers.

5:5 Servicing the clutch components

Dismantling:

Lay the clutch assembly on the bench with the pressure plate upwards. Press down on the plate and the thrust washer and, using circlip pliers, remove the circlip which retains the release bearing. Take careful note of the washers and which way round they are fitted. Remove the release bearing.

Release bearing:

Do not use petrol or any solvent to clean the release bearing as the prepacked grease must not be washed out. An excessively worn bearing cannot be repaired and should be replaced by a new component of the same part number.

FIG 5:7 Turning the bearing through 90°

FIG 5:8 Turning the bearing into engagement with the fork lever

Diaphragm spring:

Check for wear and cracks. Scoring and wear at the inner ends of the fingers up to a depth of 0.30mm (0.012in) is acceptable. If the spring is cracked or excessively worn, a new or exchange replacement assembly will be required. Ensure that the new clutch is the same type as that removed.

Pressure plate:

Cracks, deep scores or uneven wear dictate rejection and the fitment of a new assembly of the same type as that removed. Concavity across the operating face of up to 0.30mm (0.012in) is acceptable.

Driven plate:

Renew the plate if the linings are broken, burned or contaminated with oil. Do not attempt to clean off contamination. Check for wear and renew the plate if the thickness over the linings is down to 6.5mm (0.25in). Reject the plate if the wear is uneven.

Mount the plate on a mandrel between centres and check the run out with a dial gauge. Maximum permissible runout is 60mm (0.023in). It will be noticed that the steel disc is divided into leaves and the linings are riveted to these alternately. The leaves are bowed and offset to provide a cushioning effect and the offsetting must be evenly balanced.

Check hub splines for wear. The plate should slide freely on the input shaft without undue play. Check the hub shock absorbing springs for wear and breakage.

The linings may have a high polish and be perfectly capable of transmitting power. If the grain of the lining material is visible the linings are good, but if the linings are a dark brown with an opaque glaze, they are probably contaminated with burnt oil and the plate must be renewed. It is not advisable to attempt to rivet new linings into place.

A new replacement plate must be of the correct type. Note, in particular, that the number of splines in the bore of the hub differs between earlier and later type clutches.

Reassembly:

Follow the reverse of the dismantling sequence. Apply molybdenum disulphide grease sparingly to the diaphragm spring finger tips before fitting the release bearing.

5:6 Fault diagnosis

(a) Noisy clutch

1 Worn pilot bush in flywheel boss
2 Worn release bearing
3 Broken springs in driven plate hub
4 Broken driven plate disc or linings

(b) Clutch judder

1 Defective engine and transmission mountings
2 Pressure plate face worn and uneven
3 Diaphragm spring distorted
4 Driven plate disc distorted
5 Grease or oil on linings

(c) Dragging or incomplete release

1 Excessive clutch clearance
2 Driven plate or input shaft running out of true
3 Driven plate segments or linings unevenly set
4 Input shaft spigot bearing tight
5 Stiffness of clutch pedal, cable or release mechanism
6 Sticky linings
7 Distorted clutch cover or pressure plate

(d) Slipping

1 See 3 and 5 in (b)
2 Lack of free play in clutch pedal
3 Linings burned or broken, contact faces defective

NOTES

CHAPTER 6

MANUAL TRANSMISSION

6:1 Description

The manual transmission operates in conjunction with the clutch which is covered in **Chapter 5**. It may have either four speeds and reverse or five speeds and reverse. All forward speeds have synchromesh engagement. Final drive to the rear wheels is through a conventional type of bevel and pinion arrangement and a differential which may be of either conventional design or of a self-locking (limited slip) type. The drive shafts are covered in **Chapter 8, Section 8:4**.

Either of two types of four-speed or either of two types of five-speed gearboxes may be fitted to the models covered by this manual. A cross-section through the earlier five-speed gearbox is included in **FIG 6:1** and through the later type five-speed gearbox in **FIG 6:2**. In each case the later type of gearbox is stiffened to accommodate the higher torques provided by the bigger engines installed in later models. It will be noted that a one-piece transmission casing is provided for the earlier type transmission while, on the later type, the gearbox casing and the final drive/bellhousing casing are separate components. It will also be noted that, as indicated by the position of the ballbearings, the axial location of the input and pinion shafts is, on the later type

gearbox, at the front of these shafts and not, as on the earlier type, at the rear. The speedometer drive arrangement also differs notably between the earlier and later type box. On a later version of the stiffened type gearbox, pressure lubrication is provided by a pump incorporated into the gearbox front cover (see **Section 6:9**). 1976 models incorporate a new guide tube for the clutch release bearing, an easy to remove drive shaft seal, and an electronic speedometer transmitter. 1977 models have modified synchronisation in first and second gears.

The transmission assembly is attached to the forward face of the engine and cannot be removed from the vehicle separately. After removal of the engine and transmission as a unit, the transmission is separated from the engine.

Overall transmission ratios differ between models and special competition and racing ratios have also been produced.

6:2 Maintenance

Every 12,000 miles (20,000km) drain the oil from the transmission and refill with an SAE 90 Hypoid transmission lubricants of reputable brand. In the case of limited slip differentials, refer to **Section 6:6** for

FIG 6:1   Longitudinal section through earlier five-speed manual transmission

Key to Fig 6:1   1 Shift rod   2 Front cover and oil seal   3 Speedometer driven gear   4 Speedometer drive gear   5 Pinion shaft   6 Synchronising ring   7 Spider   8 Shift fork   9 Sliding sleeve   10 Fifth-speed gear   11 Input shaft 12 Differential carrier   13 Spider gear   14 Side gearshaft   15 Oil seal   16, 17 Clutch release bearing   18 Housing 19 Clutch plate splines   20 Pinion shaft gear for first-speed and reverse   21 Intermediate plate   22 Castellated nut   **A** First-speed fixed gear   **B** Second-speed fixed gear   **C** Third-speed fixed gear   **D** Fourth-speed free running gear   **E** Fifth-speed free running gear   **S** Pinion positioning gasket

FIG 6:2   Longitudinal section through later five-speed manual transmission

Key to Fig 6:2   1 Front cover   2 Reverse gear   3 Fifth-speed fixed gear   4 Roller bearing   5 First-speed fixed gear 6 Gearbox casing   7 Second-speed fixed gear   8 Third-speed free running gear   9 Synchronising ring   10 Synchronising hub (spider)   11 Fourth-speed free running gear   12 Ballbearing   13 Roller bearing   14 Flange nut   15 Input shaft 16 Transmission casing   17 Breather   18 Seal   19 Speedometer drive gear   20 Spider, fifth-speed and reverse gears 21 Flange nut   22 Fork, fifth-speed and reverse   23 Fifth-speed free running gear   24 Roller bearing   25 Fork, first-speed and second-speed   26 Selector shaft   27 Bearing retaining plate   28 Ball sleeve   29 Pinion shaft   30 Differential assembly   31 Castellated nut   **S** Pinion positioning shim

70

recommended lubricants. Drain off the old oil while the transmission is hot. Clean the drain plug of any adhering steel particles.

The drain (lower) and filler/level (upper) plugs are located on the lefthand side of the transmission casing just forward of the ribbed differential cover. The correct oil level is up to the bottom of the filler plug orifice. Both plugs should be tightened to a torque of 2.0 to 2.5kgm (14.5 to 18.0lb ft).

6:3 Removing and installing the transmission
Removal:

Remove the engine and transmission unit as described in **Chapter 1, Section 1:3**, taking particular care (see operation 8 of the removal procedure) to check that all pipes, controls and wiring connections which bridge the chassis and engine have been removed, uncoupled or disconnected.

Separation of the transmission from the engine:

With both the engine and the transmission assembly supported, remove the nuts, bolts and washers which attach the transmission casing to the engine. Taking care that the gearbox input shaft is not strained in any direction, separate the transmission from the engine and clutch.

Refitting the transmission to the engine:

Lightly coat the gearbox input shaft splines with multi-purpose grease. Press about 2cc of molybdenum disulphide grease into the bore of the pilot bearing after checking that it is serviceable (see **Chapter 1, Section 1:9**). Ensure that the input shaft is not strained in any direction when entering it into the clutch hub and pilot bearing. Torque tighten the attachment nuts and bolts to 2.5kgm (18lb ft).

Refitting:

Refitting of the engine/transmission unit into the vehicle is the reverse of the removal sequence (see **Chapter 1, Section 1:3**).

6:4 Dismantling the transmissions

Servicing Porsche transmissions demands a high degree of experience and mechanical skill and the use of many special tools not normally available. The relative positions of the pinion and crownwheel (ring gear) must be set with great accuracy. Any error in these settings may lead to rapid tooth wear and noisy running.

Due to manufacturing tolerances, renewal of such parts as the easing(s), the differential carrier, the intermediate plate, the pinion shaft and its bearings and the crownwheel will upset the relative positions just mentioned and it will be necessary to go through the whole procedure for meshing the drive gears. It is possible to dismantle and reassemble the transmission without the need for adjustment, provided that all shims and spacers are refitted in their original positions. It is also possible to renew parts which obviously have no effect upon the meshing of the drive gears.

The following instructions, which are given primarily to help those who have the requisite experience, access to

FIG 6:3 Section through detent components in intermediate plate

Key to Fig 6:3 1 Intermediate plate 2 Fourth and fifth selector shaft 3 Ball 4 Detent bush 5 Detent spring of second- and fifth-speed 6 Detent pin 7 Ball 8 Second and third selector shaft 9 Detent bush 10 Detent pin 11 First and reverse selector shaft 12 Ball 13 Detent bush 14 Detent spring for reverse 15 Plug

FIG 6:4 Section through detent components in gearbox casing

Key to Fig 6:4 1 Gearbox casing 2 Half-round dowel pin 3 Third-speed and fourth-speed selector fork rod 4 Short detent 5 Roll pin 6 Pin 7 Sleeve 8 Spring 9 Long detent 10 Roll pin 11 Fifth-speed and reverse selector fork rod

FIG 6:5   Input shaft section and components (earlier five-speed gearbox)

Key to Fig 6:5   1 Input shaft (with fixed gear for second-speed)   2 Gear of third-speed (fixed)   3 Thrust washer   4 Gear of fourth-speed (free running)   5 Sliding sleeve   6 Spider   7 Gear of fifth-speed (free running)   8 Thrust washer (5.9mm) 9 Roller bearing   10 Nut   11 Oil seal race   12 Splined end for clutch plate   13 Needle bearing inner race   14 Needle bearing cage   15 Brake band   16 Synchronising ring   17 Needle bearing inner race   18 Needle bearing cage   19 Nut lockplate   20 Spigot for flywheel bearing

the necessary tools and to appropriate precision measuring equipment, must be supplemented by the operator's own notes and sketches.

Earlier five-speed gearbox:

1 Drain off the oil and remove starter. Prise up flange caps if fitted. Hold input shaft splines securely and engage fifth gear. Remove the retaining bolts and withdraw the final drive flanges. Remove side cover and withdraw the differential assembly.

2 Remove the support from the front cover 2 (see **FIG 6:1**). Remove front cover with care as reverse gears may fall out. Remove the selector fork screw. Remove the gear and fork.

3 Engage the fifth speed and lock the pinion with tool P37. Remove bolt 22 from pinion shaft. Drive out locking pin from nut, remove the nut and the first speed gear.

4 Select neutral. From the underside of the casing remove the plate and guide fork. Pull out the inner shift rod through the rear access hole. Insert a screwdriver in the guide fork hole and select fifth speed. **Gears cannot be withdrawn or inserted unless transmission is in this position.**

5 Tap the intermediate plate with a soft-faced hammer and detach it complete with gears. **Check gasket thickness for correct assembly.** Hold the plate in a vice with soft jaws and prise off the spider wheel. Remove the first speed gear and needle bearing from the pinion shaft. Shift into neutral.

6 Remove the plug and detent spring (refer to **FIG 6:3**). Withdraw the selector shaft and detent ball for first and reverse gear. Mark the forks to avoid confusion and remove the shafts, forks and detents.

7 Tap the dowels forward and remove the throttle linkage. Place the intermediate plate under a press with gears downwards and press out input and pinion shafts simultaneously. Balls may fall out of input shaft bearing. Prise out the circlips from the centre web if the bearings are to be renewed.

8 Heat the casing to 120°C (248°F) and tap out the bearing races one at a time using tool P254 and a soft-faced hammer.
Clean the parts and check for damage, cracks or wear. Tooth breakage and subsequent jamming may cause casing cracks and possible damage to bearing bores. Check the bearings when clean and dry.

Later five-speed gearbox:

1 Drain off the oil and remove the starter. Use tool P37a to block the input shaft. Engage fifth gear. Refer to **FIG 6:2** and remove the front cover 1.

2 Remove the castellated nut 31 from the input shaft and the flanged nut 21 from the pinion shaft. Identify the needle bearing of the fifth-speed free gear which must be reassembled with the same gear. Remove the guide fork cover and gasket from the bottom of the gearbox casing. **Engage neutral.**

3 Remove the nuts from the casing. Pull the casing and selector fork rod (fifth and reverse) and the selector

72

FIG 6:6 Components of pinion shaft (earlier five-speed gearbox). Numbered items are to rear of intermediate plate

Key to Fig 6:6 1 Thrust washer (6.6mm)   2 Needle bearing inner race   3 Needle bearing cage   4 Second-speed gear (free running)   5 Synchronising assembly   5a Energiser   5b Stop   5c Brake band   5d Synchronising ring   5e Retainer
6 Spider   7 Sliding sleeve   8 Synchronising assembly   9 Needle bearing inner race   10 Needle bearing   11 Third-speed gear (free running)   12 Thrust washer   13 Fourth-speed gear (fixed)   14 Spacer bush   15 Fifth-speed gear (fixed)
16 Spacer   17 Shim   18 Retaining ring   19 Roller bearing   20 Pinion shaft

fork rod and selector shaft off the studs (tap lightly if necessary) noting that **fifth and reverse must be in neutral** or the casing cannot be removed.

4 Remove the third and fourth detent plug. Withdraw the spring and detent. Remove the bolt from the first and second selector fork, gently spread the clamping piece with a screwdriver.

5 Remove the input and pinion shaft retaining plates. Withdraw the input and pinion shafts complete with the third and fourth selector rod and the first and second selector fork from the final drive casing.

6 Remove the first and second detent plug. Withdraw the spring and detent. Remove the first and second selector fork. **Identify and retain the shims fitted between the casing and the retaining plates.**

7 If the detent components are to be removed, refer to **FIG 6:4** and drive out the roll pins 5 and 10 (since the detent components are under spring load, the roll pins must be removed before the half-round dowel pin). Drive out the half-round dowel pin 2.

8 Heat the gearbox casing to 120°C (248°F), identify and drive out the bearing races using tool US8050. Check the parts and the bearings as described earlier for the unstiffened type gearbox.

Earlier four-speed gearbox:

When dismantling the earlier type four-speed transmission, refer to the the procedure for the earlier type five-speed transmission. For reference purposes it will be found that the Sportomatic four-speed gearbox closely resembles this manual four-speed box and **FIGS 7:1** and **7:4** in **Chapter 7** should be referred to.

Later four-speed gearbox:

When dismantling the later type four-speed transmission, refer to the procedure for the later type five-speed transmission. Engage fourth gear (instead of fifth) in operation 1. Differences due to there being four and not five forward gears will be self-evident.

FIG 6:7 Input shaft and components (later five-speed gearbox)

Key to Fig 6:7 1 Flange nut   2 Roller bearing   3 Bearing inner race   4 Ballbearing   5 Bearing retaining plate
6 Bearing inner race   7 Thrust washer   8 Fourth-speed free running gear   9 Needle bearing   10 Needle bearing race
11 Sleeve   12 Spider   13 Third-speed free running gear   14 Needle bearing   15 Needle bearing race   16 Thrust washer
17 Second-speed fixed gear   18 Roller bearing   19 Input shaft

FIG 6:8 Pinion shaft and components (later five-speed gearbox)

Key to Fig 6:8 1 Roller bearing 2 Thrust washer 3 First-speed free running gear 4 Needle bearing 5 Sleeve
6 Synchronising hub 7 Second-speed free running gear 8 Needle bearing 9 Needle bearing race 10 Thrust washer
11 Third-speed fixed gear 12 Spacer 13 Fourth-speed fixed gear 14 Bearing retaining plate 15 Bearing inner race
16 Ballbearing 17 Roller bearing 18 Speedometer drive gear 19 Pinion shaft

FIG 6:9 Examples of synchronising assembly components

Key to Fig 6:9 1 Circlip 2 Synchronising ring 3 Brake band (one only for first-speed) 4 Brake band anchor block (second-speed) 5 Thrust block (second-speed) 6 Brake band anchor block (first-speed) 7 Thrust block (first-speed, 'hooked') 8 Second-speed free running gear 9 First-speed free running gear

6:5 Servicing the gearbox shafts

This section covers the input and pinion shafts of the earlier type five-speed gearbox in some detail and **FIGS 6:5** and **6:6** relate directly to this gearbox. When dealing with the four-speed version of this box, refer in addition to **Chapter 7, Section 7:9**.

FIGS 6:7 and **6:8** relate directly to the later, stiffened, five-speed gearbox. The servicing procedures for the stiffened shafts are similar to those described for the earlier types but, where relevant, notes on differences and on tool numbers are given later.

Input shaft, earlier type:

Refer to **FIG 6:5**. Take careful note of which way round the components are fitted.

1 Unlock and remove nut 10 after checking the shaft runout. Press the roller bearing 9 off the shaft. Mark the needlebearing cages for position and pull all components off the shaft.

2 The inner half of the front bearing race is hard against gear 1. Drift it away a little and use a puller to remove it taking care not to damage the gear.

Clean parts and check for wear or damage. Runout must be checked before shaft is dismantled because tightening nut 10 may alter it. Assemble bearings on shaft and mount in V-blocks. Check runout of pilot spigot 20. Maximum permissible is 0.10mm (0.004in). Excessive runout up to 0.30mm (0.012in) may be corrected cold under a press, using tools VW405 and VW406.

Check the spigot for wear. Check the clutch plate splines for radial play. Oil seal race 11 must be smooth and unmarked. Running surfaces of gears and bearings must be unworn. Also check those parts which are to be press fitted on the shaft. Gear 1 is integral with the shaft. If worn, renew the shaft. Check synchromesh parts for wear and renew parts, particularly if gear changing has been noisy.

Fit all components dry. Gear 2 has its small collar facing the shaft flange. Following with thrust washer 3 and inner race 13. Fit cage 14, gear 4 and spider 6. **Used bearings must be fitting in original positions.** Fit sleeve 5 followed by bearing 17 and 18 and gear 7. Fit

FIG 6:10 Components of the later differential assembly

Key to Fig 6:10 1 Roll pin 2 Shaft 3 Anchor piece 4 Mating gear 5 Retainer 6 Side gear 7 Taper roller bearing 8 Shim 9 Washer 10 Lockplate 11 Bolt 12 Ring gear 13 Differential carrier 14 Pin 15 Spacer 16 Magnetic carrier disc

thrust washer 8 and roller bearing 9 with the cover ring of the cage facing towards the clutch plate splines. Press the bearing into place using a tubular extension to avoid damaging the threads at the front end of the shaft. Fit a new lockplate 19 with its inner tab in the groove in the shaft and under the inner race of the bearing. Oil the face and the threads of the nut and fit it with the spherical part uppermost. Tighten to 10 to 12kgm (72 to 86lb ft). Bend up the locking tab. Check the mating numbers then press the inner half of the front bearing race into place.

Pinion shaft, earlier type:

Refer to **FIG 6:6**. The un-numbered components are forward of the intermediate plate. Take careful note of which way round the components are fitted.

Place the shaft, pinion downwards under a press, using tool P225 as an abutment to the roller bearing so that the shaft may be pushed through the gear and bearing assemblies. Mark the positions of the needle bearing cages for correct reassembly and take great care of the shims 17 as they control the basic location of the pinion.

After cleaning look for wear and damage. Check the shaft for the condition of the splines and the pinion for worn, cracked or broken teeth. Check synchromesh parts for wear, particularly if gear changing has been noisy. Dismantle these by removing the retaining plate 5e with circlip pliers. Make a note of the positions of the bands 5c, energisers 5a and stops 5b. When installed, diameter of ring 5d should be 76.30 ± 0.18mm (3.004 ± 0.117in).

Remember that the pinion and crownwheel (ring gear) are a matched pair and are marked as such. If no parts are renewed which affect the endwise location of the pinion

shaft, there there is no problem in reassembling, but otherwise refer to **Section 6:7**.

1 All parts must be fitted to the pinion shaft in a dry state. Press roller bearings into place with the thin coverplate of the cage facing away from the pinion. Fit shims 17 as removed or as calculated (see **Section 6:7**).

2 Fit the spacer 16. Fit the fifth-speed gear 15 with the small collar facing away from the pinion. Fit the spacer bush 14, followed by the fourth-speed gear 13 with the collar against the bush.

3 Fit the thrust washer 12 and the needle bearing inner race 9. Fit the bearing cage 10. Reassemble the synchromesh parts and fit the third-speed gear 11 followed by the spider 6. **Always fit used needle-bearing cages in their original positions.**

4 Fit the inner race 2, bearing cage 3 and sliding sleeve 7. Fit gear 4. Fit the bevelled thrust washer 1 with its wide face against the needlebearing. Follow up with the thin spacer, but note that starting with transmission No 100.407, the washer and spacer were replaced by a single washer 6.60mm (0.26in) thick. Using a tubular drift, press on the inner half race for the front bearings. This must be marked with the mating number without the letter X.

Input shaft, later type:

Take careful note of which way round the components are fitted. To remove the roller bearings, use press tools VW412, VW401 and VW402 for the rear bearing and VW407 and VW415a for the forward bearing. Keep the needle bearings identified to their own gears. Use press

FIG 6:11   Half cross-section through a limited slip differential assembly

Key to Fig 6:11   1 Thrust washer   2 Outer disc (dished profile)   3 Outer discs   4 Pressure ring   5 Differential casing
6 Mating gear (four per set)   7 Shaft (two per set)   8 Circlip   9 Ring gear   10 Bolt   11 Locking plate   12 Inner disc
13 Inner discs   14 Casing cover   15 Side gear and shaft   16 Threaded block

tools VW412, VW416b and VW402 to fit the forward
bearing and VW407, VW401 and VW454 to fit the
rear bearing. Torque tighten the flange nut to 16 to 18kgm
(116 to 130lb ft) and (on assembly) the castellated nut to
12 to 14kgm (87 to 101lb ft). Lock the flange nut by
peening.

Pinion shaft, later type:

Take careful note of which way round the components
are fitted; in particular on 1977 models where the
asymmetrical pointed teeth of the first/second gear

operating sleeve must face towards the first gear wheel.

To remove the roller bearings, use press tools VW412,
P255a and VW401 for the front bearing and VW407 and
VW415a for the rear bearing. Keep the needlebearings
identified to their own gears. A suitable puller is required
to withdraw the speedometer drive gear and the new gear
must be heated to 120°C (248°F) before it is pressed into
position. Refit the bearings using press tools VW412,
VW244b and VW401. Torque tighten the flange nut
(on assembly) to 24 to 26kgm (174 to 188lb ft) and lock
by peening.

Synchronisers:

To dismantle a synchroniser assembly, remove the circlip type retainer (e.g. 5e in **FIG 6 : 6** or 1 in **FIG 6 : 9**) with circlip pliers. Note carefully which way the bands, rings, etc. are fitted and identify them to their gears. Ensure that new parts match those being rejected. Refer to **FIG 6 : 9** and note that the first-speed gear up to 1977 models has only one brake band 3 and that one of the blocks is 'hooked.' Correct assembly positioning of these parts is very important.

Using a micrometer, check the diameters of the installed synchronising rings. Depending upon the transmission type and the speed gear, this diameter should be either 76.30 ± 0.18mm (3.004 ± 0.007in) or 86.37 ± 0.17mm (3.4004 ± 0.0067in).

The clearance between the first/fifth selector fork and its sleeve must not exceed 0.50mm (0.02in).

Pinion shaft positioning:

The pinion and crownwheel (ring gear) are manufactured as a matched set and cannot be renewed individually. The positioning of the pinion in relation to the ring gear is critical and, on initial assembly of the transmission, was set accurately by the fitment of shims of selected thickness at the datum casing face. The pinion is located by the ballbearing included in the shaft assembly. If no new critical components are required, the unit may be reassembled with the original shims. If the pinion/ring gear set, the ballbearing or the main casing is renewed, the pinion shaft position must be reset as described in **Section 6 : 7**.

6 : 6 The differential gearing

A cross-section through an earlier type Sportomatic differential and final drive assembly is shown in **Chapter 7, FIG 7 : 4**. The components of a later type differential are shown in **FIG 6 : 10**. The design is conventional with two side gears 6 splined to the output shafts and two mating gears 4 running on shaft 2. The carrier runs on two taper roller bearings 7 which are preloaded by washers 9 and shims 8. Bolts 11 retain the ring gear to the carrier and its meshing with the pinion is adjustable. **Chapter 7, FIG 7 : 4** shows that the output flanges 5 are retained by bolts 4 which engage with retainers 6 (5 in **FIG 6 : 10**). Note that, in this case, an extension on each bolt locates with the cross-shaft and that there is no anchor piece 3 or pin 1 (see **FIG 6 : 10**) as in the later type unit. Items 14, 15 and 16 are only fitted in conjunction with the electronic speedometer.

Removal:

Refer to **Chapter 7, FIG 7 : 4**. Remove both bolts 4 and withdraw the flanges 5. Remove the side cover 24 and withdraw the differential assembly.

Dismantling:

Refer to **FIG 6 : 10**. Drive out and discard pin 1 (if fitted). Drive out shaft 2. Remove the anchor piece 3 (if fitted). Withdraw the gears and retainers. Using thrust piece P263 and a puller, withdraw the roller bearings. Identify each washer 9 and shim(s) 8 to the side to which they were fitted. **Do not get them mixed.** Untab and withdraw the bolts 11. Remove the ring gear 12.

Check all parts for serviceability. If a new ring gear is required, a new matching pinion shaft must also be fitted. If new bearings are required, the outer races must also be renewed and this will entail heating the casing to 120°C (248°F). Check the condition of the input shaft seal and renew if necessary.

Assembly:

This is the reverse of the dismantling sequence. Use Molykote or an equivalent lubricant on the spherical surfaces of the side and mating gears. Centre the side gears by temporarily fitting the drive flanges. Use a new pin 1 (if fitted). Torque tighten bolts 11 to 12kgm (86lb ft) and lock by tabbing. Lubricate with transmission oil of the type specified for the type of transmission.

Fitment:

Reverse the removal sequence. Torque tighten the side cover retaining nuts to 2.2 to 2.5kgm (16 to 18lb ft), the drive flange retaining bolts to 4.5 to 5.0kgm (32.5 to 36.0lb ft) on unstiffened type transmissions and to 2.6 to 3.0kgm (19 to 22lb ft) on later, stiffened, transmissions.

Limited slip differential:

A cross-section through a limited slip differential is shown in **FIG 6 : 11**. The disc sequence shown (one dished profile outer disc, two inner discs, two outer discs, one inner disc—reading inwards at each side) provides a 50% locking effect. The locking effect can be modified to 40%, 75% or 80% by changing the 'mix' of inner and outer discs and, if a different % is required, the appropriate discs should be obtained from a Porsche agent together with their fitment sequence.

To dismantle, remove the ring gear and the two Allen type screws. **Note the sequence of the discs.** They must be refitted in the same order or the locking effect will not be the same. On reassembly, apply Molykote G or LM348 to all disc surfaces, pressure rings and differential shafts. Ensure that each dished profile outer disc is next to the casing or to the casing cover. When assembled but before fitting the ring gear, hold the flange section in a soft-jawed vice and measure the torque required to turn a drive flange. This torque should be 4 to 8kgm (30 to 57lb ft) for a 50% and a 40% assembly or 6 to 12kgm (43 to 85lb ft) for a 75% and an 80% assembly. If the torque is outside the relevant range, fit thicker or thinner disc(s) to bring the torque within the specified range. Torque tighten the ring gear retaining bolts to 15kgm (108lb ft).

Recommended lubricant for limited slip transmissions is Shell Transmission Oil S 1747A. The equivalent in other countries is: USA, Shell HDR Gear Oil 90EP; Canada, Shell HDR Gear Oil 90; Australia, Shell SCL Gear Oil 90.

Adjustments:

If either new bearings, a new carrier or a new casing have been fitted, adjust the bearing preload. If any of these parts or if a new gear ring and pinion have been fitted, adjust the backlash after setting the pinion position. The procedures are described in **Section 6 : 7**.

6 : 7 Gear and backlash settings

This section is applicable to both the manual and to the Sportomatic transmissions.

FIG 6:12 Bearing preload and ring gear backlash adjustment

Key to Fig 6:12   **AA** Differential centreline   **B** Pinion   **C** Ring gear   1 Shims and washer (**S1**)   2 Shims and washer (**S2**)   **E** Pinion setting dimension (see text)

FIG 6:13   Pinion setting data

Key to Fig 6:13   **R** Design dimension (see tabulation)   **r** Deviation   1 Actual deviation in 0.01mm units   2 Pinion and ring gear matching set no.   3 Desired backlash (mm)

Refer to **FIG 6:12**. The total thickness of shims 1 and 2 determines the preload on the taper roller bearings in which the differential unit runs. The individual thicknesses of 1 and 2 determines the backlash between the ring gear **C** and the pinion **B**. **E**, the position of the pinion in relation to the ring gear centre line **AA**, is a calculated dimension and the pinion is set to this by selecting the appropriate thickness of the gasket or shim at the face arrowed **S** in **FIGS 6:1** or **6:2** or in **Chapter 7, FIGS 7:1, 7:2, 7:3** and **7:4**. **FIG 6:13** illustrates diagrammatically the geometry of the pinion and ring gear engagement. Manufacturing tolerances preclude **E** in **FIG 6:12** from being precisely equal to the design dimension **R** in all cases. The difference (**r**) between **R** and **E** is marked on the matched pinion as shown at 1. The **N** figure is always positive (since 1970) and indicates, in 0.01mm units, the amount by which **E** deviates from **R**. The values of **R** are tabulated later in this section. **E** is **R** + **r**. The pinion shaft is positioned by selecting the appropriate thickness of **S** so that the measured value of **E** is equal to the calculated value.

Pinion shaft positioning:

Refer to this heading in **Section 6:5** and, if new critical components have been fitted, proceed as follows. Refer to **FIGS 6:12** and **6:13**. Check that the pinion and ring gear numbers match. Note **r** the **N** figure. Read off **R** (which differs for different types of transmission) from the following tabulation. Calculate **E** which equals **R** plus **r**.

Transmission and type

No.		R
Earlier manual, type 911	..	63.20mm (2.488in)
Earlier Sportomatic, type 905	..	54.20mm (2.134in)
Later manual, type 915 ..	..	66.30mm (2.610in)
Later Sportomatic, type 925	..	59.70mm (2.350in)

In place of the differential assembly, install dummy carrier tool P258 with its dial gauge set to measure **E**. As a datum use the thickness of **S** (see **FIGS 6:1, 6:2** or **Chapter 7, FIGS 7:1, 7:2, 7:3** and **7:4**) originally fitted. Measure the deviation of **E** from the calculated figure and increase or decrease the thickness of **S** by the amount of the divergence. Recheck the setting.

Determining the total thickness of S1 plus S2:

So that the pinion is not engaged with the ring gear, the gearbox must be separated from the main casing for the following procedure. The oil seal must be removed from the side cover.

Check that the outer races are fully seated in the casing and in the side cover. On later (stiffened) models note whether SKF or FAG bearings are fitted. Select shims 8 in **FIG 6:10** so that the thickness of these shims plus that of the spacer 9 is 3.5mm (0.138in) and fit them to the ring gear side of the carrier. These are 1 (**S1**) in **FIG 6:12**. On the opposite side fit a spacer plus shim thickness of 3mm (0.118in). These are 2 (**S2**). Fit the bearings and install the differential. Fit the side cover without a gasket. Lightly tighten it down using only two nuts opposite each other and, using feeler gauges, measure the gap between the cover and the casing. The required gap is 0.15mm (0.006in). If it differs from this, reduce or increase the **S1** thickness until the required gap is obtained. Fit all the cover retaining nuts and tighten down to 2.3kgm (17lb ft). Fit the drive flanges and their retaining bolts torque tightened to the figure quoted in **Section 6:6**.

Using a torque meter on the drive flange at the cover side, measure the drag of the differential/final drive assembly. This should be within the range of 18 to 24kgcm (16 to 21lb in) on unstiffened transmissions and 25 to 35kgcm (22 to 30lb in) on stiffened transmissions fitted with SKF bearings or 40 to 65kgcm (35 to 57lb ft) if fitted with FAG bearings. If necessary, adjust the preload shim thickness to bring the drag within the relevant specified range.

Backlash basic setting:

Remove the differential assembly. Withdraw the bearings and identify the spacing washers to their

FIG 6:14 Front cover (later transmissions) and speedometer drive components

Key to Fig 6:14   1 Reversing light switch   2 Switch actuating pin   3 Seal   4 Retainer   5 Thrust washer   6 Speedo-meter drive   7 Retainer   8 'O' ring   9 Positioning piece   10 Worm shaft   11 Seal   12 Selector rod sleeve   13 Bush
14 Front cover

respective sides. Measure the total thickness (**S1** plus **S2**) and proportion the shims so that **S1** is 0.10mm (0.004in) thinner than half the total of **S1** plus **S2**. **S2** will now be 0.10mm (0.004in) thicker than half the total of **S1** plus **S2**. Round off **S1** and **S2** if necessary but do not depart from the total thickness of **S1** plus **S2**.

Backlash, final setting:

Reassemble and fit the differential (with the oil seal fitted to the side cover). Fit the drive flanges and torque tighten the retaining bolts. Fit the gearbox less its front cover but with the pinion shaft correctly positioned. Use clamping tool P259 (earlier models), P259a (later manual), or P357a (later Sportomatic) on the forward end of the pinion shaft to block it. Using a suitable dial gauge set up at the radius of the ring gear tooth mid-face (the official dial gauge holder, etc. are part of the clamping tool toolset) measure the pinion/ring gear backlash. This should be within the range of 0.12 to 0.18mm (0.0047 to 0.0071in). This is ± 0.03mm (0.0012in) of the 0.15mm (0.006in) nominal backlash shown at 3 in **FIG 6:13**. If the backlash is outside this range, transfer shimming from **S1** to **S2** or vice versa but, again, do not depart from the **S1** plus **S2** total.

6:8 Front cover and intermediate plate

Earlier type front cover:

The front cover (2 in **FIG 6:1**) fitted to earlier type gearboxes is similar to the front cover fitted to Sportomatic transmissions and reference may be made to **Chapter 7, Section 7:9**.

Later type front cover:

The front cover fitted to later type manual gearboxes (1 in **FIG 6:2**) is shown in **FIG 6:14**. This shows the components of the speedometer drive and the location of the reversing light switch. If the bush 13 has to be renewed, heat the cover to 120°C (248°F) and drive out the bush with a suitable mandrel. With the cover again at this temperature, drive in the new bush. If a new seal 3 is being fitted, use tool P374. If a new seal 11 is being fitted, use tool P369.

The oil pump which is incorporated into the front cover is covered in **Section 6:9**.

Intermediate plate:

A separate intermediate plate (21 in **FIG 6:1**) is only relevant to earlier type manual transmissions and is equivalent to that fitted to Sportomatic transmissions. Reference may consequently be made to **Chapter 7, Section 7:9**.

6:9 The oil pump

If fitted, the pump is incorporated into the front cover as shown in **FIG 6:15**. It is driven from the forward end of the input shaft by a simple dog arrangement.

Dismantling and reassembling:

Remove the cover 1. Carefully remove and retain the gasket(s). Withdraw the gears. The relief valve assembly 4, 5 and 7, the suction tube 8 and the delivery tube can only be removed after the cover has been separated from the gearbox.

FIG 6:15 Gearbox front cover oil pump (2.7 litre Carrera)

Key to Fig 6:15 1 Pump cover   2 Pump gear   3 Pump gear   4 Relief valve ball   5 Relief valve spring   6 Bush   7 Relief valve plug   8 Oil suction tube   Front cover casing

If the bushes have to be renewed, note their orientation and mark the alignment of the oil holes. Use mandrel P368 to drive in the new bushes which must be correctly positioned and fully entered. The milled ends of the oil pockets must point towards the pressure chamber or oil pump gears respectively.

When fitting the pump cover, tighten the retaining nuts diagonally and keep checking that the pump gears remain free. If necessary, reduce or increase the thickness of the gasket(s) to give an axial clearance of 0.05mm (0.002in) between the gears and the cover. Finally, torque tighten the cover nuts to 1kgm (7lb ft). Torque tighten plug 7 to 2.5kgm (18lb ft). If the suction tube was removed, ensure that the 'O' ring is refitted. Torque tighten the Allen retaining bolts to 0.9kgm (6.5lb ft).

On refitment of the front cover to the gearbox, ensure that the pressure line passes through the hole in the third/fourth gearchange fork.

6:10 Reassembling the transmission

General:

Reassembly of the transmission is substantially the reverse of the dismantling sequence and the following notes will augment the operator's own notes and sketches made during dismantling. It is assumed that the **Section 6:5, 6:6, 6:7, 6:8** and **6:9** procedures (as may have been relevant or necessary) have been correctly carried out. As the work proceeds, lubricate parts and assemblies with the transmission oil specified for the type of transmission.

Earlier (unstiffened) transmission:

Torque tighten bolt 4 in **FIG 6:1** to 11 to 12kgm (80 to 86lb ft) while blocking the input shaft with P37. Torque tighten the detent plug 15 in **FIG 6:3** to 2.5kgm (18lb ft).

FIG 6:16 Supporting the shafts in P260 (earlier gearboxes)

FIG 6:17 Adjusting the selector forks (later gearboxes)

Key to Fig 6:17 1 Install flush 2 Mounting plate P260a

FIG 6:18 Components of gearlever and linkage

Key to Fig 6:18 1 Gearlever knob 2 Gearlever 3 Boot 4 Base 5 Spring seat 6 Spring 7 Spring seat 8 Stop plate 9 Guide bush 10 Guide bracket 11 Stop plate thrust spring 12 Guide pin 13 Retainer 14 Ball socket 15 Shift rod joint 16 Tapered screw 17 Shift rod 18 Boot 19 Bolt 20 Clamp 21 Lockwasher 22 Nut 23 Shift rod coupling

Use plasticine to check that there is clearance of at least 1mm (0.04in) between the teeth of the first speed and reverse gears under the conditions which bring them closest together. Check that the first and reverse selector control forks have a side clearance of 2 to 3mm (0.08 to 0.12in) with those for the second and third. Torque tighten the first and reverse selector fork screw to 2.5kgm (18lb ft).

It is not possible to set the remaining forks accurately without supporting the shafts with tool P260 as shown in FIG 6:16. Adjust the position of the second and third and fourth and fifth speed forks so that the sliding sleeves are exactly central between the synchronising rings. After a shift test, tighten the fork screws to 2.5kgm (18lb ft), making sure that the control forks clear each other by 2 to 3mm (0.08 to 0.12in).

Take shift rod 1 in FIG 6:1 and assemble the shift lever and pin, making sure that the pin and hole tapers are correct. Fit the cotterpin.

Insert the shift rod into the casing and install the intermediate plate and gears, fitting the correct gaskets under the plate as determined in Section 6:7. It is essential to select fifth speed for this operation and care must be taken not to damage the input shaft oil seal. Shift back into neutral. Set the shift lever between the selector control forks and pushrod into the rear bore. Fit a new gasket and install the guide fork, locating the lever in the fork correctly. Fit the front cover. The hole in the breather must point forward at an angle of 45° from the transmission centre line.

If the reversing light switch was removed, make sure when refitting it, that the operating pin is fitted with the rounded end entering first.

Later (stiffened) transmissions:

The torque tightening figure specified for the differential side cover, the front cover and the guide fork cover is 2.2 to 2.5kgm (16 to 18lb ft). The figure for the guide fork nut is 0.8 to 0.9kgm (5.8 to 6.5lb ft); for the detent nut (transmission casing) is 1.5 to 1.8kgm (11 to 13lb ft); and for the fork nuts, 2.4 to 2.6kgm (17 to 19lb ft). Torque tighten the bearing retaining plate nuts to 2.1 to 2.3kgm (15 to 17lb ft) and ensure that the correct thickness of shimming is fitted to suit the pinion shaft positioning. Adjustment of the selector forks is described later. When installing the idler gear shaft, turn the shaft until the pin in the casing prevents it from turning further. Use tool P37a to block the input shaft and engage fifth gear so that the input shaft castellated nut and the pinion flange nut may be tightened to the figures specified in Section 6:5.

To adjust the selector forks, install mounting plate P260a as shown in FIG 6:17. Block the input shaft with P37a, engage fifth speed and torque tighten the input shaft nut. Turn the first/second fork rod left to the stop and then slightly back until the unmachined flat inner surface is almost vertical. Do not turn back beyond the middle point or fully to the right. Position the first/second selector fork so that the sleeve is exactly in the middle between the synchronising rings and tighten the bolt. Adjust the third/fourth fork in the same way. Position the third/fourth guide flush with the fork and check that this is 2 to 3mm (0.08 to 0.12in) clearance between third/fourth and first/second guides. They must not touch.

6:11 Gearchange linkage

The components of a manual transmission lever and linkage are shown in **FIG 6:18**. The lever knob is pressed onto the lever.

Uncoupling and removing the linkage:

Pull off the knob, lift off boot 3 and the tunnel cover and release the base 4. Remove the tunnel cover in the rear compartment, push the boot 18 forwards, loosen clamp bolt 19 and drive rod 17 off the coupling 23. Pull off the clamp and boot. Cut the locking wire and remove screw and socket 15. With the engine/transmission unit removed, rod 17 may be withdrawn.

Installation:

This is the reverse of the uncoupling and removal sequence. Torque tighten screw 16 to 1.5kgm (11lb ft) and relock with wire.

Coat the working faces of coupling 23 with lithium grease. Tighten the bolts for gearlever base to 2.5kgm (18lb ft). Tighten the bolts securing guide bracket 10 to 1kgm (7lb ft). Adjust the linkage as described later.

Adjusting the linkage:

Through the aperture in tunnel, loosen bolt 19. Put the gearlever in neutral and press it to the right as far as it will go. With the transmission in neutral, move coupling 23 as far to the left as it will go and tighten the clamp bolt to 2.5kgm (18lb ft), using a serrated lockwasher under the nut.

Try all gears and check for play in the linkage. Gear lever play should be the same in all gears in every direction.

6:12 Fault diagnosis

(a) Difficulty in changing gear

1 Bent or worn gearshift mechanism
2 Shift rod coupling wrongly set
3 Faulty or worn synchronising mechanism
4 Faulty clutch or release bearing
5 Stiffness of clutch pedal, cable or release mechanism
6 Input shaft spigot bearing tight
7 Excessive clutch clearance
8 Faulty selector rod detent or springs

(b) Noisy gearchanging

1 Check 3 to 7 in (a)
2 Wrong grade of transmission oil

(c) Slipping out of gear

1 Check 8 in (a)
2 Excessive end float of free running gears
3 Worn synchronising teeth
4 Selector fork wrongly positioned
5 Gearshift mechanism worn
6 Worn bearings

(d) Noisy transmission

1 Check 2 and 6 in (c)
2 Incorrect or insufficient lubricant
3 Worn drive gears and differential
4 Insufficient preload on differential bearings
5 Drive gears incorrectly meshed

NOTES

CHAPTER 7

THE SPORTOMATIC TRANSMISSION

7:1 Description

The Sportomatic semi-automatic transmission is alternative to the manual transmission covered in **Chapter 6**. The differential and final drive is substantially the same as for manual transmission models. **Chapter 6, Sections 6:6** and **6:7** and **Chapter 8** are relevant to both types of transmission.

The Sportomatic transmission comprises an engine driven three-element hydraulic torque converter, a single dry plate clutch (which operates automatically) and either a four-speed and reverse or a three-speed and reverse gearbox. The gearbox itself is non-automatic and the four-speed versions are similar to the unstiffened and stiffened versions of the four-speed manual gearboxes. Cross-sections through three versions of earlier and later type Sportomatic transmissions are shown in **FIGS 7:1, 7:2** and **7:3**. **FIG 7:4** shows a horizontal section through the earlier four-speed gearbox and differential. The clutch and torque converter are not included in this illustration. Later transmissions are stiffened to accommodate the higher torques provided by the bigger engines installed in later models. The three-speed gearbox is available only in the stiffened version.

The engine drives the torque converter casing which, internally, carries impeller blading. This (via stator blading) directs oil against the turbine blading and transmits torque to the driven rotor. The clutch is interposed between the turbine and the gearbox input shaft. The pneumatically operated 'automatic' clutch is arranged to disengage while a gearchange is being made. The clutch operation is triggered by the driver's initial movement of the manual gearchange lever. This, electrically, actuates an air valve and powers a vacuum-servo unit which operates the clutch. Pneumatic power for the vacuum-servo is provided by the difference between atmospheric pressure and the partial vacuum derived from the engine induction manifold. The system is shown diagrammatically in **FIG 7:5**.

The torque converter provides intermediate 'gear ratios' between the mechanical ratios of the gearbox. Maximum torque multiplication occurs when the turbine is stationary and the impeller is being driven at increasing engine speed (vehicle moving off). The stator element redirects the oil flow from the turbine so that it re-enters the impeller at the most effective angle. The stator hub incorporates a one-way drive and, as the turbine picks up speed and the slip between it and the impeller becomes

FIG 7:1 Cross-section through earlier four-speed transmission

Key to Fig 7:1 1 Selector shaft 2 Oil seal 3 Speedometer gearshaft 4 Speedometer drive gear 5 Input shaft 6 Pinion shaft 7 Synchronising ring 8 Sliding sleeve 9 Selector fork 10 Spider 11 Fourth-speed gear 12 Differential case 13 Pinion gear 14 Pinion gearshaft 15 Pump 16 Turbine 17 Stator 18 Freewheeling unit 19 Turbine shaft bush 20 Oil restrictor in turbine shaft 21 Oil seal 22 Freewheeling unit support 23 Clutch pilot needle bearing 24 Oil seal 25 'O' ring 26 Clutch release bearing 27 Clutch carrier and turbine shaft 28 Clutch plate 29 Clutch pressure plate 30 Oil seal 31 Nut **S** Gasket(s) see text

FIG 7:2 Cross-section through later four-speed transmission

Key to Fig 7:2 1 Speedometer drive 2 Front cover 3 Flange nut 4 Reverse gear 5 Input shaft 6 Ballbearing 7 Intermediate plate 8 Second-speed gear 9 Third-speed gear 10 Third and fourth sleeve 11 Third and fourth sleeve 12 Third and fourth sleeve 13 Fourth-speed gear 14 Clutch fork 15 Oil seal 16 Clutch plate/turbine shaft 17 Oil seal 18 Torque converter housing 19 Torque converter 20 Speedometer drive shaft 21 Ballbearing 22 Clamping plate 23 Roller bearing 24 Selector shaft 25 Roller bearing 26 Anchor block 27 Oil seal 28 Needle bearing sleeve 29 Ballbearing 30 Stator support **S** Gasket(s) see text

FIG 7:3   Cross-section through three-speed transmission

Key to Fig 7:3   1 Speedometer drive   2 Front cover   3 Flanged nut   4 Reverse gear   5 Input shaft   6 Ballbearing
7 Intermediate plate   8 Second-speed gear   9 Third-speed gear   10 Transmission casing   11 Third-speed fork   12 Third-speed
sleeve guide   13 Spacer   14 Washer   15 Clutch fork   16 Oil seal   17 Turbine shaft   18 Oil seal   19 Torque converter
housing   20 Torque converter   21 Speedometer drive shaft   22 Ballbearing   23 Clamping plate   24 Roller bearing   25 Inner
shift lever   26 Roller bearing   27 Anchor block   28 'O' ring   29 Needle bearing   30 Ballbearing   31 Stator support
S Gasket(s) see text

less, the torque multiplication reduces progressively until, when their speeds become substantially equal, the unit acts as a fluid coupling and the free wheel stator hub permits it to rotate with the other two elements.

Oil for the torque converter is common to the engine lubrication system and is fed to it under pressure from a pump driven by the lefthand camshaft. The gearbox lubrication is entirely separate and operates on the same transmission oil as that for manual transmission gearboxes.

Gearlever symbols are: **P** (Parking lock), **R** (Reverse), **L** (Low), **D** (for city driving), **D3** (for normal highway speeds) and **D4** (for high-speed motorways) or, in the case of the three-speed gearbox, **D3** combines normal and high-speed driving. A gear may remain engaged for brief stops but, otherwise, engage **P**. **Do not touch the gearlever except when actually changing or engaging gear. Do not change down when the engine speed is very high or overspeeding will occur.** If the oil temperature warning light comes on, change down to a lower gear. An inhibitor (bypass) switch prevents the starter motor from operating except when **P** is engaged. **Engage P only when the vehicle is stationary** and then apply the handbrake.

The transmission assembly is attached to the forward face of the engine and cannot be removed from the vehicle separately. After removal of the engine and transmission as a unit, the transmission is separated from the engine.

7:2 Maintenance

Gearbox lubrication:

Refer to **Chapter 6, Section 6:2** and renew the oil at the same mileage intervals as those specified for the manual transmission models.

Torque converter oil:

Renewal of the engine oil (see **Chapter 1, Section 1:2**) covers the torque converter oil. Note, however, that if the torque converter has been drained, some 4 pints (2.3 litre) of additional engine oil will be required to refill the system (see **Section 7:7**).

Clutch free play:

Check this every 6000 miles (10,000km) and adjust as described in **Section 7:7**.

Control valve and air filter:

Every 6000 miles (10,000km) adjust the control valve and clean the filter as described in **Section 7:5**.

Gearlever microswitch:

Every 6000 miles (10,000km), clean and, if necessary, adjust the contacts as described in **Section 7:6**.

FIG 7:4 Horizontal cross-section through earlier four-speed transmission

Key to Fig 7:4 1 Side bearing   2 Oil seal   3 Washer   4 Bolt   5 Axle flange   6 Threaded piece   7 Side gear   8 Pinion gear   9 Pinion gearshaft   10 Reverse gearshaft   11 Thrust washer   12 Caged needle bearing   13 Gear for reverse   14 Retaining ring   15 Gear for reverse   16 Caged needle bearing   17 Thrust needle bearing   18 Thrust ring   19 Ring gear (crownwheel)   20 Pinion shaft   21 Transmission side cover   22 Bolt   23 Differential case   24 Side cover   25 Bypass switch   26 Speedometer drive   27 Reversing light switch   28 Parking lock cap   **S** Gasket(s) see text

7:3 Removing and installing the transmission

Refer to **Chapter 6, Section 6:3**. The notes regarding removal and refitment of the engine/transmission unit are also relevant to models with Sportomatic transmissions. Separation of the Sportomatic transmission from the engine and refitment to the engine are covered in **Section 7:4**.

7:4 Separating and refitting the transmission

On earlier models, refer to **FIG 7:6**. Remove the electrical wiring from the temperature gauge sensor **A** and the temperature switch **B**. Loosen hose clamp 1 and uncouple hose 2 and pipe 3 from the sensor unit **C**. Detach the vacuum hose 4 from the clutch vacuum-servo unit. On later models the sensor and switch are fitted to the torque converter casing.

Unhook and withdraw the rear throttle control rod. Through the large apertures in the torque converter casing, remove the angled 12-point bolts which secure the torque converter to the coupling plate. Remove the bolts and nuts joining the engine to the transmission. As the units are separated, take care that the torque converter remains in its housing. A short length of flat steel strip may be bolted to one of the casing bolt holes to keep the torque converter in place.

When refitting the engine to the transmission, use a torque of 4.7kgm (34lb ft) on the attaching nuts and bolts. The 12-point bolts for securing the torque converter to the coupling plate must be tightened to 2.4 to

2.6kgm (17 to 19lb ft). Set the clutch free play as described in **Section 7:7**.

7:5 Servicing the control valve and sensor control valve:

No procedures are prescribed for the overhaul or repair of this unit and a faulty valve must be renewed. To remove it, detach the battery leads. Remove the air cleaner assembly after detaching the oil tank breather hose and the small hose for the breather valve. Refer to **FIG 7:6**. Withdraw the rubber cap from solenoid 6. Remove the splitpin and pull off the wire connector.

Detach the hoses from the valve and release the bracket from its support.

When fitting a control valve, coat the sliding surface of the cam, and drag spring where fitted, with molybdenum disulphide grease. Adjust the valve as described later. Make sure the cable connector is well seated. Redrill the splitpin hole if necessary.

Cleaning the air filter:

Remove the filter 7 in **FIG 7:6**. Refit after washing off in petrol and drying thoroughly with compressed air.

Control valve adjustment:

Do this every 6000 miles (10,000km) or when required as in preceding notes. Control linkage and engine idling speed must be correctly adjusted first.

Electric circuit ---·---
Negative pressure (hatched)
Atmospheric pressure (dotted)

FIG 7:5   Diagrammatic layout of Sportomatic transmission

Key to Fig 7:5   1 Microswitch in gearlever   2 Bypass switch   3 Gear selector shaft   4 Reverse light switch and 'park' position contact   5 Shift rod P and R   6 Vacuum servo unit   7 Transmission clutch   8 Torque converter   9 Reverse light   10 Crankshaft   11 Control valve   12 Adjusting screw   13 Vacuum reservoir   14 Electric solenoid switch   15 Cam and plunger   16 Inlet manifold   17 Check valve   18 Auxiliary valve   19 Main valve   a Wire from fuse 1   b Wire from ignition switch   c Wire to starter terminal 50   d Wire to intermediate fuse 8/15 A

FIG 7:6   Control valve and earlier location of temperature sensor and switch

Key to Fig 7:6   A Temperature sensor   B Temperature switch   C Housing   1 Hose clamp   2 Hose   3 Pipe   4 Hose   5 Valve   6 Solenoid   7 Air cleaner   8, 9 Hoses   10 Adjusting screw

FIG 7:7   Control valve adjustment

Key to Fig 7:7   1 Control valve plunger   2 Drag spring, early models   3 Correct clearance of 1.5mm (0.059in)   4 Socket head bolt   5 Plate on throttle cross-shaft   6 Cam   7 Inlet manifold

FIG 7:8 Details of the gearlever and microswitch

Key to Fig 7:8 1 Gearlever 2 Retaining pin 3 Stop ring
4 Microswitch 5 Ball 6 Spring 7 Gearlever lower part
8 Position of switch when engaged with pin 9 Parts to be
lightly lubricated 10 Spring and guide pin

Upshift on acceleration is adjusted as follows:

Where CIS equipment is fitted, it will be necessary in
order to gain access to remove the following after
disconnecting the battery: the air cleaner cover, the
heater blower, holder, and detach number 3 cylinder
injection line at the injector, and remove number 3
cylinder intake pipe.

1 Refer to **FIG 7:7**. Clearance at 3 must be 1.5mm
(0.06in) when the throttles are set for idling. Cam 6
must be fully returned.
2 Put a 4mm (0.16in) shim under the lefthand idling
stop screw (see **Chapter 2**). Adjust the cam so that
the cam or the drag spring where fitted just touches
the control valve plunger 1.

FIG 7:9 Clutch and torque converter components

Key to Fig 7:9 1 Torque converter 2 Turbine shaft and
clutch carrier plate 3 Clutch driven plate 4 Clutch pressure
plate

3 Remove the shim. In this position the original
clearance of 1.5mm (0.06in) may be different, but a
minimum clearance of 1.0mm (0.04in) must be
maintained.

Downshift on deceleration is adjusted as follows:

1 Drive the car or run it onto a roller stand. As a rough
guide on a standing vehicle, set the handbrake, let the
engine idle and engage a gear. The time lag between
releasing the gear lever and the perceptible impact of
engagement must be 0.30 to 0.50 seconds.
2 Check under driving conditions by running at
4500rev/min in 'D'. Take the foot off the throttle and
shift down to 'L'. The clutch should engage without a
time lag, but the rear wheels must not lock. If necessary, adjust the time lag as follows:
3 Remove the plastic cover from the control valve
adjusting screw 10 in **FIG 7:6**. Turn the screw in to
give a softer, delayed clutch engagement. Turn the
screw anticlockwise to give a harder and more
instantaneous clutch engagement. Do not turn more
than $\frac{1}{4}$ to $\frac{1}{2}$ a turn at a time. Refit the plastic cover.

Temperature switch and gauge sensor:

The location of these on earlier models is shown in
FIG 7:6. They may be removed without taking the power
unit out of the car by following the instructions for
removing the engine and transmission as described in
Chapter 1 up to the point where the unit is lowered a
little. The switch and sensor are then accessible from
above. Pull the cables off and remove the unit.

When refitting, heat and quench the copper gaskets to
anneal them. Tighten the switch and sensor to 4.5 to
5.0kgm (33 to 36lb ft). On later models the switch and
sensor are fitted to the torque converter housing.

7:6 Servicing the gearchange lever and microswitch

Refer to **FIG 7:8**. Remove and refit the microswitch as
follows:

1 Lift the rubber boot and remove the tunnel covering.
Release the base flange from the tunnel and lift
slightly.
2 Detach the microswitch cables in the tunnel and lift
away the lever and base.
3 Drive off the gear lever knob and pull the boot and
switch off the lever.

Clean dirty switch contacts or, if unserviceable, renew
the switch. Reassemble by pushing the switch on to the
lever with the split facing forward. Push far enough to
engage pin 2. Check the contact gap with the lever in
neutral. The gap must be 0.30 to 0.40mm (0.012 to
0.016in). Adjust the gap by bending the outer contact
tabs. Fit the switch top and boot. Refit the knob. Connect
the cable connectors and fit the assembly to tunnel. The
earth lead from the switch goes under the front lefthand
bolt. Tighten the 8mm bolts to 2.5kgm (18lb ft) and the
6mm bolts to 1kgm (7.2lb ft).

Overhauling the gearchange lever base:

Apart from the microswitch, the rest of the assembly
resembles that for the manual gearbox lever, so refer to

Chapter 6, Section 6:11 for instructions. Having fitted the plastic ball socket to the lever, lightly grease the stop ring 3 and push onto the lever. Grease spring 6 and insert it into lower part 7, grease the ball and lever and insert it into the lower part. Fit the retaining pin 2. It must enter easily to prevent the switch malfunctioning. Install the switch and knob.

7:7 Servicing the torque converter and clutch

Cross-sections through the torque converter and clutch are included in **FIGS 7:1, 7:2** and **7:3**. Cut-away sections are shown in **FIG 7:9**.

FIGS 7:10 and **7:11** are relevant to the clutch controls.

Clutch free play:

Check this every 6000 miles. Depressurise the vacuum-servo unit by pressing the accelerator linkage operating lever towards full throttle. Push the clutch intermediate lever 2 towards the righthand rear wheel (see **FIG 7:10**). Free play at this point should be at least 5mm (0.20in). If play is less, readjust as follows:

1 Remove engine/transmission unit (see **Section 7:3**). Remove the clevis pin from fork 3.

2 Pull the actuating rod of vacuum-servo unit 4 right out to the stop. Push the intermediate lever 2 towards the servo unit as far as possible.

3 The holes in the fork must be further away from the servo unit than the hole in the intermediate lever by 12 to 15mm (0.47 to 0.59in). Refit the clevis pin, using a new splitpin. Tighten the locknut on the rod. Check the control valve adjustment as described in **Section 7:5** then refit power unit.

Removing the torque converter and clutch:

With the engine detached from transmission as described in **Section 7:4**, withdraw the torque converter. **Oil will run out.** Cover the converter to keep out dirt. Remove the external and internal nuts securing the converter housing to the transmission casing. Release the front end of the clutch rod 5 from the intermediate lever 2 (see **FIG 7:10**). Part the housing from the casing while disengaging the clutch release bearing from its fork.

Remove the socket head bolts from the clutch pressure plate flange, loosening them a turn at a time diagonally to prevent distortion. Withdraw the pressure plate, noting that the release bearing may fall out. Remove the clutch driven plate. Remove the socket head bolts from the free-wheel support, insert two long bolts in opposite holes and drive out the support with the oil seal.

Remove the circlip from turbine shaft 2 in **FIG 7:9**. Support the housing on blocks and drive out the turbine shaft. Using a punch at alternating points, drive out the shaft bearing and push out the oil seal.

Inspecting converter and clutch:

Refer to **Chapter 5** for instructions on checking the clutch condition, but note that the minimum thickness over the linings (uncompressed) is 5.5mm (0.217in). Lateral runout must not exceed 0.50mm (0.02in).

Torque converters cannot be repaired. Renew a damaged or unserviceable unit.

FIG 7:10 Components of the clutch operating mechanism

Key to Fig 7:10   1 Mounting stud   2 Intermediate lever   3 Clevis   4 Servo unit   5 Clutch rod

Check the clutch face of turbine shaft and carrier assembly. Renew the assembly if it is heavily scored. Check the needle bearing and inspect the hub seat and oil passage. If worn, the needle bearing and oil seal may be extracted with a puller and a new bearing driven in with tool P361. The oil seal is fitted with tool P362. Grease the bearing with molybdenum disulphide grease, using it sparingly so that the clutch plate will not be contaminated.

Check the ballbearing in its housing when it is dry after cleaning. To fit a new bearing, heat the housing to 120°C (248°F) and drive it in with tool P359. Renew the smaller oil seal by driving it in with tool P359. Oil the sealing lip.

Check the freewheel support and turbine shaft bushing for wear. Check the oil passages. A defective support must be renewed as an assembly complete with bushing and sealing sleeve.

FIG 7:11   Clutch intermediate lever

Key to Fig 7:11   1 Lockring   2 Washer   3 Grommet   4 Spacer   5 Bush   6 Intermediate lever   7 'O' ring   8 Thrust ring   9 Spring

FIG 7:12 Earlier type gearbox with front cover removed

Key to Fig 7:12 1 Reverse selector fork   2 Parking lever and pawl   3 Pinion shaft bolt   4 Roll pin   5 Reverse sliding gear   6 Circlip

Reassembling:

Secure the freewheel support with three bolts and drive in the turbine shaft using tool P362. Remove the bolts and support and fit the circlip onto the shaft. Refit the freewheel support, tightening the sockethead bolts diagonally to 1.4kgm (10lb ft). Fit new 'O' rings to the bolts. Refit the seal and oil its lip.

Centre the clutch driven plate with a suitable mandrel (see **Chapter 5**). Lightly coat both sides of the diaphragm spring segments with molybdenum disulphide grease and work the release bearing in diagonally from the inside. Fit the clutch pressure plate, tightening the bolts diagonally a turn at a time to 1.4kgm (10lb ft). Make sure plate is seating on the dowels and that the release bearing is free.

Refitting:

Use molybdenum disulphide grease to coat the contact faces of the clutch release fork and bearing, also the pilot at the rear end of the gearbox input shaft. Fit the engine mounting bolt and spring washer into housing adjacent to temperature sensor body. **The vacuum-servo unit prevents the fitting of the bolt later on.** Bring the mounting flanges together while guiding the clutch release bearing into the fork. Tighten the large nuts to 4kgm (29lb ft) and the smaller nuts to 2.2kgm (16lb ft).

The torque converter must hold a small quantity of oil during assembly. Put about 0.50 litres of engine oil in a new converter. The equivalent is 1 US pint and slightly less than 1 Imp. pint. Slide the converter on to the freewheel support and turbine shaft. Refit the engine to the transmission.

Refilling the torque converter with oil:

On completion of a torque converter and clutch overhaul it is necessary to fill the torque converter and the oil pipes. The converter must be full of engine oil before checking the tank level by dipstick. If there is any doubt about this, detach the oil return pipe from the converter at the tank, run the engine and check that oil flows from the pipe.

7:8 Servicing the clutch controls:

Intermediate lever:

Components of the lever are shown in **FIG 7:11**. To remove the lever, detach the clutch rod and actuating rod clevis. Remove circlip 1, washer 2, grommet 3, spacer 4 and lever 6. Lift off 'O' ring 7, thrust ring 8 and spring 9.

Renew the pivot shaft and bush 5 if worn. Renew the lever pin if its eyes are worn. To remove and refit the

FIG 7:13 Cross-section through earlier four-speed input shaft

Key to Fig 7:13   1 Input shaft   2 First-speed fixed gear   3 Second-speed fixed gear   4 Thrust washer   5 Third-speed free running gear   6 Sliding sleeve   7 Spider   8 Fourth-speed free running gear   9 Thrust washer   10 Roller bearing   11 Nut   12 Oil seal location   13 Splines (clutch plate hub engagement)   14 Needle bearing   15 Needle bearing cage   16 Brake band   17 Synchroniser ring   18 Needle bearing   19 Needle bearing cage   20 Lockplate

FIG 7:14   Cross-section through earlier four-speed pinion shaft

Key to Fig 7:14   1 First-speed free running gear   2 Spider   3 Brake band   4 Second-speed free running   5 Third-speed fixed gear   6 Fourth-speed fixed gear   7 Spacer   8 Roller bearing   9 Pinion shaft   10 Thrust washer   11 Needle bearing   12 Needle bearing cage   13 Sliding sleeve   14 Synchroniser ring   15 Needle bearing   16 Needle bearing cage   17 Spacers   18 Retaining ring   **L** Ballbearing location

shaft and dowel pin, heat the casing to 120°C (248°F). Install to dimensions given in **FIG 7:11**. Coat the shafts with molybdenum disulphide grease. Fit the spring as shown at A. Fit the thrust ring with the cavity over the dowel pin and the end of the spring. Fit the 'O' ring, the lever and the remaining parts. Install the circlip.

Clutch fork:

Detach the rear end of the clutch rod 5 from the release fork lever (see **FIG 7:10**). The fork is carried on the shaft located in the transmission casing. holes being covered on outside by caps. Prise out the caps with two screwdrivers. Drive out the roll pin securing the fork to the shaft. Drift out the shaft and remove the fork and washers.

If worn, renew the shaft bushes, driving them below the outer surface so that the caps may be refitted. Reassemble the fork and shaft so that the holes for the roll pin are aligned. Fit the roll pin. Use molybdenum disulphide grease on the shaft and its bushes.

7:9 Overhauling the transmission:

Refer to the opening paragraphs of **Chapter 6, Section 6:4**. These apply with equal force to the Sportomatic transmissions and the following instructions are given to assist those who have the requisite experience, access to the necessary tools, a press, an oven and to appropriate precision measuring equipment. Make notes and sketches to supplement the text. In particular note which way round components are fitted. Do not transpose shims or washers (see **Chapter 6, Section 6:5**).

Dismantling, all transmissions:

The following initial dismantling operations (which assume that the transmission is to be completely dismantled) are common to the three-speed and to the earlier and later types of four-speed transmissions.

1 Release the clutch intermediate lever from the vacuum-servo clevis (see **FIG 7:10**). Release the servo unit and bracket from the transmission casing.
2 Remove the transmission front support. Remove the parking lock cap screw from just above the tachometer elbow drive. Withdraw the spring and ball. Remove the bypass switch. Remove the front cover.
3 Remove the torque converter and clutch as described in **Section 7:7**. Remove and dismantle the differential and final drive as described in **Chapter 6, Section 6:6**.

Dismantling the earlier four-speed gearbox:

FIGS 7:1 and **7:4** relate to this gearbox.

1 Refer to **FIG 7:12** and remove the parking lockpin and ball from reverse selector fork 1. Remove circlip 6 and pull off the reverse sliding gear 5 and fork. Detach the springs and lift off the parking lock lever and pawl 2.
2 Select fourth speed by turning the selector rod clockwise and pulling it forward. Fit tool P37 to the splines at the rear end of the input shaft to prevent turning and unscrew bolt 3. Remove the splined muff.
3 Remove roll pin 4 and unscrew the castellated nut. Remove the reversing light switch and the actuating pin. Remove the selector shaft guide fork and

FIG 7:15 Later type gearbox with front cover removed

Key to Fig 7:15　　1 Reverse gear　　2 Flanged nut
3 Reverse idler gear assembly　　4 Reverse selector gear
5 Parking lock springs　6 Parking lock pawl　7 Speedometer
drive gear　8 Bolt　9 Parking lock lever　10 Reverse gear
fork　11 Snap ring

continue with removal of the intermediate plate as described for the earlier five-speed gearbox in **Chapter 6, Section 6:4**. Identify and retain the gasket(s) in **FIGS 7:1** and **7:4**.

4 Carry on dismantling as instructed for the five-speed transmission. When identifying the gears, remember there is one speed less, so that called a second-speed gear in the five-speed transmission is the first-speed gear in the four-speed gearbox, and so on.

5 A cross-section through the input shaft is shown in **FIG 7:13**. The gear for first-speed is splined to the shaft and is mounted to the rear of the intermediate plate, the shaft carrying no gear in front of the plate as it does in the five-speed box. The gear may be pressed off the shaft together with the inner race half of the ballbearing. When refitting this gear, its small collar faces outward.

6 A cross-section through the pinion shaft is shown in **FIG 7:14**. The relevant **R** dimension (see **Chapter 6, FIG 6:13**) is tabulated in **Chapter 6, Section 6:7** and the pinion positioning procedure is as described in **Chapter 6, Sections 6:5** and **6:7**.

FIG 7:16　Three-speed gearbox input shaft

Key to Fig 7:16　1 Spacer　2 Nut　3 Lockplate　4 Roller bearing　5 Washer　6 Spacer　7 Sliding sleeve　8 Sleeve guide
9 Third-speed free running gear　10 Needle bearing　11 Needle bearing race　12 Thrust washer　13 Second-speed fixed gear
14 Input shaft with integral first-speed gear

FIG 7:17　Three-speed gearbox pinion shaft

Key to Fig 7:17　1 Ballbearing inner race　2 Spacer　3 Roller bearing　4 Thrust washer　5 First-speed free running gear
6 Needle bearing cage　7 Needle bearing race　8 Sliding sleeve　9 Sleeve guide　10 Second-speed free running gear　11 Needle
bearing　12 Needle bearing race　13 Thrust washer　14 Third-speed fixed gear　15 Spacer　16 Spacer　17 Shim(s)　18 Roller
bearing　19 Pinion shaft

94

FIG 7:18 Front cover

Key to Fig 7:18 1 Speedometer drive retaining bolt 2 Washer 3a Elbow adaptor 3b Seal 3c Guide bush 3d 'O' ring
4 Gearshaft 5 Seal 6 Thrust washer 7 Bush 8 Front cover

Dismantling the later four-speed and the three-speed gearboxes:

FIGS 7:2 and **7:3** relate to these gearboxes.

1 Refer to **FIG 7:15**. Engage fourth gear by turning the selector rod to the right and pulling it forwards (see arrows). Detach the parking lock springs and remove the pawl and lever.

2 Use tool P37 to block the input shaft. Remove bolt 8 and gear 7. Remove ring 11. Remove parking lock 9. Push in the detent pin and remove the reverse gear selector and rod 10.

3 Remove the splined bush and the reverse idler gear assembly 3 together with the needle bearing cages and thrust bearing cage. Remove nut 2. Remove the bypass

and reversing light switches and their contact plungers.

4 Withdraw the shaft assemblies and intermediate plate. Identify and retain gasket(s) **S** in **FIG 7:2** or **7:3**. Using tool P353a, press the pinion and input shaft assemblies from the intermediate plate as described in **Chapter 6, Section 6:4** for the earlier five-speed box.

5 The components of the three-speed input and pinion shafts are shown in **FIGS 7:16** and **7:17** respectively. The components of the four-speed version will be identified from **FIG 7:2** in conjunction with these illustrations. The relevant **R** dimension (see **Chapter 6, FIG 6:13**) is tabulated in **Chapter 6, Section 6:7** and the pinion positioning procedure is as described in **Chapter 6, Sections 6:5** and **6:7**.

FIG 7:19 Intermediate plate

Key to Fig 7:19 1 Bolt 2 Washer 3 Clamping plate 4 Ballbearing 5 Support plate 6 Snap ring 7 Reverse idler gearshaft 8 Thrust washer 9 Reverse gear/ballbearing assembly 10 Roller bearing outer race 11 Dowel 12 Spring anchor stud 13, 14 and 15 Bushes 16 Intermediate plate

Synchronisers:

Refer to **Chapter 6, Section 6 :5**. Take particular care to note which way round the single brake band in the first-speed gear is fitted as **this is not the same for all boxes.**

Front cover:

Refer to **FIG 7:18**. This shows a later Sportomatic version. Differences between this and other models will be self-evident. To withdraw the speedometer drive, remove retaining bolt 1. Remove the reverse idler thrust washer 6 by prying it out. Extract bush 7 after heating the

cover to 120°C (248°F). Heat the cover to this temperature before pressing in a new bush or, using tool P362, driving in washer 6. When reassembling, ensure that the blind hole in bush 3c aligns with the hole for the retaining bolt 1. If seal 5 is being renewed, use P218 to drive in the new part. Torque tighten bolt 1 to 1.6 to 1.8kgm (12 to 13lb ft).

Intermediate plate:

Refer to **FIG 7:19**. This shows a later Sportomatic version. Differences between this and other models will be self-evident. Heat the plate to 120°C (248°F) before removing shaft 7, bearing/reverse gear 9, roller bearing outer race 10 or dowels 11. Heat the plate again to this temperature before fitting those new parts. If new detent bushes are being fitted, use mandrel P262 and drive in bush 15 until the mandrel bottoms. Drive in bush 14 to the second mark on the mandrel and bush 13 to the first mark on the mandrel. Use tool P372 to align bearing 4 and torque tighten the bolts which retain clamping plate 3 to 2.1 to 2.3kgm (15.0 to 16.5lb ft). Bolts 1 should also be tightened to this torque. Dowels 11 should protrude by 5.5mm (0.22in) on each side of the plate. Use press tools VW407 and P255 to assemble the reverse gear into a new bearing to form assembly 9.

The differential gearing:

Refer to **Chapter 6, Section 6:6.**

Gear and backlash settings:

Refer to **Chapter 6, Section 6:7.**

Reassembling the earlier four-speed gearbox:

Reverse the dismantling procedure. Torque tighten the reversing light and bypass switches to 4.5 to 5.0kgm (33 to 36lb ft), the input shaft nut and the pinion shaft bolt to 11 to 12kgm (80 to 87lb ft), the input shaft castellated nut to 10kgm (72lb ft), and also refer to **Chapter 6, Sections 6:10** (earlier five-speed box). Refer also to **Sections 7:5, 7:6, 7:7** and **7:8.**

Reassembling the later four-speed and three-speed gearboxes:

Reverse the dismantling procedure. Use tools VW401, VW426 and VW412 when pressing the input and pinion shafts into the intermediate plate. Use tools P360 and P364 to fit a new input shaft seal. Note the following torque tightening figures. Reversing light and bypass switches, 3.5 to 4.0kgm (25 to 29lb ft); input shaft flanged nut and pinion shaft bolt, 11 to 12 kgm (80 to 87 lb ft); input shaft front nut, 10 to 12kgm (72 to 87lb ft); selector fork bolts, 2.2 to 2.6kgm (16 to 19lb ft), and refer to **Sections 7:5, 7:6, 7:7** and **7:8.**

7:10 The torque converter pump

The dual rotor pump is driven by the lefthand camshaft. A non-adjustable relief valve is incorporated. The function of the pump is to keep the torque converter full of oil drawn from the main oil tank. This oil is drawn from the tank at a 30mm higher level than is the engine oil supply. The difference in level ensures that a leaking converter will not result in failure of the engine lubrication. Functioning of the pump may be checked by disconnecting the oil return line from the converter at the oil tank while the engine is running.

Access to the pump requires removal of the lefthand road wheel and the lefthand heat exchanger. Spare rotors and shaft are only supplied in sets. Check that the 'O' ring

is in good condition and use new gaskets when re-assembling the pump. Assemble with internal parts wetted with engine oil and ensure that the outer rotor is fitted with the bevelled diameter into the pump body. The alignment dowel should project from the housing face by 4mm (0.157in). The driving roll pins should project by 8mm (0.315in) from the end face of the camshaft.

7:11 Fault diagnosis

(a) Clutch slip

1 Oily linings
2 Defective clutch or operating linkage

(b) Clutch slips after gearshift

1 Control valve out of adjustment

(c) Too fast or slow clutch engagement after downshift

1 Control valve needs adjusting

(d) Clutch will not disengage

1 Clutch linkage wrongly adjusted
2 Leaking hoses or vacuum reservoir, blocked hoses
3 Defective servo unit
4 Defective bearing for input shaft spigot
5 Control valve solenoid faulty, break in circuit
6 Dirty gearlever switch contacts, poor earthing

(e) Engine dies on gearshifting, idling cannot be adjusted

1 Check 2 and 3 in (d)
2 Leaking check valves in inlet manifold

(f) Clutch not engaging after downshift, engages too rapidly on opening throttle

1 Gearshift switch contacts sticking or shorted
2 Shortcircuited wire between switch and solenoid
3 Sticking solenoid in control valve

(g) Car leaps when gearlever is released with engine idling and gear engaged

1 Idling speed too high
2 Control valve wrongly adjusted

(h) High pitched whine from converter

1 Too little oil in converter
2 Oil pressure too low
3 Loss of oil through pump hub of converter
4 Converter seams leaking

(i) Poor acceleration from good engine and transmission system

1 Defective torque converter
To check this, apply handbrake, select D4 (D3 on the three-speed gearbox) and open throttle. The stall speed should be 2400 to 2800rev/min. Keep the temperature below the red section on the dial.

NOTES

CHAPTER 8

REAR AXLE AND SUSPENSION

8:1 Description

The layout of the system is shown in **FIG 8:1**, each independent suspension unit consisting of a radius arm 1 bolted at the rear end to the flange of control arm 3. The front end of the radius arm is coupled to the outer splined end of torsion bar 2, the inner end of the bar being fixed.

Triangulated control of the suspension is maintained by arm 3, the inner end being pivoted in a bracket on the body. Drive from the transmission is taken through drive shaft 4, each shaft being provided with two constant speed joints. Telescopic hydraulic dampers 5 are fitted. These straddle the body and each rear suspension assembly. Depending upon the vehicle model and whether a different make may have been optionally selected for fitment, dampers of Boge, Koni or Bilstein manufacture may be installed. Note, however, that dampers of Koni manufacture cannot be installed on Targa models. Eccentric bolts 6 and 7 allow adjustments to be made to wheel camber and toe-in as described in **Section 8:10**. An anti-roll bar is not standard but may have been fitted as an optional extra.

8:2 Maintenance

Wheels and tyres:

Regularly check and re-inflate the tyres to the pressure tabulated in **Technical Data** in the **Appendix**.

Periodically check the treads and sidewalls of the tyres for damage. A damaged tyre should be renewed; this is particularly vital if the car is to be driven at high speeds.

Suspension:

Every 6000 miles (10,000km), check over the suspension generally. Ensure that the dampers are securely mounted and that all rubber bushes are serviceable.

Drive shafts:

No routine maintenance to the drive shafts is required except for checking that the rubber boots are not torn or perished.

8:3 Dampers

Dampers fitted to later models are of larger diameter and increased length and are not interchangeable with those fitted to earlier models. Defective dampers cannot be overhauled or repaired by an owner and must be replaced by new units. Ensure that the new dampers are the same make and type as those originally fitted. If dampers of another manufacture are to be fitted, consult a Porsche agent regarding the availability of the acceptable alternative(s) noting that **Koni dampers cannot be installed on Targa models**. Dampers are colour coded

FIG 8:1 Layout of the rear suspension system and camber and toe-in adjusters

Key to Fig 8:1 1 Radius arm 2 Torsion bar 3 Suspension control arm 4 Drive shaft (early type) 5 Damper 6 Camber adjuster 7 Toe-in adjuster

as follows: Boge, black; Koni, red; and Bilstein, green. A cross-section through a damper is shown in **FIG 8:2**.

Damper removal:

The car should preferably be standing on its wheels. If it is on stands, lift the suspension arm with special tool P289 or use a jack at the rear of the arm. From inside the engine compartment, remove the mounting cap, hold the damper rod with a spanner fitted to the flats and remove the retaining nut, washer and grommet. Release the lower end from the suspension arm by removing bolt 12 in **FIG 8:3** or nut and bolt 13 and 14 in **FIG 8:4** and withdraw the damper.

Damper fitment:

Hold the new damper vertically in a vice and reciprocate the top end several times to 'bleed' the unit. Fitment is now the reverse of the removal sequence. If the original damper is being refitted, ensure that the buffer 6 in **FIG 8:2** is serviceable and that all grommets are in good

condition. Torque tighten the nut and bolt (**FIG 8:4**) to 7.5kgm (54lb ft) or the bolt (**FIG 8:3**) to 12.5kgm (90lb ft). Tighten the upper retaining nut to 2.5kgm (18lb ft). This will partially compress the grommet.

8:4 Drive shafts

Later type drive shafts are lighter than those fitted to earlier models and have narrower constant velocity joints of 32mm (1.26in) width. The later type of shaft may be fitted to earlier models but new supporting plates and new bolts will be required to match.

Removal:

1 Raise the car and remove the rear wheels. Refer to **FIG 8:4**. Remove and discard the splitpin 16 and remove nut 15. The flange should be held with tool P36b and the nut removed with tools P296, P44a and P42a.

2 Remove the bolts 11 from both flanges and dismount the shaft. Discard the gaskets 7.

FIG 8:2 Cross-section through a rear damper, top end to the left

Key to Fig 8:2 1 Nut 2 Washer 3 Grommets 4 Vehicle body 5 Grommet bush 6 Rubber buffer 7 Rod 8 Cover tube 9 Stop disc 10 Plunger 11 Cylinder 12 Check valve 13 Grommet 14 Grommet bush

FIG 8:3   Components of a hub and suspension assembly (later type)

Key to Fig 8:3   1 Brake line   2 Clip   3 Brake hose   4 Bolt   5 Lockwasher   6 Brake caliper   7 Splitpin   8 Nut   9 Washer   10 Screw   11 Brake disc   12 Bolt   13 Washer   14 Damper   15 Drive shaft splined stub   16 Hub   17 Bolt   18 Lockwasher   19 Cover   20 Splitpin   21 Nut   22 Washer   23 Expander   24 Spring   25 Handbrake cable   26 Spacer tube   27 Washer   28 Nut   29 Spring washer   30 Bolt   31 Backing plate with handbrake shoes   32 Nut   33 Toothed washer   34 Washer   35 Bolt   36 Washer   37 Nuts   38 Toothed washers   39 Toe-in adjuster   40 Camber adjuster   41 Nut   42 Washers   43 Bolt   44 Control arm   45 Ballbearing   46 Rubber mounts   47 Radius arm

Dismantling and reassembling:

Remove the clips from the rubber boots and the circlips from the shaft ends. Press the constant velocity joints from the shafts. Clean all parts and check for wear.

Fit new dust boots. Slide the wire retainer and joint onto the shaft and fit new circlips. Fill each joint with 70g (2.5oz) of molybdenum disulphide grease. Apply any surplus to the flange side. Clean the boot and flange face from grease. Apply MMM EC.750M.2G51 adhesive between the flange and large boot diameter. To fit the boot clips, drill 2mm (0.08in) holes at each end and draw together with pliers. Lock by bending the tab over. Tap down flat.

Refitting:

Fit new gaskets 7. Lightly oil the stub shafts and insert them into the wheel hubs. Check that the flange faces are free of grease. Use only bolts marked either 130-140 or 12K on Schnorr washers that have their hollow sides facing the base plates. Torque tighten the bolts to 4.3kgm (30lb ft) on earlier shafts or to 8.3kgm (60lb ft) on later, lighter joint, shafts. Tighten the axle nut to a torque of 30 to 35kgm (220 to 250lb ft) and lock with a new splitpin.

8:5   Removing and refitting a control arm

It is officially specified that, on earlier models (those fitted with fabricated arms), the engine/transmission assembly should be removed (see **Chapter 1, Section 1:3**) before carrying out the following procedure. Depending, however, upon the experience of the operator and the equipment available, removing the pivot bolt (removal operation 5) may be carried out after releasing the relevant mountings, pipes, controls, etc. and raising the engine/transmission assembly sufficiently to provide the necessary clearance. The engine/transmission assembly removal requirement is not specified for models fitted with the type of arm shown in **FIG 8:3** (cast aluminium arms).

Removal:

1 Mount the rear of the car on stands and remove the road wheels. Remove the brake caliper and brake disc as described in **Chapter 11, Section 11:5**.
2 Using tool P289, refer to **Section 8:3** and uncouple the lower end of the damper from the control arm. Dismount the drive shaft as described in **Section 8:4**. Drive out the wheel hub (2 in **FIG 8:4**) using tool P297 and, if necessary, remove the bearing inner race of bearing 5.

FIG 8:4   Cross-section through a rear hub

Key to Fig 8:4   1 Brake disc   2 Wheel hub   3 Cover   4 Stub shaft   5 Ballbearing   6 Handbrake carrier plate   7 Gasket
8 Drive shaft constant velocity joint   9 Plate   10 Schnorr washer   11 Bolt   12 Suspension control arm   13 Bolt   14 Nut
15 Nut   16 Splitpin   17 Shroud   18 Circlip

3 Remove the splitpin and nut from the handbrake cable and withdraw the cable. Remove the retaining bolt from the shield plate. Remove the retaining bolts and dismount the carrier plate and shield plate. Remove the handbrake cable guide.

4 Remove the hexagon nuts and washers 32, 33 and 34 from the bolts which attach the radius arm 47 in **FIG 8:3** to the control arm 44. Remove the bolts. Remove the nuts and washers 37 and 38 from the eccentric bolts 39 and 40. Remove the bolts.

5 Remove the self-locking nut 41 and remove the pivot bolt 43. Dismount the control arm assembly. Service the arm and hub as described in **Section 8:6**. If necessary, remove the radius arm as described in **Section 8:8**.

Refitment:

Follow the reverse of the removal sequence. Raise the control arm until its lower edge is in line with the upper edge of the radius arm and, **in this position**, fit a new nut 41 and tighten it to a torque of 12kgm (87lb ft). Connect the control and radius arms and torque tighten the retaining nuts and bolts to 9kgm (65lb ft). Tighten the camber adjustment nut to 6kgm (43lb ft) and the toe-in adjustment nut to 5kgm (36lb ft). Tighten the brake support and the shield plate retaining bolts to 2.5kgm (18lb ft). Use new splitpins where applicable. The refitment procedure for the drive shafts is covered in **Section 8:4**. The procedure for refitment of the brake caliper, bleeding the system and adjustment of the handbrake are described in **Chapter 11, Sections 11:5, 11:7** and **11:8**. Adjust the wheel camber and toe-in as described in **Section 8:10**.

8:6 Servicing a control arm

An unserviceable hub bearing (45 in **FIG 8:3**, 5 in **FIG 8:4**) may be renewed without dismounting the control arm. After removing the drive shaft, brake disc and hub and knocking out the old bearing, press in a new bearing using tool P298b and the drive shaft as shown in **FIG 8:5**. Once removed, a hub ballbearing must not be refitted.

For full servicing, dismount the arm as described in **Section 8:5**. An unserviceable hub bearing may be removed and a new bearing pressed in. If a suitable press is not available, use tool P298b as described earlier.

Possible accident distortion of an arm may be checked using gauges P295b and P295c. Do not attempt to salvage an arm which is distorted or cracked.

The flanbloc pivot bearings (fabricated type arms) can only be removed by breaking them up. Always renew radial ball thrust bearings on fabricated type arms noting that the housing must be heated to approximately 120°C (250°F) before inserting the new bearing. The rubber mounts (46 in **FIG 8:3**) fitted to the pivots of later type aluminium arms cannot (if pressed out) be refitted and new mounts must be obtained.

8:7 Removing, refitting and adjusting torsion bar

The torsion bar, shown at 2 in **FIG 8:1** may be removed as follows:

1 Raise the car and remove the rear wheel. Lift the radius arm with a jack or with the aid of tool P289 as shown in **FIG 8:6**. Release the damper lower mounting bolt or bolt and nut (see **Section 8:3**).

2 Refer to **FIG 8:3**. Release the radius arm from the control arm 44 by removing the bolts 35 (2 off) and the adjusting bolts 39 and 40. All these bolts are attached by nuts and washers 32, 33, 34, 37 and 38.

3 Refer to **FIG 8:6** and remove the four cover bolts shown and withdraw the single spacer fitted to the lowermost bolt. Prise off the cover with a screwdriver.

4 Lower the jack or remove the lifting tool P289. Remove the body plug from inside the body and withdraw the radius arm.

5 Withdraw torsion bar taking care not to damage its protective coating.

A broken bar is removed by withdrawing opposite bar and pushing out parts with a steel rod. **Do not attempt to identify the bar by scratches or centre-punch marks.** Check the rubber support for deterioration. Check the torsion bar for cracks, rust or worn splines.

FIG 8:5   Pressing in a new hub bearing

FIG 8:6   Removing a radius arm cover

Key to Fig 8:6   A Special tool P289

Renew if necessary. Ends of bars are stamped 'R' for righthand side and 'L' for lefthand side. **They are pre-stressed and must not be interchanged.**

When refitting, coat the bar and its splines with multi-purpose lithium grease. Adjust as described later. Coat the rubber support with rubber grease and fit it. Refit the radius arm and cover and start the three bolts which can be reached. Lift the radius arm until the fourth bolt and spacer can be fitted. Tighten these bolts to 4.7kgm (34lb ft). Refit to the control arm as described in **Section 8:5**. Adjust the wheel tracking and camber as in **Section 8:10**.

Adjusting a torsion bar:

The car must be standing level. Check with a spirit level on door sill. The radius arm must be hanging free and detached from the control arm. Check the angle of the radius arm with a clinometer placed along the top edge.

The correct angle is 39°. Adjustment is by vernier splines on the torsion bar. There are 40 splines at the inner end and 44 at the outer end. If the bar is turned one spline onwards at the inner end, the change in angle is 9°. If the radius arm is reset in the opposite direction by one spline, the change is 8° 10'. The total movement of the radius

FIG 8:7 Anti-roll bar. Arrows show correct angle for top shackle eyes

FIG 8:8 Rear height adjustment

Key to Fig 8:8   a, b, b1 See text

arm is thus only 50'. This is the minimum re-adjustment possible. Adjust to the nearest degree. After completing the assembly of the control arm, adjust the rear wheel tracking and camber as described in **Section 8:10**.

8:8 Radius arms

Lefthand radius arms are shown 1 in **FIG 8:1** and 47 in **FIG 8:3**. They link the 'springing' function of the torsion bars with the suspension control arms. Radius arms are bolted to the control arms. The procedure for uncoupling and recoupling the radius arms to the control arms is included in **Section 8:5**. The procedure for dismounting and refitting a radius arm is included in **Section 8:7**.

8:9 Anti-roll bar

Rear anti-roll (stabiliser) bars are not standard equipment on the models covered by this manual. As an optional extra, a bar may or may not have been fitted to the model being dealt with. If installed, the bar is fitted transversely and forward of the suspension control arms.

Removal and fitment:

The outer ends of the bar are connected by shackles to ball-studs on the arms. To remove the bar, prise the upper eyes of the shackles off the ball-studs with a large screwdriver. Remove the bearing caps (four bolts) and lift away the bar. Check the rubber bearing bushes for wear. Place the bar on a flat surface and check that the ends lie in the same plane. Look for cracks and rust which may lead to premature failure. Check shackle bushes and fit new ones dry, making sure thay are the right size for the bar diameter. There are grommets in the upper eyes and these may be renewed by lightly lubricating new ones and pressing them in with a vice. When installing the shackles make sure that they are correctly angled to point as shown in **FIG 8:7**. Lubricate the grommets with molybdenum disulphide grease.

To refit bar, reverse the dismantling procedure, pressing the upper eyes of the shackles into place with a screwdriver.

8:10 Rear wheel alignment

Checking alignment must be carried out in association with front wheel alignment, the total effect giving the best road-holding and cornering characteristics to the car. It is desirable to have the checking and setting made on accurate equipment and with the car properly prepared. The fuel tank must be full and the spare wheel fitted. All parts of the suspension must be in good mechanical condition and adjustment. Wheel rims must not runout excessively, tyres must not be unevenly worn and they must be correctly inflated. It is assumed that the rear torsion bars are correctly set as described in **Section 8:7**.

Refer to **FIG 8:1** and slacken the eccentric bolt nuts 6 and 7 and the retaining nuts, one of which can be seen to the left of the eccentric bolts. Turn the tracking and camber eccentric until the values specified in **Technical Data** in the **Appendix** are obtained on the equipment.

When installing the camber eccentric, make sure it points downwards so that there is adequate clearance for adjustment. If it is found that the eccentric binds at one end or the other of the slot, turn it through 180°. After adjustment, tighten the nuts.

8:11 Height adjustment

Refer to **FIG 8:8**. Have car correctly prepared as described in **Section 8:10** and standing on level ground. Bounce the car at the rear several times to allow suspension to settle naturally. Note that dimension '**b**' cannot be measured directly because the torsion bar is eccentrically mounted in its bush and cover. Dimension '**b1**' is calculated as follows: Measure wheel centre height '**a**' and add 12mm (0.47in) to give value '**b**'. Subtract from this figure half the diameter of the radius arm cover (30mm or 1.18in). The result is '**b1**'.

The measured height '**b1**' must not differ from the calculated height by more than ± 5mm (0.197in), and the height difference between the righthand and lefthand sides must not exceed 8mm (0.315in). If the correct setting cannot be obtained, check both the height adjustment of the front suspension and the adjustment of the rear torsion bar.

8:12 Fault diagnosis

(a) Noise from axle

1 Worn wheel bearings
2 Worn constant velocity joints
3 Worn axle splines
4 Loose axle nuts
5 Damper mountings defective (or loosely fitted)
6 Broken stabiliser bar or faulty mountings.
7 Loose radius or control arm
8 Control arm pivot mounting worn
9 Worn torsion bar splines or bushes
10 Brake backplate loose

(b) Poor handling, bad road holding

1 Check 6, 7, 8 and 9 in (a)
2 Torsion bars 'settled' or broken
3 Radius arm setting incorrect
4 Incorrect wheel alignment
5 Incorrect height adjustment
6 Dampers inoperative, rubber buffers worn
7 Faulty transmission mountings

CHAPTER 9

FRONT SUSPENSION

9:1 Description

Two types of front suspension are fitted to models covered by this manual. In both types the layout incorporates MacPherson type struts with forward facing steering arms. Earlier models are provided with telescopic self-levelling struts with which torsion bars are not incorporated. Later models are provided with torsion bars and conventional dampers unless the self-levelling type of struts have been optionally ordered on relevant models.

Self-levelling type suspension:

This system is shown in **FIG 9:1**. The strut provides the suspension 'spring' function and also acts as a damper. A cross-section through this type of hydro-pneumatic strut is shown in **FIG 9:2**.

Gas in the high pressure chamber is isolated from the oil by a diaphragm shown as a thick black line. Oil and gas are not separated in the low pressure chamber. Gas pressure acting on the piston rod area takes 90% of the weight of the empty car. Pump rod 12 forms a hydraulic pump in conjunction with piston rod 11.

Road bumps cause the pump to transfer oil through valves 7 and 9 from the low pressure cylinder to the high pressure cylinder. The pressurised gas is further compressed, which raises the car to a predetermined level.

The pump action also acts as a damper. At a predetermined height, port 5 is cleared by the damping piston and normal suspension movements continue, the ports being too small to affect them. The pump rod is reduced in diameter higher up so that no pumping can take place. This prevents excessive raising of the suspension.

The struts will bring the car up to normal level within 300 to 1500 yards on smooth roads and much shorter distances on rough roads. The level remains constant if the load is not altered after parking.

Torsion bar suspension:

In this system each suspension strut incorporates a single function telescopic hydraulic damper (see **FIG 9:3**) and torsion bars provide the 'springing' function.

Hubs and suspension control arms:

The wheel hub stub axles are integral with the struts. Each strut unit is ball jointed at its lower end to a transverse suspension control arm which is 'keyed' to a control arm. Struts are located at their upper ends in body mountings which can be moved to allow adjustment of wheel camber and caster angles. Wheel toe-in is adjusted by altering the 'lengths' of the steering linkage tie rods. Each wheel hub runs on two taper roller bearings.

FIG 9:1 Layout of front suspension and steering linkage (hydro-pneumatic type struts shown)

Key to Fig 9:1 1 Boot 2 Strut top location 3 Self-levelling hydro-pneumatic strut 4 Boot 5 Steering gearbox 6 Brake caliper 7 Triangulation link 8 Crossmember (fabricated type) 9 Ball joint 10 Brace 11 Tie rod 12 Tie rod clamp

Anti-roll bar:

Depending upon the model, an anti-roll bar may or may not be fitted and may be of differing diameters. **FIG 9:4** shows the location of an anti-roll bar.

9:2 Maintenance

Wheels and tyres:

Regularly check and re-inflate the tyres to the pressure tabulated in the **Technical Data** section of the **Appendix**. Periodically check the treads and sidewalls of the tyres for damage. A damaged tyre should be renewed.

Suspension and hubs:

Every 6000 miles (10,000km), look over the suspension generally. Check the wheel bearings for play and, if necessary, adjust as described in **Section 9:4**.

9:3 Suspension struts

Self-levelling struts:

A cross-section through a self-levelling hydro-pneumatic suspension strut is shown in **FIG 9:2**. Their operation is described in **Section 9:1**.

As there are no height adjusters on this system, wheel alignment must be entrusted to a Porsche service station. The agent must also be consulted if the strut gives trouble.

It is most important to check ground clearance during servicing operations. If the car is lifted so that the wheels are clear of the ground, pressure in the struts is equalised. When the car is lowered, the strut will then support only the basic load and the car will drop below the normal static load position. The procedure for checking the suspension height is described in **Section 9:9**.

Damper struts:

A cross-section through a damper suspension strut is shown in **FIG 9:3**. Damper struts may be of Boge, Bilstein or Koni manufacture depending upon the model or which make of damper may have been optionally selected. Note, however, that **dampers of Koni manufacture cannot be installed on Targa models.**

Suspension strut removal and fitment:

1 Remove the brake caliper as described in **Chapter 11, Section 11:4**. Remove the wheel hub as described in **Section 9:4**. Remove the brake shield plate.

2 Uncouple the tie rod ball joint from the strut steering arm as described in **Chapter 10**, **Section 10:6**. On cars fitted with the damper type struts, refer to **Section 9:7** and **FIG 9:8** and remove the torsion bar and adjusting lever 6.

3 Uncouple the suspension strut from the suspension arm and separate them by pushing the arm downwards. If the strut is fitted with the type of ball joint shown in **FIG 9:5**, unscrew the nut 1 and tap out the double wedge bolt 2 to separate the strut from the suspension control arm. The other type of fitting is that shown in **FIG 9:6**, which consists of three bolts securing the lower end of the strut to the control arm. From inside the luggage compartment, remove the retaining nut, etc. and withdraw the strut downwards. If necessary, pull off the spacer ring.

If accident damage to a suspension strut of either type is suspected, have the geometry and function serviceability checked on the relevant gauges by a Porsche agent.

Do not attempt to salvage a strut with a damaged, cracked or distorted stub axle, steering arm or strut body. Renew torn or perished rubber parts.

From chassis No 301800, damper repair kits can be installed in damper type struts. This saves a renewal of the whole strut, but it entails the local or home manufacture of a suitable peg tool to open the damper.

1972 models have a modified ball joint mounting which is attached to the strut by a double-wedge arrangement as shown in **FIG 9:5**. The former clamping arrangement is no longer used. A special adaptor tool with four lugs spaced at 90° is necessary to remove the nut 6. The part number is P2806. To remove the ball joint, refer to **FIG 9:5** and proceed as follows:

1 Separate the suspension strut from the control arm as detailed in the preceding instructions.

2 From beneath the control arm, extract splitpin 4, remove lockplate 5 and, with the special adaptor tool and a wrench, unscrew nut 6. Using a soft-faced mallet, tap out the ball joint and remove it from the control arm.

3 Reassemble in the reverse order and coat the double-wedge bolt with multi-purpose grease before assembling. Install it so that the retaining nut 1 is forward and the notch on the face of the double-wedge and the wedge contour are directed towards the stub axle. Renew splitpin 4 and lockwasher 5.

4 Tap the double-wedge with a hammer before finally tightening the nut to a torque of 2.2kgm (16lb ft).

Refitting the strut:

This is the reverse of removal, noting the following points where relevant to the type of strut used.

Fit 'O' ring R32-2.5 on to the axle when installing ring 10 (see **FIG 9:6**). Heat the ring to 150°C (300°F) and push it into place.

Fill rubber boots on new ball joints with 6.5g (0.2oz) of multipurpose molybdenum disulphide grease. **The taper of the ball stud must be grease-free.** Tighten the stud nut to 4.5kgm (32.5lb ft). Use new lockplates and tighten the steering lever bolts to 4.7kgm (34lb ft). Fit the rubber buffer dry. Fit the top nut of strut on a new safety plate with its tab upwards. Tighten the nut to 8kgm (58lb ft).

FIG 9:2 Section through the self-levelling hydro-pneumatic suspension strut

Key to Fig 9:2   1 Low pressure chamber   2 Low pressure cylinder   3 High pressure chamber   4 High pressure or damping cylinder   5 Relief port orifice   6 Overload valve   7 Suction valve   8 Piston ring seal   9 Pressure valve   10 Damping valve   11 Piston rod   12 Pump rod

Use the following torques:

Ball joint to control arm nuts 7.5kgm (54lb ft). Use washers and new splitpins. Tie rod ball joint nut 4.5kgm (32.5lb ft) using a new splitpin. Brake carrier plate bolts on new lockplates 4.7kgm (34lb ft). Caliper bolts on spring washers 7kgm (50.5lb ft). Gland nut for brake pipe at caliper 2kgm (14.5lb ft). Shroud bolts 2.5kgm (18lb ft).

Adjust the wheel bearings as described in **Section 9:4**. Bleed the brakes as described in **Chapter 11**, **Section 11:7** and check the wheel alignment as described in **Section 9:10**.

FIG 9:3 Section through the damper strut fitted to torsion bar suspension models

Key to Fig 9:3   1 Hexagon nut   2 Safety plate   3 Washer   4 Bracket (on vehicle)   5 Rubber bush   6 Rubber buffer
7 Piston rod   8 Shielding tube   9 Stop disc   10 Oil seal   11 Cylinder   12 Strut tube   13 Piston   14 Bottom valve
15 Steering lever and ball

Checking the strut:

Alignment of the damper and stub axle is checked on special tool P.286. Renew the strut if the outside is covered in oily dirt. Hold strut vertically in a vice and pump it a few times. Then give long full strokes up and down and check for free play at any point. Excessive free play calls for strut renewal.

Damper type strut adjustment:

Koni adjustable dampers are standard on 911S cars and are optional on other models except Targa. To adjust outside car, mount vertically, press top end right down and turn gently to left until lugs engage inside damper and mark position. Check damper action by pumping top end up and down. If more damping is needed, press down and engage lugs at mark and then turn top tube to left for harder setting and to the right for a softer setting. Make sure both dampers have the same setting. To adjust Koni dampers when installed in car, raise front end and remove wheels. Hold up control arm with a jack and remove nut from top end of strut (inside luggage compartment). Adjust as just described. When finished, fit top nut on a new safety plate with tab upwards. Tighten nut to 8kgm (58lb ft).

9:4 Hubs

A cross-section through a hub is shown in **FIG 9:6**.

FIG 9:4   Front anti-roll bar

Key to Fig 9:4   A Crossmember brace clamp   B Control arm location

Removal:

Remove the brake caliper as described in **Chapter 11, Section 11:4**. Prise off cap 6, loosen the socket-headed screw and remove nut 7 and washer 8. Pull off the hub 3. Press out and discard the bearing outer races and the inner oil seal. If the brake disc is to be removed, mark it so that it may be refitted in its original relative position. Removal of the bearing may be eased by heating the hub to 120° to 150°C (250° to 300°F).

Clean out the old grease from the hub and check the flange for cracks, distortion or loose studs. Clean the bearings and check them in a dry state. Renew if rough, but note that renewed parts must be of same manufacture if mixed with original parts. Various makes of bearing have been fitted, such as SKF, FAG or Timken. **Do not mix parts of one make with those of another.**

Reassembly:

Heat the hub to 120° to 150°C (250° to 300°F) and press in the outer race of the inner bearing. Insert the inner race and press in the oil seal until it is flush with hub. Fit the outer race of the outer bearing.

Refit the brake disc with the marks made earlier, align and fit the bolts from the inside. Tighten the nuts on the spring washers to 2.3kgm (16.5lb ft). Fill the hub with 50cc or 43g (3cu in or 1.5oz) of multipurpose lithium grease, pressing it well into the bearings. Smear grease on both lips of the oil seal. Refit the hub to the axle stub.

Tighten the clamping nut to about 1.5kgm (10.8lb ft) while turning the hub to seat the rollers in their races. Slacken the nut until it is possible to move the washer 8 in **FIG 9:6** with a screwdriver (see **FIG 9:7**). There must be no free play in the bearings. Lock the nut by tightening the socket-head screw to 2.5kgm (18lb ft). Check that the adjustment is still correct.

Coat the nut and washer with lithium grease. Fit the cap without filling it with grease. Refit the caliper as described in **Chapter 11, Section 11:4**. Bleed the brakes as described in **Chapter 11, Section 11:7**.

9:5 Control arms

A control arm, fabricated type crossmember and associated parts are shown in **FIG 9:8**.

FIG 9:5 Front axle ball joint (later type)

Key to Fig 9:5 1 Nut, M8 2 Washer 3 Double wedge bolt 4 Splitpin 5 Lockplate 6 Nut 7 Ball joint 8 Strut

FIG 9:6 Section through front hub, showing bearings and seal

Key to Fig 9:6 1 Shield plate 2 Brake disc 3 Hub 4 Seal 5 Taper roller bearing 6 Cap 7 Clamping nut 8 Washer 9 Taper roller bearing 10 Distance ring 11 Damper strut 12 Steering lever 13 Ball joint (earlier type)

Control arm removal:

1 Refer to **Section 9:8** and remove the anti-roll bar if one is fitted. Remove the torsion bar adjusting screw 5 in **FIG 9:8**.

2 Refer to **Section 9:3** and uncouple the lower end of the suspension strut from the control arm. Withdraw the torsion bar adjusting lever 6 from the bar and remove the OWA-seal 4.

3 Remove bolt 3a. Remove the bolts which retain the control arm rubber mount cover bracket 1. Dismount the bracket. Press the control arm and torsion bar out of the reinforcing support member.

4 If distortion of the arm is suspected, have it checked in gauge P288. Inspection of the torsion bar is covered in **Section 9:7**.

Control arm fitment:

If a new torsion bar is being fitted or if both arms have been removed, confirm that the correctly handed bar (L, lefthand; R, righthand) is being fitted. Lightly coat the bar with lithium grease (particularly the splines) and fit the bar into the arm. Ensure that the end cap 7 in **FIG 9:8** is in position. Proceed by reversing the removal sequence and referring to **Sections 9:7** and **9:3**. Torque tighten bolts 10 to 4.7kgm (34lb ft) and bolts 3a to 9kgm (65lb ft). Adjust the suspension height as described in **Section 9:7** and check the wheel alignment as described in **Section 9:10**.

FIG 9:7 Checking adjustment of front hub bearings by moving thrust washer with a screwdriver

FIG 9:8 The modified control arm and crossmember introduced on 1968 models. The arm has integral rubber mountings

Key to Fig 9:8 1 Cover bracket 2 Control arm (left) 3 Crossmember 3a Crossmember bolt 4 OWA-seal 5 Adjusting screw 6 Adjusting lever 7 End cap 8 Torsion bar 9 Brace, bolt and washers 10 Bolt and washer

9:6 Crossmember

1974 Carrera models are provided with light-alloy crossmembers with detachable braces. The fabricated type of crossmember (with welded on braces) fitted to other models is 3 in **FIG 9:8**. Removal of the crossmember will normally only be necessary if, following an accident, distortion is suspected.

Removal and fitment:

Remove the control arms as described in **Section 9:5**. Detach the axle shield. Remove the two bolts which retain the steering gearbox (see **Chapter 10, Section 10:7**) to the crossmember. Remove the bolts which retain the crossmember to the body and dismount the crossmember.

A cracked or distorted crossmember should be renewed.

Fitment is the reverse of the removal sequence. Make sure that the crossmember is correctly seated in the

FIG 9:9 Fitting a torsion bar adjusting lever

Key to Fig 9:9 A Levering the control arm downwards
B See text

alignment studs in the body. Torque tighten the steering gearbox bolts (use new spring washers) to 4.7kgm (34lb ft).

9:7 Torsion bars

Torsion bars are prestressed. They are handed and marked L and R. Do not fit a lefthand bar to a righthand control arm or vice versa.

Removal:

Remove the adjusting screw 5 in **FIG 9:8**. Pull the adjusting lever 6 off the torsion bar and withdraw the OWA-seal 4. Remove the bolts 10 and dismount the bracket 1. Using an appropriate punch and taking care not to damage the splines, drive the bar forwards out of the control arm.

Check the bar for damaged splines, rust or chipped lacquer finish and renew if necessary.

Fitment:

Lightly coat the bar (particularly the splines) with lithium grease, check that the correctly handed bar is being fitted and insert the bar into the control arm from the front. Fit the OWA-seal. Refer to **FIG 9:9** and lever (see arrow **A**) the arm downwards as far as the suspension strut will allow. With the end cap 7 in **FIG 9:8** fitted, slide the adjusting lever 6 onto the bar leaving as little clearance at **B** in **FIG 9:9** as possible. Coat the adjusting bolt threads with molybdenum disulphide grease and lightly tighten it in place. Check that the end cap is properly seated. Fit the cover bracket and torque tighten the retaining bolts to 4.7kgm (34lb ft).

FIG 9:10   Measuring the suspension 'height'

Key to Fig 9:10   **A, B** and **C**   See text

Adjustment:

Refer to **Section 9:9**. The bolt 5 in **FIG 9:8** is screwed inwards until the suspension height specified for the model is achieved.

9:8 Anti-roll bar

The anti-roll bar fitted to later models is shown in **FIG 9:4**. The bar is mounted in rubber bushes and is clamped to the braces of the crossmember. The bar diameter differs between Carrera (20mm) and other models (16mm). If a replacement bar is required, ensure that it is of the same diameter as that removed.

To dismount the anti-roll bar, remove the stone guard, dismount both clamps **A** and withdraw the bar rearwards from the locations **B**. Fitment is the reverse of this sequence. Use rubber lubricant in the bushes.

9:9 Suspension height

The front suspension 'height' is dimension **C** in **FIG 9:10**. It is the difference between the wheel centre to ground dimension **A** and the control arm pivot centre (centre of the torsion bar if fitted) to ground dimension **B**. When measuring the suspension height it will be advantageous to use conical plugs as shown in **FIG 9:11**.

Vehicles fitted with damper struts and torsion bars:

On models produced up to 1974, **C** should be 108 ± 5mm (4.25 ± 0.2in) and on models produced in 1974 and onwards, **C** should be 113 ± 5mm (4.45 ± 0.2in). The difference in **C** between the lefthand and righthand sides should be kept to within 5mm (0.2in).

Vehicles fitted with self-levelling hydro-pneumatic struts:

1 Distribute a load of 100kg (220lb) in the luggage compartment so that both front wheels are evenly weighted.

2 Drive the car onto a level surface and, referring to **FIG 9:10**, measure the distance **A** from the ground to the front wheel centre. Distance **B** should be equal to **A** minus 124mm (5in), that is **C**, the distance between wheel centre and the mounting point centre of the traverse control arm. Special cone-shaped plugs (P301b) are used by the service agents which fit into the box section as shown in **FIG 9:11** to give an accurate datum point. Work on both sides of the vehicle.

3 Raise the car with a jack under the front centre until distance **B** is attained. Now measure, and make a note of the reading, the distance between ground and the bottom edge of the front fender on both sides. To eliminate tyre deflection when the jack is lowered, measure also the distance between the wheel flange and ground; measure again when the jack has been lowered and deduct the difference from that obtained between ground and fender.

FIG 9:11   Using cone-shaped plugs (arrowed) to measure centre point to ground dimension

4 Remove the ballast from the boot, load the car with passengers and drive the vehicle on a straight but rough road for a distance of 2km (1.25 miles), without hard braking.

5 The driver and passengers must stay in the car, which is also parked on a level surface, and another person must measure the distance between lower edge of wing and the ground. The values should not have differed by more than 10mm (0.4in) either way.

9:10 Wheel alignment

First class gauges and optical equipment is essential for accurate measurement and adjustment of toe-in and camber and caster angles. Specification figures are quoted in the **Technical Data** section of the **Appendix**.

Toe-in adjustment:

Toe-in is adjusted by altering the 'lengths' of the tie rods. Loosen the clamps 12 in **FIG 9:1** and rotate the tie rods 11 in the appropriate direction. Maintain symmetry by adjusting both tie rods by equal amounts until the specified toe-in is achieved. Retighten the clamps to a torque of 2.5kgm (18lb ft).

Caster and camber angles:

Adjustment is made by repositioning the suspension strut top location. From inside the luggage compartment mark the position of the single-hole and double-hole plates, loosen the retaining screws using tool P291 and reset the dish ring together with the strut end. Movement **across the direction of vehicle travel adjusts the camber angle** and movement of 1mm (0.04in) corresponds to 0.1° of strut attitude. Movement **along**

the direction of vehicle travel (fore and aft) adjusts the caster angle. Retighten the screws to a torque of 4.7kgm (34lb ft).

9:11 Fault diagnosis

(a) Wheel wobble

1 Unbalanced wheels and tyres
2 Worn steering ball joints
3 Incorrect steering geometry
4 Weak or incorrectly set torsion bar
5 Worn hub bearings

(b) Erratic steering

1 Check (a)
2 Bent suspension components
3 Worn ball joints and control arm mountings
4 Uneven tyre wear or pressures
5 Defective strut

(c) Excessive pitching, rolling or 'bottoming'

1 Check 4 in (a) and 5 in (b)
2 Buffer rubbers missing or faulty
3 Broken anti-roll or torsion bar

(d) Rattles

1 Check 3 in (b) and 3 in (c)
2 Loose strut
3 Loose crossmember or control arm

(e) Incorrect suspension 'height'

1 Check 4 in (a)
2 Defective hydro-pneumatic strut

CHAPTER 10

THE STEERING

10:1 Description

The layout of the steering gearbox, its linkage to the steering arms and the coupling of the column shaft to the gearbox unit are included in **Chapter 9**, **FIG 9:1**.

The steering gearbox unit is a rack and pinion type in which the pinion is actuated by the steering column assembly and slides the rack in the selected direction. The ends of the rack are linked with the steering arms by tie rods. It will be noted that the front suspension/steering design does not incorporate a kingpin and that what would be the kingpin inclination is the inclination of the line through the top of the support of the suspension strut and the suspension arm ball joint.

The steering gearbox unit is mounted directly onto a supporting crossmember the ends of which carry the suspension arm pivots. The steering shaft couples to the centre of the gearbox unit and lefthand or righthand drive mounting of the steering column is accommodated via substantial angulation of the intermediate shaft. The tie rods are adjustable to allow adjustments to be made to wheel alignment (see **Chapter 9**, **Section 9:10**).

10:2 Maintenance

As the steering gearbox is packed with a special grease at the time of manufacture, or after a complete overhaul, there is no provision for subsequent extra lubrication. The same applies to the universal joints and ball joints in the steering system. There is no need for routine adjustment at any point.

Every 12,000 miles (20,000km), look over the steering gear generally. Ensure that all couplings and joints are secure and tight. Check the condition of the rubber boots as, apart from age deterioration these are subject to being damaged by road surface debris. Cracked or torn boots should be renewed at the earliest opportunity.

The procedure for the adjustment of wheel alignment is described in **Chapter 9**, **Section 9:10**.

10:3 The steering wheel

A cross-section through the steering wheel is included in **FIG 10:1**.

Removal:

1 Set the road wheels in the straightahead position. Disconnect the battery earth lead(s). Release the horn button by turning it anticlockwise or, on later models, release the horn bar. Withdraw the horn contact pin.
2 Remove the wheel retaining nut and collect the washer. Mark the relative position of the wheel in

FIG 10:1   Cross-section through the earlier type steering wheel assembly

Key to Fig 10:1   1 Upper shaft   2 Ballbearing   3 Front compartment wall   4 Panel   5 Nut (caged)   6 Fillester screw (switch shrouds)   7 Contact ring   8 Contact finger   9 Seal   10 Steering post extension   11 Screw   12 Shear bolt   13 Fillester screw (contact ring)

relation to the shaft so that it may be refitted in its original position. Pull off the steering wheel.

Refitment:

1 Confirm that the road wheels are in the straightahead position. Position the spring and support ring on the wheel hub and fit the steering wheel with the wheel and shaft marks aligned. The wheel spokes should be horizontal and the direction indicator flasher striker should be pointing towards the switch.

2 Fit the washer and tighten the retaining nut on earlier models (those with a horn button) to a torque of 8kgm (58lb ft) or, on later models (those with a horn bar), to 7.5kgm (54lb ft). Check that the flasher return striker operates correctly.

3 Lightly grease the horn contact ring, insert the contact pin and fit the horn button by turning it clockwise or, on later models, refit the horn bar.

10:4 The steering column

A cross-section through the earlier type steering column is shown in **FIG 10:1**. The components of the

later type steering column (with collapsible, energy-absorbing hub) are shown in **FIG 10:2** and it may be noted that models not initially fitted with this collapsible type of column may have it fitted retrospectively.

Column removal:

Depending upon the model, access to the intermediate shaft and universal couplings requires removal of air box, ductings, hoses and blower unit and associated electrical connections. The following procedure relates to models fitted with normal equipment. **If an air conditioning system is installed, refer to Chapter 13, Section 13:8 before proceeding.**

1 Disconnect the battery earth lead(s). Remove the luggage compartment carpet. Remove the panel from the front of the fresh air box.

2 Remove the fresh air box by: pulling out the frame and grille after removing four crosshead screws; removing the two crosshead screws which retain the box; detaching the control box hoses, the electrical connections from the air box and the wire cable from

FIG 10:2 Components of the later type steering wheel assembly

Key to Fig 10:2   1 Horn bar (pull to remove)   2 Nut   3 Washer   4 Steering wheel with energy-absorbing hub   5 Oval head screw   6 Lockwasher   7 Contact ring   8 Fillester head screw   9 Lockwasher   10 Hub cover   11 Fillester head screw   12 Lockwasher   13 Contact plate   14 Fillester head screw   15 Lockwasher   16 Contact tab   17 Fillester head screw   18 Switch housing top   19 Switch housing bottom   20 Nut   21 Stud   22 Shear bolt (M8)   23 Lockwasher   24 Ignition steering lock   25 Fillester head screw   26 Ignition/starter switch   27 Nut   28 Bolt   29 Universal joint   30 Shear bolt   31 Lockwasher   32 Shear bolt   33 Lockwasher   34 Steering shaft tube   35 Fillester head screw   36 Lockwasher   37 Direction indicator/dimmer switch   38 Fillester head screw   39 Lockwasher   40 Wiper/washer switch   41 Lockwasher   42 Lockwasher   43 Retaining ring   44 Steering shaft   45 Ballbearing   46 Contact ring   47 Circlip   48 Ballbearing   49 Circlip

the flap lever on the air box; pushing off the retaining clip from the outer cover.

3 Remove the intermediate shaft coverplate. Remove the **upper** nut and bolt from the intermediate shaft **upper** universal joint. Remove the **lower** nut and bolt from the intermediate shaft **lower** universal joint.

4 Remove the fillester headed bolts (see **FIG 10:3**) which retain the lower steering shaft bearing cap and remove the bearing cap. Withdraw the lower universal joint from the lower steering shaft and dismount the intermediate shaft complete with the upper and the lower universal joints.

5 Remove the steering wheel as described in **Section 10:3**. Using a suitable extractor as shown in **FIG 10:4**, withdraw the column sleeve. Remove the circlip from the steering shaft and drive the shaft out upwards.

6 Remove the circlip from the grooved ballbearing/ steering outer tube and drive out the bearing downwards.

Note that if the steering/ignition switch and/or the steering shaft tube is to be dismounted, the light switch and the tachometer must be removed. Refer to **FIG 10:5** and drill or grind off the shear bolts. Access to the bolts

FIG 10:3 Uncoupling the lower universal joint

Key to Fig 10:3   1 Universal joint lower bolt
2 Bearing cap nuts

FIG 10:4 Withdrawing the bearing sleeve (earlier type column)

FIG 10:5 The shear bolts (later type column)

which retain the steering tube (later model illustrated) is shown in **FIG 10:6**.

Column refitment:

Follow the reverse of the removal sequence. Refer to **Section 10:5** when refitting the intermediate shaft and couplings. Note the following points. Pack bearings with a lithium based multi-purpose grease. On the later type column, drive the bearing into place with a piece of pipe of 24mm (0.945in) internal diameter by 28mm (1.102in) external diameter and ensure that the pipe section only contacts the bearing inner race. Adjustment of heater valves is described in **Chapter 4, Section 4:2**. Tighten the new shear bolts until their heads break off.

10:5 The intermediate shaft and couplings
Removal:

The procedure for the removal of the intermediate shaft and its universal couplings is covered by operations 1 to 4 of the steering column removal sequence described in **Section 10:4**.

Refitment:

Do not attempt to salvage a bent or damaged shaft. If there is any backlash in a universal joint, it should be renewed.

FIG 10:6 Access to the steering tube bolts (later type column)

To refit the intermediate shaft assembly, reverse the removal sequence. Use new self-locking nuts and torque tighten them and the fillester headed bearing cap retaining nuts to 2.5kgm (18lb ft). Tighten the bearing cap retaining nuts before tightening the universal joint clamping nuts and bolts.

10:6 The steering linkage

A tie rod couples each steering arm to each end of the steering unit rack. The arrangement is shown in **Chapter 9, FIG 9:1**. Alteration of the effective 'length' of the tie rods allows wheel alignment to be adjusted. The steering arm to tie rod connection is through a ball joint and the tie rod to steering unit is through a yoke coupling.

Removal:

Unlock and remove the castellated nut which retains the ball joint to the steering arm. Using a suitable extractor (the official tool is VW266h), separate the ball joint stud from the arm. Unlock and remove the coupling bolt from the tie rod yoke. Withdraw the tie rod. If necessary the ball joint or the yoke may be removed after loosening the relevant clamp bolt.

Refitment:

To refit the tie rod, follow the reverse of the removal sequence. Torque tighten the ball joint retaining nut to 4.5kgm (32.5lb ft). Apply molybdenum disulphide grease to the yoke coupling bolt and torque tighten it to 4.7kgm (34lb ft). Use new splitpins.

If the 'length' of either tie rod was disturbed, adjust the wheel alignment as described in **Chapter 9, Section 9:10**.

10:7 The steering gearbox
Removal:

Refer to **Section 10:4** and uncouple the lower universal joint from the lower steering shaft. Remove the rubber boot from the lower steering shaft, unlock and remove the two bolts which retain the pinion flange to the coupling. Withdraw the lower steering shaft and coupling.

Separate the tie rod ball joints from the steering arms as described in **Section 10:6**. Remove the bolts which retain the steering gearbox to the crossmember 8 in **Chapter 9, FIG 9:1**. Remove the righthand crossmember brace. Dismount the steering gearbox by withdrawing it to the right.

Dismantling:

1 Hold the assembly between the padded jaws of a vice to avoid cracking the casing. Release the rubber bellows outer clamps to expose the tie rod bushing holders. Use a 42mm wrench to unscrew the bushing holder. It will be advisable here to use two wrenches, one to unscrew a holder, the other to hold the holder on the opposite side to prevent the steering rack from turning. Remove the tie rods and bushes.
2 Refer to **FIG 10:7** and dismantle in the numerical sequence shown; 1 to 20 is fairly straightforward.
3 Use a puller to extract the rack bushing 21. Withdraw the bearing 17 from the pinion 18 by removing the

FIG 10:7   Components of the steering gearbox

Key to Fig 10:7   1 Bolts M8   2 Spring washer   3 Cover   4 Shims   5 Spring   6 Pressure block   7 Self-locking nut M10
8 Coupling flange   9 Washer   10 'O' ring   11 Bolt M8 × 18   12 Spring washer   13 Cover   14 Shims   15 Snap ring
16 Thrust washer   17 Ballbearing   18 Pinion   19 Rack   20 Lock ring   21 Rack bushing   22 Needle bearing   23 Steering
housing.

FIG 10:8 Measure distance from top of bearing to top of housing to determine correct position of bearing

FIG 10:9 Measure distance from top of ballbearing to contact surface of housing to determine shim pack

FIG 10:11 Checking steering gear drag

FIG 10:10 Measure distance from top of pressure block to contact surface of housing to determine shim thickness. This measurement minus 0.2mm (0.008in) will give correct end float

snap ring 15 and thrust washer 16 and forcing the pinion through the bearing under a flypress or any other small press.

4 Drive the needle bearing 22 out of the housing with special drift P362 or an equivalent tool.

Reassembly:

1 Fill the steering and rack housing with multi-purpose molybdenum disulphide grease and drive in the needle bearing until the top edge of the bearing is 3mm (0.12in) below the top edge of the housing (see **FIG 10:8**).

2 Fit the pinion 18 complete with bearing 17 thrust-washer and snap ring and measure the distance between ballbearing and contact face of housing (see **FIG 10:9**). This clearance must be taken up by the shims 14. Free play between the cover 13 and bearing should be not more than 0.05mm (0.002in).

3 Continue the reassembly and measure the distance between pressure block 6 and the housing flange face (see **FIG 10:10**). This clearance must be taken up by the shims 4 but allow for a maximum free play between the block and cover 3 of 0.2mm (0.008in).

4 Temporarily fit the shims and covers and check the gear drag over the entire working length of the steering rack (see **FIG 10:11**). A drag of 6 to 8kgcm (5 to 7lb in) must be attained. If the drag cannot be attained renew the spring 5.

5 Remove the covers and smear the contact surfaces with gasket compound. Tighten the bolts 1 and 11 to a torque of 1.5kgm (10lb ft).

6 Lubricate 'O' ring 10 when fitting and fit a new self-locking nut 7 (size M10), tighten to a torque of

4.7kgm (33lb ft). Ensure the lockplates 20 seat correctly when refitting.

7 Refit the tie rod bushing holders and tighten them to 7kgm (50lb ft).

8 Check the eyebolts for faulty bushes and look for cracks and deterioration of the bellows. **FIG 10:12** shows the correct settings for the eyebolts, and although this may be done by measurement it is better to use the setting fixture P.285a. The angles are important to ensure free movement of the tie rods.

9 Fit the bellows to the housing. Put gasket compound on the eyebolt threads, the end faces of the rack and on both faces of the stop plate and lockwasher. Fit eyebolts, set them correctly and tighten nuts to 6.5kgm (47lb ft), locking them when secure.

Installing:

Reverse the sequence of operations followed when the steering gearbox was removed but do not, at this stage, reconnect the tie rods to the steering arms. Remove the horn button or the horn bar and, using a torque meter on the steering wheel retaining nut, measure the drag in a similar manner to that shown in **FIG 10:11**. The drag should be about 10kgcm (8.75lb in) with the tie rods disconnected. If this check is satisfactory, connect the tie rods to the steering arms as described in **Section 10:6**. The steering unit retaining bolts should have new lockwashers fitted and torque tightened to 4.7kgm (34lb ft). Fit the crossmember brace without strain and torque tighten the nut to 6.5kgm (47lb ft) and the bolt to 4.7kgm (34lb ft). Adjust the wheel alignment as described in **Chapter 9**, **Section 9:10** if new parts were fitted to either the steering unit assembly or to the tie rods.

10:8 Fault diagnosis

(a) Wheel wobble

1 Unbalanced wheels and tyres, uneven pressures
2 Free play in steering gear and connections
3 Front end damaged, incorrect steering angles
4 Incorrect toe-in adjustment
5 Worn or slack hub bearings
6 Faulty damper strut
7 Insufficient drag in steering gear

(b) Steering wander

1 Check 2, 3, 5 and 7 in (a)
2 Smooth front tyres, pressures too high or too low

(c) Heavy steering

1 Check 3 in (a)
2 Low or uneven tyre pressures
3 Too much drag in steering gear
4 Insufficient lubricant
5 Steering gearbox mountings out of line
6 Weak or broken torsion bars
7 Faulty steering shafts and joints
8 Defective bearing assembly in post extension

(d) Lost motion

1 Check 2 in (a)
2 Loose steering wheel
3 Worn ball joints
4 Steering gearbox loose on mountings
5 Worn steering gearbox
6 Universal joints loose on steering shafts

(e) Steering pulls to one side

1 Check 3 in (a) and 2 in (c)
2 One front brake binding
3 Broken or sagging front or rear suspension

NOTES

CHAPTER 11

THE BRAKING SYSTEM

11:1 Description

The layout of the braking system is shown diagrammatically in **FIG 11:1**. A dual line hydraulic system is employed. This operates the front brakes (via lines 4 and 5) and the rear brakes (via lines 15, 16 and 5) from the tandem piston master cylinder 2. In the event of a rear brake line failure, the front brakes can be temporarily operated normally and vice versa. Each hydraulic system has its own fluid supply source. These supplies are amalgamated into a two-part reservoir 3 which is topped up through a single filler orifice.

Both front and rear brakes are disc type. Each disc is straddled by a twin piston caliper in which each piston actuates a friction pad. Compensation for pad wear down to the pad wear limit thickness is automatic and does not require routine attention. Pads are renewed when the wear limit thickness of the friction material is reached. Each caliper is provided with a fluid bleed nipple and the procedure for bleeding the system when this operation is necessary is described in **Section 11:7**. Discs are provided with air cooling passages to ensure that they do not heat up excessively under heavy and continuous use of the brakes.

The handbrake is mechanically actuated by a system of cables and operates on the rear wheels only. The cable mechanism expands two brake shoes on each wheel onto the internal diameter of a drum which is integral with each rear brake disc. Pull-off springs retract the shoes when the handbrake lever is released. Routine adjustment is required to compensate for wear of the shoe friction linings. The hand throttle lever and the heater control lever(s) are incorporated in the handbrake lever mounting.

11:2 Maintenance

General:

At least every 12,000 miles (20,000km), check the system for damaged pipes and hoses and confirm that the warning devices are operative.

Reservoir fluid level:

The fluid level in the reservoir will drop as the caliper pistons take up progressively advanced positions to compensate for wear of the pad friction linings. It is important to distinguish between this normal drop in fluid level and any excessive drop which results from

FIG 11:1 Diagrammatic layout of the braking system

Key to Fig 11:1   1 Brake pedal   2 Master cylinder   3 Fluid reservoir   4 Front brake feed pipe (metal)   5 Flexible hose   6 Front caliper   7 Front brake disc   8 Rear caliper   9 Rear brake disc   10 Handbrake lever   11 Handbrake cables   12 Front brakes fluid feed   13 Rear brakes fluid feed   14 Brake warning light switch   15 Rear brake feed pipe (metal)   16 Lefthand and righthand rear brake feed pipe (metal)   17 Handbrake shoe adjuster   18 Handbrake shoes   19 Bleed nipple   20 Handbrake equaliser

FIG 11:2   Wear limit of caliper pads

Key to Fig 11:2   1 Spring pins   2 Retaining pins   3 Cross spring   4 Arrows indicate pad wear limit

leaks from seals or pipe connections which must be corrected without delay.

At least every 12,000 miles (20,000km), check the fluid level and top up as necessary. The correct fluid level is approximately 2cm (0.80in) below the top ridge of the reservoir. Use only ATE Blue fluid or an equivalent of reputable brand and be careful not to spill fluid onto the paintwork as it has solvent properties. Clean off round the reservoir cap before unscrewing it.

Brake pads:

The rate of wear of the pad friction linings will depend greatly upon the driving conditions and methods employed. Subject to the severity with which the brakes have been used, visually check the thickness of the pad linings at least every 12,000 miles (20,000km).

Renew pads when the friction lining thickness has worn down to 2mm (0.08in). The procedure is described in Section 11:3.

Handbrake:

When, due to wear of the shoe linings, the travel of the handbrake lever becomes excessive, adjust as described in Section 11:8.

Brake pedal free play:

Every 12,000 miles (20,000km) or more frequently if necessary, check and, if necessary, adjust the pedal free play. The procedure is described in **Section 11:6**.

11:3 Brake pad renewal:

The wear limit of pads is reached when the pad backing plate touches the cross spring or when the pad friction lining has worn down to 2mm (0.08in) as indicated between the arrows in **FIG 11:2**.

The overall thickness, the friction lining plus the backing plate, of a new pad is approximately 15mm (0.60in). Pads with different types of linings (touring, competition, etc.) are available and all pads in both the front or in both the rear calipers should be of the same type. Although it is possible to renew one pad only, it is recommended that all four front pads or all four rear pads are renewed together. Front and rear pads are not identical and are not interchangeable.

Serviceable pads which are being withdrawn as part of a caliper removal procedure must be marked so that they may be refitted in their original positions. It is not permissible to change their positions.

Changing pads:

1 Jack up car and remove wheels. Extract spring pins 1 and push out retaining pins 2 (see **FIG 11:2**), pressing down on the cross spring 3 and pushing pins inwards.

2 If pads are still usable, mark their positions for correct re-installation before withdrawing them.

3 The next operation may cause overflowing of the fluid reservoir so drain the relevant section of it. Press both pistons into their bores, either with tool P83 or with a lever of hardboard. Do not use steel tools which may damage the disc or pistons.

4 Clean out the pad cavities with methylated spirits and a soft-edged tool. **Do not use other solvents.** Check the condition of the dust cover and clamping ring. Renew hardened or cracked covers.

5 Polish the brake discs with fine emerycloth and smooth out any inner and outer ridges on each face.

6 Fit the pads and check that they are free to move in the cavities. Reassemble in the reverse order, fitting new spring pins in the retaining pins if the original pins are distorted or worn. Put clean fluid in the reservoir and depress the brake pedal several times to set the pistons in the correct positions. Recheck the fluid level in the reservoir.

Do not use the brakes heavily during the first 200km (125 miles) if new pads are fitted. Condition the pads by moderate pedal pressure, with intervals for cooling, unless an emergency occurs. The pads, with careful bedding in, will then give effective braking without fade.

11:4 Front brakes

Removing a caliper and disc:

1 Remove the pads (operations 1 and 2 in **Section 11:3**). Block brake pedal in slightly depressed position, then detach fluid pipe at the banjo connection behind the caliper.

FIG 11:3   Removing the bolts which secure the brake carrier to the front axle

2 Remove the two caliper mounting bolts on the inner side of the brake assembly and pull off the caliper.

3 Prise off the hub cap. Slacken the socket head screw in the clamping nut on the end of the axle, unscrew the nut and remove the thrust washer. Parts are shown in **Chapter 9**, **FIG 9:6**. Pull off the disc and hub. If tight, do not hammer on the disc but use a puller.

4 From behind the axle remove the disc shroud. Unlock and remove the bolts and lift off the brake carrier (see **FIG 11:3**).

FIG 11:4   A front caliper and brake disc assembly

Key to Fig 11:4   1 Disc   2 Intermediate plate (between the caliper halves)   3 Disc shroud   4 Caliper base housing   5 Pad segment   6 Cross spring   7 Spring pin   8 Retaining pin   The bleed nipple is arrowed

FIG 11:5 Prising out spring ring that secures caliper piston dust cover

Dismantling a caliper:

1 Do not separate the caliper halves unless there has been leakage. Loosen bleed screw arrowed in **FIG 11:4** and use gentle air pressure (1atm or 14lb/sq in) to eject any residual fluid from the caliper.

2 Remove the clamping ring and dust cover (see **FIG 11:5**). Depress one piston with tool P83 or use a clamp. Place a block of wood in the slot and blow out the opposite piston with air pressure of 2atm or 29lb/sq in, raising the pressure if necessary. **Serious injury may result if fingers are not kept out of slot during this operation.**

3 Remove the piston seal from inside the cylinder bore with a plastic or wooden tool, so that the groove and

FIG 11:6 Using 20° plate to set piston step in relation to caliper and to disc rotation

bore are not damaged. Restore the removed piston and seal and the clamp in order to remove the opposite piston. Clean all parts in methylated spirit (industrial alcohol). **Do not use any other type of solvent or the rubber seals will be damaged.** Check the cylinder bores and pistons for wear, scoring or pitting, and renew faulty parts. **Renew all seals as a matter of course.** It is dangerous to refit any doubtful parts. The components of the automatic pad adjustment cannot be renewed. Always fit a new piston if the automatic action is defective.

Reassembling a caliper:

1 Use ATE brake cylinder paste to coat the cylinder and piston parts. Insert the seals in the cylinder grooves.

2 Note the cut-away step on the piston pressure face. Use aligning tool P84, or make up a thin sheet metal gauge with an included angle of 20°, as shown in **FIG 11:6**, to set the piston correctly. Insert the piston carefully so that it does not tilt or jam, and align it so that the stepped down part faces the disc rotation as shown. Use a clamp to press the piston into place. The aligning tool must rest against the upper edge of the brake pad slot. If the caliper is installed, a piston may be turned by clamping the opposite piston and ejecting the required piston until it can be turned by hand.

3 Wipe off surplus assembly grease and fit the dust covers dry.

4 If the caliper was separated into halves because of 'O' ring leakage, clean the faces with methylated spirit (industrial alcohol), fit new rings and assemble with new bolts, nuts and spring washers, using genuine Porsche spares. Tighten to half the required torque and then fully tighten. Torque for front calipers is 3.5kgm (24.5lb ft). Do not omit the packing plate from between the halves of the caliper.

5 Fit the disc to its hub, if it was removed, with the marks aligned and tighten the nuts to 2.3kgm (16.5lb ft). Refit the hub as described in **Chapter 9** and adjust the bearings. Use a dial gauge to check the lateral runout of the disc faces as described in **Section 11:5**.

6 Fit the caliper using new spring washers and tighten the retaining bolts to 7kgm (50.5lb ft). Fit the brake pads in their original positions (see **Section 11:3**). Bleed the hydraulic system (see **Section 11:7**).

Brake discs:

If necessary, separate the disc from its hub after marking for correct reassembly.

The servicing of both front and rear brake discs is covered at the end of **Section 11:5**.

11:5 Rear brakes

Removing:

1 Jack up the car and remove the rear wheels after chocking the front wheels and releasing the handbrake.

2 Remove the brake pads (see **Section 11:3**). From behind, remove the disc shrouds. Block the brake pedal in a slightly depressed position and detach the fluid pipe from the caliper. Detach the caliper.

3 Remove the two countersunk screws adjacent to the wheel studs and pull off the disc.

4 Refer to **FIG 11 : 7**. Remove the castellated nut 1 and its washer. From behind, pull out the handbrake cable. Remove the expander 2 and its spring.

5 Turn the retainer 3 to release it from its pin, remove the spring and pull out the pin from rear. Lift the upper shoe with a screwdriver, withdraw the adjuster 4 and unhook the spring from between the shoes.

6 Release the retainer from the lower shoe. Remove both shoes in a forward direction and unhook the second return spring.

Servicing a caliper:

For this operation, follow the instructions for front brake calipers in **Section 11 : 4**. There is a packing plate 10.6mm (0.417in) thick between the caliper halves. Bolt torque for the caliper halves retaining bolts is 1.8kgm (13lb ft).

Checking parts:

Clean and examine all mechanical parts for wear. Renew any broken or distorted springs and check that the adjuster works freely. Discard oily brake linings as it is not possible to clean them satisfactorily. Worn linings must be replaced by Porsche-approved makes.

Reassembling:

1 Insert the handbrake cable and fit the washer against the spacer tube. Fit the inner expander struts. Fit the special return spring 5 to both shoes with coils pointing inwards (see **FIG 11 : 7**).

2 Slide the shoes rearwards onto the brake carrier plate and fit the retaining pins, springs and retainers 3. Fit the inner expander of the handbrake into the seats in the shoes.

3 Lift the upper shoe with a screwdriver and fit the adjuster 4. The sprocket should be downwards in the righthand brake and upwards in the lefthand brake. Fit the return spring at the adjuster end of the shoes.

4 Slacken the adjusting nut on the handbrake cable fully back. Fit the expander spring, the second half of the expander 2 and tighten the castellated nut, until one of its slots clears the splitpin hole. Fit a new splitpin. Make sure the expander struts are correctly seated in the shoes.

5 Refit the disc and check for runout as described later. Fit the intermediate plate between the caliper and the rear axle control arm. Fit the caliper and tighten the retaining bolts to 6kgm (43.5lb ft). Fit the pads in their original positions. Bleed the hydraulic system (see **Section 11 : 7**) and adjust handbrake (see **Section 11 : 8**).

Handbrake carrier plate:

Removal and refitment of the carrier plate are covered in **Chapter 8**.

Brake discs:

A ventilated disc is shown in **FIG 11 : 4**. Note the plate 2 between the caliper halves. Disc thickness is 19.8 to 20.0mm (0.780 to 0.787in) both front and rear.

Smooth, rounded concentric scoring is normal, but sharp ridges, cracking and pitting call for disc renewal or regrinding. This is also the remedy for excessive runout or excessive variation in thickness.

FIG 11 : 7 Handbrake assembly with drum removed. Dotted lines show correct alignment of coils of right-hand spring

Key to Fig 11 : 7 1 Nut for cable 2 Brake shoe expander assembly 3 Shoe retainer 4 Shoe adjuster 5 Interrupted return spring

When regrinding, remove no more than 0.70mm (0.028in) equally from each side, the minimum permissible disc thickness being 18.6mm (0.732in). Surface finish must be within 0.006mm (0.0002in). Deviation in thickness 0.03mm (0.001in) maximum. Runout up to 0.05mm (0.002in) measured on faces 10mm (0.4in) inside the outer edge.

Wear limit of disc thickness is 1mm (0.04in) from each face. If worn symmetrically, the lowest limit of disc thickness is 18mm (0.71in).

To check front disc runout when installed, remove the brake pads (see **Section 11 : 3**) and adjust the front

FIG 11 : 8 The disc regrind datum faces are arrowed

Key to Fig 11 : 8 a See text 1 Front disc 2 Rear disc

FIG 11:9   Components of the tandem piston (dual line) master cylinder

Key to Fig 11:9   1 Cylinder   2 Secondary piston return spring   3 Spring seats   4 Supporting washers   5 Primary and separating cups   6 Filler disc   7 Secondary piston   8 Stroke limiting bolt   9 Sleeve   10 Primary piston return spring   11 Primary piston   12 Secondary cup   13 Stop plate   14 Lock ring   15 Dust boot   16 Cap screw   17 'O' ring   18 Spring   19 Piston 20 Piston cup   21 Grommet   22 Washer   23 Gasket   24 Stop bolt   25 Circuit failure sender wheel bearings. Set up a dial gauge so that its plunger bears on the disc face about 10 to 15mm (0.40 to 0.60in) below the outer edge. It is advisable to check both faces. Maximum permissible runout when mounted in 0.20mm (0.008in), and discs with excessive runout must be reground or renewed.

To check the rear discs, remove the pads and fit up a dial gauge as before. The disc must be fully tightened onto the hub by refitting the wheel nuts on steel spacers, so that the nuts may be tightened to 10kgm (12.25lb ft). To avoid warping, tighten evenly and diagonally. Runout must not exceed the figure given for front discs.

When regrinding discs it is most important to preserve the original symmetry. This is the reason for taking an equal amount off each side. To ensure that this may be checked by the operator, the following dimensions are given. Measurement 'a' in FIG 11:8 is tabled together with the original disc thickness, and a simple calculation will enable the check to be made.

When the thickness of a new front disc is 19.8 to 20.0mm (0.780 to 0.787in), dimension 'a' is 35.0 ± 0.10mm (1.378 ± 0.004in).

With the same thickness of a new rear disc, dimension 'a' is 65.0 ± 0.10mm (2.559 ± 0.004in).

Pad thickness:

All the preceding limits for wear and regrinding apply only if the pad thickness is not allowed to fall below 2mm (0.08in). **This is important if the brakes are to function correctly.**

Disc balance:

Discs are balanced at the factory by inserting spring clips into the ventilating slots. **Do not remove these clips.**

Disc cleanliness:

Using the car on dirty roads may lead to clogging of the ventilating slots. When washing the car, use a hose to clear the slots to ensure adequate cooling.

11:6 The master cylinder

Observe scrupulous cleanliness when working on any part of the hydraulic system and use only ATE Blue Fluid or an equivalent of reputable brand. Note that **brake fluid will damage paintwork.**

The components of the tandem piston dual line master cylinder are shown in FIG 11:9. Each piston serves a separate hydraulic section. One section operates the front brakes and the other operates the rear brakes. In the event of a pipe or seal failure in one section, the other section will continue to operate normally. Note that each section of the master cylinder is separately connected with the partitioned reservoir. A disc on the master cylinder pushrod operates the brake warning lights.

On certain models a brake circuit failure sender (25 in FIG 11:9) is provided. This device closes an electrical circuit to a warning light in the event of either front or rear brake hydraulic circuits becoming inoperative. This device is obligatory fitment on vehicles imported into the USA and must be checked every 6000 miles (10,000km) as described later.

FIG 11:10 Correct clearance (free play) between master cylinder piston and pedal pushrod is 1mm (0.04in)

Removing the master cylinder:

1 Jack up the car. Detach the accelerator pedal from the rod by pulling the pedal back. Remove the mat and floorboard. From behind the brake pedal, pull rubber boot off the master cylinder (see part 15 in FIG 11:9).

2 Drain both sections of the brake fluid reservoir (see FIG 11:1) beneath car, remove the shield from the suspension crossmember. Detach the pipes and switch wires from the master cylinder.

3 Loosen the clamps and withdraw the hoses connecting the reservoir to the cylinder. Release the cylinder flange from body (2 nuts) and withdraw the cylinder.

Dismantling:

Refer to FIG 11:9. Hold cylinder lightly in a vice fitted with soft jaws.

1 Prise out ring 14. Remove stop plate 13 and piston 11 complete with all cups, washers, spring and stop 9.

2 Remove the stop bolt 24 of secondary piston 7 and use gentle air pressure of 1atm (15lb/sq in) to blow out the piston and cups. Cover any holes in the cylinder which would allow air to escape. Remove spring 2 and the associated washers.

3 Hold the neck of the primary piston 11 between soft jaws in a vice and unscrew the stroke limiting bolt 8, keeping the spring compressed to reduce the load on the threads. Separate the parts.

4 On relevant cars, remove the warning sender 25 and the cap screw 16 and blow out parts 19 and 20 with gentle air pressure blocking any air escape holes.

Cleaning and inspection:

Wash all parts in methylated spirit (industrial alcohol). **Use no other solvents as they may lead to rapid deterioration of the rubber parts.** Dry the housing and clear all parts with compressed air. Renew all rubber parts at every overhaul. They are available in kit form.

Check the piston and cylinder bore surfaces for wear, scoring or corrosion. Renew if not smooth and highly polished.

Reassembling the master cylinder:

Do not let mineral oil contact any of the internal parts. Observe absolute cleanliness at all times. Reassemble in the reverse of the dismantling order. Lightly coat the bore, the piston and the cups with ATE brake cylinder paste. When inserting the cups, take care not to turn back the

FIG 11:11 Slackening handbrake cable adjuster behind rear brake (left). Using screwdriver to turn brake shoe adjuster for handbrake (right)

sealing lips. Make sure that the cups face correctly as shown in the illustration, with the lips entering first, except for the rear cup of piston 7 where the lip faces the opposite direction (towards the rear of the master cylinder).

Insert the secondary piston and filler disc, primary cup, supporting washer, spring seat and spring, with the large coil of the spring entering first. Using a piece of clean plastic rod, push the piston down the bore until it clears the hole for the stop bolt. Fit the bolt and washer, tightening to 1.0 to 1.2kgm (7.2 to 8.7lb ft). Check that the bolt is properly seated ahead of the piston and that the piston moves freely to the bottom of the bore.

Fit the filler disc, primary cup and supporting washer to the primary piston. Use the stroke limiting bolt to secure the spring, spring seat and stop sleeve to the piston. Insert the assembly into the bore and fit the lock ring, making sure that it is well seated.

On relevant models, coat the warning system plungers with ATE brake cylinder paste before fitting. Use a new 'O' ring under the cap screw and tighten to 1.5kgm (11lb ft). Fit a new 'O' ring to the sender unit and tighten to the same torque.

Installation:

Apply sealer to the cylinder mounting flange and check that the pushrod enters the cylinder. Attach the flange to body, using new spring washers. Tighten the retaining nuts to 2.5kgm (18lb ft). Inside the car, check the pushrod clearance shown in **FIG 11:10**. To adjust to 1mm (0.04in) specified, loosen the locknut and turn the pushrod as necessary, then tighten the locknut. Reconnect pipes and switch wires.

Check that the vent hole in the reservoir cap is clear. Fill the reservoir (see **Section 11:2**). Bleed the brake system (see **Section 11:7**). Check the operation of the brakes, check for leaks with the pedal depressed firmly and check the stoplights. Refit the undershield, tightening nuts to 6.5kgm (47lb ft) and the bolts to 4.7kgm (34lb ft).

Circuit failure sender:

On relevant models, check the warning system every 6000 miles (10,000km) or whenever the hydraulic system has been disturbed. Confirm that the warning lamp is operative by switching on the ignition and applying the handbrake. If the lamp does not light up, check the bulb. Test the sender as follows.

Depress the brake pedal to the brake actuation point. A second operator must now simulate failure of one braking circuit by slackening a bleed screw on one of the brake calipers. Further depression of the brake pedal to actuation point for the other brake circuit should cause the control lamp to light up. Tighten the bleed screw and release pedal.

Repeat the operation but select a bleed screw in the second circuit. If the lamp does not light up during one of the tests, check the sender unit on the master cylinder and renew if necessary. If the sender unit is found to be serviceable, check the wiring continuity and correct the fault.

Stoplight switch:

This is mounted on a bracket to one side of the brake pedal and pushrod. Remove the two screws and detach the wires to release the switch.

To adjust the switch, place a packing piece 4mm (0.157in) thick under the pedal stop. This will be equivalent to a pedal pad travel of 21mm (0.827in). Adjacent to the cable connections on the switch is a screw and locknut. Slacken the nut and turn the screw to the point where the stoplights just go on. Tighten the locknut and recheck the action.

11:7 Bleeding the hydraulic system

This procedure, for which two operators are required, is only necessary if air has entered the system. This may result from the level of the fluid in the reservoirs having fallen too low; because the system has been drained of old fluid or because part of the system has been dismantled. It is important to keep the reservoirs topped up during the bleeding procedure to avoid further air from entering the system. Do not re-use fluid which has been bled from the system as it will have become aerated. Use fresh fluid straight from the supply tin. The bleed screws are shown in **FIGS 11:1** and **11:4**. Proceed as follows.

Sequence:

If only one caliper has been disconnected, bleed at that point. If the master cylinder has been disconnected or if the system has been drained, bleed in the following sequence: righthand rear, lefthand rear, righthand front and, finally, lefthand front.

Procedure:

1 Remove the cap from the bleed screw and attach a length of rubber or plastic tubing. Submerge the free end of the tubing in a container which is partially filled with brake fluid. Loosen the relevant bleed screw by approximately half-a-turn.

2 Depress the brake pedal through its full travel, close the bleed screw and release the pedal slowly. Repeat this sequence until the fluid from the drain tube is free from air bubbles.

3 Close the bleed screw, remove the drain tube and refit the cap. Repeat this procedure, if relevant, on the other calipers in the order specified earlier.

FIG 11:12   Handbrake mounting and throttle and heater control levers (earlier models)

Key to Fig 11:12   1 Heater control lever   2 Hand throttle lever   3 Pressure disc   4 Cup spring   5 Self-locking nut   6 Pivot
7 Spacer sleeve   8 Friction disc   a Friction limit of heater lever is 10kg (22lb)   b Friction limit of hand throttle lever is 6kg
(13lb)   c Hand throttle lever knob is pressed on   d Heater lever knob is screwed on

11:8 The handbrake

Adjustment:

When the lever movement is excessive, adjust the
handbrake as follows:

1 Raise the car and remove the rear wheels. Release the
handbrake. Push back the pads of the rear disc brakes
so that the discs rotate freely.
2 Behind the shrouds, loosen the cable adjusting nuts to
relieve cable tension (see lefthand view, FIG 11:11).
Insert a screwdriver as in the righthand view and turn
the adjusting sprocket until the shoes lock inside the
drum and the disc is immoveable. Sprocket can be
seen at 4 in FIG 11:7. Repeat adjustment on the
opposite wheel.
3 Remove the cable slack at the adjusting nuts (see
FIG 11:11, left). Pull back the cover round the handbrake lever mounting and note two holes in the flange
near the rear bolt. Looking vertically downwards, the
ends of the cable equaliser should be visible. The
equaliser should be at right angles to the car centre
line. If not, adjust at the nuts behind the shrouds.
Tighten the adjusting nut locknuts.
4 Now back off the two sprockets by about four or five
teeth so that the discs can be turned freely. Check that
the handbrake is applied when pulled up about four
teeth, but is quite free when the lever is released.
Finally, depress the brake pedal several times to set
the pads and then check the fluid level in the reservoir.

Handbrake lever and mounting:

The handbrake lever mounting assembly also incorporates the hand throttle lever and the heater control
lever(s). FIG 11:12 relates to earlier models in which the
heater control has a single lever. Later models are
provided with twin heater control levers (see Chapter 2,
FIG 2:3) and further lever pressure plates and friction
discs is consequently incorporated into the mounting
assembly.

Removing the handbrake mounting:

1 Remove the tunnel cover and lever dust boot. Remove
the knob from the heater control lever 1. Release the
support housing from the tunnel.
2 Remove nut 5 and withdraw cup spring 4, pressure
disc 3, friction disc 8 and heater control lever 1. Note
that the numbered parts are actually at the opposite
end, so work on the end adjacent to the heater lever.
3 Lift the housing a little. The cable and equaliser beam
can be seen attached to a clevis, the clevis pin being
secured by a spring clip arrowed in FIG 11:13.
Release the clip and pull out the pin.
4 Remove the wiring from the control lamp switch and
lift away the handbrake mounting assembly.

Dismantling the handbrake mounting:

1 Remove the locking ring and withdraw the drag link
and washer from the lower end of the hand throttle
lever. Remove the nut from the pivot shaft 6 and lift off
the hand throttle lever and friction disc assembly. Pull
out the pivot shaft.

FIG 11:13   Removing   the   handbrake   mounting
assembly (later models)

FIG 11:14   Brake servo unit components

Key to Fig 11:14   1 Cap   2 Filter screen   3 Bolt   4 Spring washer   5 Washer   6 Reservoir   7 Plug   8 Nut   9 Spring washer   10 Bracket   11 Base   12 Spring clip   13 Fulcrum pin   14 Operating lever   15 Bushes   16 Circlip   17 Nut 18 Spring washer   19 Master cylinder   20 'O' ring   21 Servo unit   22 Check valve   23 Adaptor   24 Switches   25, 26 Hoses 27 Connector, straight   28 Connector, 75°   29 Adaptors

2 Remove the screw to the rear of the pivot and withdraw the control switch. Push the handbrake lever slightly to the rear and out of the housing to remove the ratchet plate.

3 Grind the rivet head off the ratchet pawl stud, drive out the stud and remove the pawl. If it is necessary to remove the handbrake lever, pull off the hand grip which is glued on. This will release the button and rod, the ring and the spring.

Reassembling the handbrake mounting:

1 After fitting the handbrake control button, glue the grip in place, making certain that no surplus glue interferes with the action of the button.

2 Grease the ratchet plate pawl and pivot shaft with multi-purpose lithium grease and insert it into place.

3 Fit the hand throttle friction discs dry. All friction assembly surfaces must be free from grease. Tighten the self-locking nut.

Installing the handbrake mounting:

Do this in the reverse order of dismantling. Do not forget to attach the wiring to the control lamp switch. Fit the heater control lever in the housing. Install the cable beam and check that the cables are correctly seated. Fit the housing to the tunnel and tighten the bolts to 2.5kgm (18lb ft). Reassemble the friction parts for the heater lever in the manner described for the hand throttle lever. Tighten the self-locking nut until the lever does not feel too stiff to move, but does not slip back when the heater is fully on. Check the adjustment of heater flaps as in **Chapter 4**. Check the adjustment of the hand throttle control as in **Chapter 2**. Check handbrake adjustment as described earlier.

Removing the handbrake cables:

1 Chock the front wheels, release the handbrake and raise the rear of the car. Remove the rear wheels.

2 Remove the handbrake housing from the tunnel. Detach the cables from the equaliser beam.

3 Block the brake pedal in a slightly depressed position to prevent draining of fluid from system and remove the pipe line from the rear caliper. Detach the caliper from its mounting.

4 Remove the countersunk screws and pull off the brake disc and spacer. Release the cable from the expander (see **Section 11 : 5**). Pull the cable out from the rear of the brake. Pull the other end out of the conduit tube in the tunnel.

Refitting the handbrake cables:

1 Feed the cable into the conduit tube while coating it with multipurpose lithium grease. Refit the cable end to the brake expander as described in **Section 11 : 5**.

2 Refit the caliper, tightening the bolts to 6kgm (43lb ft) on new spring washers. Refit the handbrake housing to tunnel. Bleed the brake system (see **Section 11 : 7**). Adjust the handbrake as described earlier.

11 : 9 Servo unit

The servo unit where fitted cannot be repaired and if defective must be renewed.

Checking servo unit:

Depress the brake pedal several times until all vacuum is exhausted from the unit, with the pedal depressed fully start the engine, the pedal will move further as vacuum takes effect if the servo unit is functioning correctly.

Malfunction of the unit can be caused by leaking vacuum line connections, a sticking check valve 22 (see **FIG 11 : 14**) or master cylinder defects. If attention to these does not correct the fault renew the unit.

Removing and refitting:

Remove the lockpin connecting the operating lever 14 to the pressure rod. Remove the screw, lockwasher and plain washer attaching the master cylinder to the luggage compartment floor plate. Drain the brake fluid carefully to avoid spillage. Disconnect the stoplight connections at the plugs 24. Disconnect the vacuum hose and brake lines. Unscrew the bolt securing the top of the strut to the unit and the securing nuts of the unit and lift away. If the unit 21 is to be renewed unscrew the nuts 17 and spring washers 18 and separate the master cylinder from the unit, discard the 'O' ring 20. Remove the nuts 8 and spring washers 9 and separate the base 11, remove the circlip 16 and lift the unit 21 away.

Reassemble and refit in the reverse order renewing the 'O' ring 20. Adjust the pressure rod and bleed the brakes (see **Section 11 : 7**).

Adjusting the pressure rod:

Pull the pedal back to the stop. Loosen the locknuts on the pressure rod and adjust the length of the rod so that the pin can enter the clevis and operating lever 14 without force with the operating lever just touching the pushrod of the servo unit without moving it and the pedal on the stop. Tighten the pressure rod locknuts.

Check the play in the unit by bleeding the brakes and with the engine stopped there should be at least 10mm (0.40in) pressure rod play at the pedal.

11 : 10 Fault diagnosis

(a) 'Spongy' pedal action

1 Leak in hydraulic system
2 Worn master cylinder
3 Leaking caliper cylinders
4 Air in the fluid
5 Insufficient fluid in reservoir

(b) Excessive pedal movement

1 Check 1, 4 and 5 in (a)
2 Excessive pad wear
3 Too much free movement in pedal pushrod
4 Defective cups and valve in master cylinder
5 Wheel bearings slack
6 Disc or caliper mountings loose
7 Excessive runout or thickness variation of discs

(c) Brakes grab or pull to one side

1 Check 5, 6 and 7 in (b)
2 Oily pads or mixed grades
3 Worn suspension or steering connections
4 Uneven tyre pressures
5 Dirt in pad slots, dust covers defective
6 20° piston step wrongly set
7 Seized piston in caliper cylinder

(d) Pedal must be pumped to get braking

1 Check 2, 4 and 5 in (a) and 4 in (b)

(e) Brakes get hot when not used

1 Check 4 and 5 in (b); 5 and 7 in (c)

2 Reservoir supply port in master cylinder blocked by
  piston cup
3 Insufficient free play in pedal pushrod
4 Rubber cups swollen due to wrong fluid
5 Handbrake adjusted too tightly, cables seized (rear)
6 Handbrake shoe return springs weak or broken (rear)

(f) Frequent topping up of fluid required

1 Check pipes, connections and cylinders for leaks

(g) Only front brakes or only rear brakes operate

1 One section of reservoir empty
2 One section of master cylinder defective
3 Broken pipe in front or in rear system

CHAPTER 12

THE ELECTRICAL SYSTEM

12:1 Description

All models covered by this manual have 12-volt electrical systems in which the negative battery terminal is earthed. A selection of wiring diagrams is included in the **Technical Data** section of the **Appendix**. Depending upon the model, a single 12-volt battery or a pair of 12-volt batteries (connected in parallel) may be fitted.

The starter motor is mounted on the transmission casing. It incorporates positive engagement of the drive pinion. The starter motor switch is combined with the ignition switch and operates a solenoid which is integral with the starter motor assembly.

The generator is housed in the hub of the engine air cooling fan which is keyed to the generator shaft. The generator and cooling fan are consequently driven by the same belt. The generator is a three-phase AC machine and incorporates a transistorised rectifier. An electronic regulator is incorporated into the charging circuit.

Headlamps may have renewable bulbs or sealed-beam or halogen lights. Flasher and reversing lights are fitted. Instrument lights may be dimmed by turning the switch knob. The revolution indicator is transistorised and is driven by electrical impulses from the ignition system. Electrical sender units operate the fuel, oil temperature and, in relevant models, the oil pressure gauges.

Although instructions for the servicing of certain of the electrical equipment units are given in this chapter, it must be accepted that it is not sensible to attempt repairs to units which are seriously defective, electrically or mechanically. Such defective equipment should be replaced by new or exchange replacement units. The testing of certain equipment requires specialist equipment, facilities and services.

12:2 The battery

Depending upon the model, a single 12-volt battery or two 12-volt batteries (connected in parallel) may be fitted. The system is negative earth. **Do not, under any circumstances, reverse the battery terminal connections.** The connections must be tight on the battery posts and a light coating of non-metallic grease should be applied to the terminal clamps and posts to retard corrosion and oxidisation. If the connections are corroded, remove the clamps and wash them in bicarbonate of soda. Dry them thoroughly, apply non-metallic grease and refit the terminal clamps tightly.

Keep the fluid in each cell topped up to about 10mm (0.4in) above the plates and separators by adding distilled water. **Never use undiluted acid. If it is necessary to prepare a new solution of electrolyte**

FIG 12:1 Fuses and relays (earlier models)

Key to Fig 12:1 1 Horn (all models) 2 (depending upon model) Fog lights/auxiliary driving lights/air conditioning *or* fog lights/auxiliary driving lights *or* fog lights only 3 Vacant *or* auxiliary driving lights/air conditioning *or* auxiliary driving lights only 4 Vacant *or* air conditioning only 5 Fuse box I 6 Fuse box II

FIG 12:2 Fuses and relays (later models)

Key to Fig 12:2 1 Air conditioning 2 Fog lights 3 Horn

due to spillage or loss, add the acid to the distilled water. It is highly dangerous to add water to acid.

If the charge state of a battery is suspect, test the electrolyte with a hydrometer. The indications from the specific gravity readings given by the hydrometer are approximately as follows:

	Specific gravity
Cells fully charged	1.240 to 1.260
Cells half charged	1.170 to 1.190
Cells discharged	1.100 to 1.120

The above readings will apply when the battery temperature is about 20°C (68°F). For the same cell condition, specific gravity will increase when the electrolyte temperature is more than 20°C and vice versa. Add 0.002 for every 3°C (5°F) above 20°C and subtract 0.002 for every 3°C (below 20°C).

If the state of a battery is low, take the car for a long daylight run or put the discharged battery on charge at 4 to 5amps. If this does not correct the battery state, have the individual cells voltage tested to ascertain whether the battery should be replaced by a new one. If a battery is to be put on charge without dismounting it from the vehicle, **disconnect both leads from the battery.**

If a battery is to stand for a long period, give it a freshening-up charge every month. If it is left discharged, it will deteriorate and be ruined.

12:3 Fuses and relays

The main fuse box(es) are located in the lefthand side of the luggage compartment and it will be noted from **FIGS 12:1** and **12:2** that their configuration is not identical in all models. On relevant models a further three fuse positions are located in the engine compartment as shown in **FIG 12:3** and in **Chapter 3, FIG 3:1**. Depending upon the model and the equipment installed, relays are located in both the luggage compartment (see **FIGS 12:1** and **12:2**) and in the engine compartment (see **FIGS 12:3, 12:4** and **12:5**).

Depending upon the model, the special equipment fitted and the optional extra equipment installed, certain fuse and relay positions may not be in use. On earlier models fuses are identified in the fuse box cover(s). On later models they are identifiable by number (No 1 is the foremost) in the relevant wiring diagram.

Never fit a replacement fuse of greater capacity than that originally fitted since, by doing so, the protection of the relevant circuit may be jeopardised. If a fuse blows repeatedly, trace the reason for it doing so without delay. A failed relay should be replaced by one of the same type.

If additional electrical equipment is being installed, it should be wired up through a fuse and, if relevant, an appropriate relay fitted to the relevant position(s). Do not connect such equipment directly across the battery posts.

12:4 The starter motor

Components of the starter motor are shown in **FIG 12:6**. When the ignition key is turned to the start position, the solenoid is energised, the plunger is drawn in and the actuating lever starts to move the actuating sleeve. When the associated locking ring has moved about 2mm or 3mm ($\frac{1}{8}$in) the balls round a groove in the shaft are freed and allow the pinion to move into engagement with the

FIG 12:3   Engine compartment console

Key to Fig 12:3 1 Console   2 Relay switch for single stage rear window defroster (not used with two stage)   3 Rev/min sensor 4 Relay switch for start enrichment (not used in carburetter engines) 5 Rev/min transducer (not used in carburetter engines except 911T USA model)   6 Control relay for two stage rear window defroster (not used for single stage)   7 Radio noise suppression 8 Regulator   9 Ignition trigger unit   10 Fuse box III

flywheel ring gear. The solenoid plunger has simultaneously closed a switch which passes current to the motor. If the engine fires, it may run up to a speed which would drive the motor by way of the pinion. To prevent this, a one-way clutch is provided. When the switch is released, the solenoid return spring starts to retract the pinion, and pressure from the engagement spring pushes the locking ring over the balls and a braking disc comes into action to slow down the armature. The one-way clutch consists of five spring-loaded rollers confined in cam-shaped recesses.

Tests for a starter which does not operate:

Check the condition of the battery and its connections. If these are in order, switch on the lights and operate the starter switch. Current is reaching the starter if the lights go dim. If the lights do not go dim, check with a voltmeter or test light if there is voltage at the solenoid when the switch is operated. If there is, suspect a defective solenoid. If there is not, suspect the ignition switch or the wiring continuity. If these are in order, remove the starter motor for further investigation and to check the brush gear.

FIG 12:4   Relays (earlier models)

Key to Fig 12:4   1 Headlight dimmer switch relay
2 Windshield defogger relay (not valid for USA)   3 Turn signal relay

FIG 12:5   Relays (later models)

Key to Fig 12:5   1 Optional equipment   2 Heated windshield   3 Emergency flasher   4 Safety belt warning system
(logic relay)

Removal:

Disconnect the battery earth cables. Detach the cables
from the starter and the solenoid. Remove the flange bolts
and disconnect the starter.

Removing and refitting the solenoid:

Remove the connector from the terminal next to the
motor body. Remove the solenoid from the drive housing.
Pull the pinion out a little and withdraw the solenoid,
while disconnecting the plunger from the actuating lever.
Solenoids are not repairable and a defective one must
be renewed.

Install the solenoid in reverse order. Hold the cable
terminals when tightening the nuts so that the studs
cannot turn. If the solenoid is new, adjust the plunger so
that the distance from the centre of the hole in the clevis

to the mounting flange is 32.4mm ± 10mm (1.276in ±
0.004in) when the plunger is in position.

When the solenoid is energised, the travel of the
plunger must be 10mm ± 0.2mm (0.394in ± 0.008in),
of which 3mm (0.118in) is engagement reserve.

Checking the brushes and the commutator:

1 Remove the cover from the end of the starter opposite
  to the pinion.
2 Lift the brush springs and pull the brushes out of the
  holders by their flexible leads. If the length of a brush
  allows a lead to touch the holder, then it is too worn
  for further use and must be renewed.
3 Clean the commutator with a stick wrapped in a
  petrol-soaked cloth. Keep dirt and excess petrol from
  the end bearing.

Check brush springs for tension. Renew brushes if
worn, oil-soaked or if their leads are loose or frayed.
Always renew brushes in sets.

If a commutator is badly scored or burned, remove the
armature and skim the commutator in a lathe. Use fine
sandpaper for polishing. Do not use emerycloth. Undercut as explained in 'Inspection and Testing'.

When refitting the brushes, make sure that they are free
in their holders and check that the flexible leads are out of
the way.

Dismantling the starter:

1 Remove the dust cap from the end opposite to the
  pinion. Remove the 'O' rings, the lock ring on the
  shaft and the spacers.
2 Detach the cable from the inner terminal of the
  solenoid. Remove the solenoid mounting screws and
  withdraw the solenoid while unhooking the plunger
  from the actuating lever.
3 Remove the two long through bolts and the end
  cover or armature support. Withdraw the brushes,
  making a note of their locations. Positive brushes
  have leads which are soldered to the field windings,
  negative brush leads going to the brush holders.
4 Remove the brush carrier plate and the metal and
  insulating washers from the armature shaft. Pull the
  complete field frame off the drive housing, taking
  care of the rubber seal and the metal plate.

FIG 12:6   Components of the starter motor

Key to Fig 12:6   1 Nut   2 Washer   3 Screw   4 Rubber block   5 Disc   6 Solenoid   7 Spring   8 Screw   9 Washer
10 Dust cap   11 'O' ring   12 Retainer   13 Shims   14 Bolt   15 Washer   16 Brush-end cover   17 Brush carrier plate
18 Negative brush   19 Positive brush   20 Brush spring   21 Grommet   22 Field frame   23 Field coil   24 Insulating washer
25 Thrust washer   26 Armature   27 Actuating sleeve   28 Actuating lever   29 Engagement spring   30 Detent balls   31 Overrun
clutch   32 Pivot bolt   33 Washer   34 Nut   35 Drive housing

5 Remove the actuating lever pivot bolt and withdraw the armature and lever. Hold the armature in a vice with soft jaws. Refer to **FIG 12 : 6** and press actuating sleeve 27 towards the overrun clutch 31 and catch the detent balls 30 as they fall out. Release the sleeve and spring 29.

6 When cleaning the parts, do not put the armature or the overrun clutch in solvent and keep the solvent away from the self-lubricating bearing bushes. Normally, during a major overhaul, it is advisable to renew these bushes. Clean off all carbon dust from the armature and from the brush carrier.

Inspecting and testing:

Check the action of the actuating lever, sleeve and clutch. Renew parts if the sleeve and lever do not move freely, or if the lever is bent. If necessary renew the brake disc. Renew the pinion and shaft if the teeth are worn.

Check the field windings for signs of excessive heat or melted solder. They must not protrude beyond the pole-pieces. Check for continuity and shorting to earth, using a 40-volt AC test lamp.

Test the armature and brush carrier plate for short to earth in the same way. The insulated brush holders must not be shorting to earth. Apply test prods to the cylindrical body of the armature and to each commutator segment in turn. The test lamp should not light.

Check the condition of the commutator. Minimum diameter is 33.5mm (1.319in) and maximum runout should not exceed 0.05mm (0.002in). Clean out excessive wear and pitting by skimming the commutator in a lathe, providing the diameter is not reduced below the stipulated figure. The mica insulation between the commutator segments must be undercut to a depth of about 0.8mm (0.03in) using a piece of fine hacksaw blade ground on the sides to the correct width. Take care not to damage the segments or the soldered joints.

Brushes which are worn, broken or which have defective leads must be renewed. Always fit a complete set. Unsolder the leads one at a time to avoid confusion, and when soldering the new leads into place do not let the solder run too far up the flexible part.

Armature shaft bushes are of the self-lubricating type, so make sure that the new bushes are well impregnated with oil. At the pinion end, drill out the rivets to release the seal and press out the bush. Press a new bush into place with a shouldered mandrel having a pilot the same diameter as the shaft until it is flush on the inside. Do not ream this type of bush after fitting. Centre a new seal with a suitable mandrel and secure the retainer with small screws, nuts and spring washers. Peening the screw ends to prevent loss of the nuts.

Reassembling:

Hold the armature in the vice and stick balls into the locking ring with grease such as Bosch Ft 2v3. Fit the actuating sleeve, brake disc and spring to overrun clutch and locking ring and push the assembly onto the shaft until balls engage the groove in the shaft. Check that the pinion and the clutch are properly seated and that the mechanical engagement parts move freely when released. Grease all parts.

Fit the actuating lever to the sleeve and push the armature and lever into the drive housing. Grease and fit the lever pivot stud. Fit the rubber seal between the solenoid and the field recesses so that its tabs seat correctly in the cutout provided. Push the field frame over the armature. Fit greased metal and insulating washers to the shaft. Fit the brush carrier plate, aligning the notch which prevents turning, in the correct position.

Seat the rubber grommet for the field lead correctly and refit the end cover. Earthing points between the brush carrier plate and the cover and between the cover and the field housing must be clean and bright. Secure the two through bolts. Fit the spacer washers and locking ring to the end of the shaft and check that the end float lies between 0.1 and 0.3mm (0.004 and 0.012in). Secure the flange of the end cap. Fit the solenoid and connect the field lead to the inner terminal.

Replacement starter motors:

Starter motor types are not identical on all models. If a new or exchange replacement starter is required, ensure that it is of the same type as that originally fitted.

12 : 5 The alternator

The alternator may be either of Bosch or of Motorola manufacture. The alternator generating capacity is not identical for all vehicle models and, if a replacement alternator is required, ensure that the new or exchange replacement machine is of the same type as that originally fitted.

The servicing of Bosch and Motorola alternators is covered separately in this section.

Servicing a Bosch alternator:

Before carrying out alternator tests, it is important to understand that it must not be run without connection to the battery, neither must the cables be removed during a running test. Be careful not to reverse the battery connections. Entrust major repairs to a Bosch service station.

Testing the system:

The control lamp should light up with the ignition switched on. If it does not, the bulb may be broken or a wire disconnected. If the lamp stays on with the ignition switched off, it indicates a defective rectifier. Disconnect the battery at once to prevent damage to the alternator and battery.

Start the engine. If the control lamp does not go out with increasing engine speed or lights up at certain speeds, the rectifier is defective.

For a quick test with the alternator installed, run the engine at a steady 3000rev/min. Switch on lamps and accessories to bring the load to 28 to 30amp. The voltage between terminals B+ and D− should lie between 13.5 and 14.5 volts.

Removing the alternator:

Remove the air cleaner. Release the clips from the upper shroud. Remove the alternator pulley nut and take off the belt (see **Chapter 4, Section 4 : 1**). Release the blower housing strap, pull the assembly rearwards and identify and detach the wires.

FIG 12:7 Removing brush plate and brushes (Bosch alternator)

Brushes:

Removing the brush plate is shown in **FIG 12:7**, but first check the brushes for freedom in their housings. Hook up the springs and check the brush length if no further dismantling is required. The minimum length is 14mm (0.55in). Unsolder the brush leads to renew brushes. Check that the brushes slide freely, rubbing the sides on a smooth file if necessary. Resolder the leads with resin-cored solder, taking care not to let solder run up the stranded, flexible connector.

Rotor:

To continue dismantling, remove the brush plate complete. Remove the six long screws and part the rotor from the stator housing (see **FIG 12:8**). The rotor may now be pressed out of the end frame for attention to the bearings and slip rings. It is not advisable to attempt repairs to the rectifier diodes which are mounted on plates at the same end as the brushes.

If the stationary windings are removed from the housing the coils may be tested. Use 40VAC and a pair of probes and check for continuity and earthing. Also check for resistance using an ohmmeter. The correct resistance is 0.26 ohm + 10 per cent.

FIG 12:8 Separating rotor and end frame from stator housing (Bosch alternator)

Using the same test voltage, check the rotor coils for earthing, putting one probe on a slip ring and the other on the pole piece. Connect an ohmmeter across the slip rings to check the rotor coil resistance. It must be 4 ohm + 10 per cent. If the slip rings are worn and pitted, skim them in a lathe, taking off the minimum amount of metal. When finished, check that runout does not exceed 0.03mm (0.001in). Minimum slip ring diameter is 31.5mm (1.24in) and maximum vertical runout of the rotor is 0.05mm (0.002in).

Bearings:

Renew bearings which are rough when spun without lubricant. In any case, renew bearings which have seen 60,000 miles (100,000km) of service. Adequately support the end frame and rotor when pressing bearings into place. Coat one side of the bearing with Bosche FT1V33 grease and fit to the end frame with the closed side entering first. Fit the retaining plate.

Cleaning:

Parts must not be soaked in solvents. Momentary exposure to solvents is permissible for cleaning purposes. Always relubricate the bearings after cleaning.

Reassembling:

Do this in the reverse order of dismantling. Check that the rotor turns freely after fitting the brushes.

Installation:

Fit the alternator to the blower housing with the marks aligned. Seat the blower housing on the dowel in the crankcase after connecting the wires to their identified connections. After fitting the pulley and belt, tighten the retaining nut to 4kgm (29lb ft).

Servicing a Motorola alternator:

The component parts are shown in **FIG 12:9**. An alternator is not self-exciting so that the necessary field current has to reach the unit by way of the generator control lamp 8 (see **FIG 12:10**) and the voltage regulator. For this reason it is important that the lamp is not burned out or of the wrong wattage. The field current is only about 2amp and is conducted to the field coils by brushes 4 and slip rings 3. An isolation diode 7 protects the alternator against overloading and also allows current to flow to the control lamp. The rectifier consists of three positive and three negative diodes 12. These pass current from the alternator to the battery or load but not in the reverse direction, so that there is no need for a cut-out.

Precautions:

Observe the following:
1 Do not earth the field exciter terminals DF of the alternator, regulator or the connecting wire.
2 Do not wrongly connect the voltage regulator and do not disconnect the regulator or the battery when the regulator is running.
3 Disconnect the battery before removing the alternator.
4 The voltage regulator must always be connected to the alternator earth.
5 For alternator tests the battery must be in good condition and fully charged. When running the

FIG 12:9   Component parts of Motorola alternator

Key to Fig 12:9   1 Isolation diode heat sink   2 Brush coverplate   3 Brush holder   4 Rear housing, supporting bearing and rotor   5 Front housing, supporting bearing and rotor   6 Positive diode heat sink   7 Negative diode heat sink   8 Stator   9 Ballbearing   10 Rotor   11 Bearing coverplate   12 Ballbearing

alternator in the car, the battery must always be connected.

6 Disconnect the battery before carrying out any arc welding on the car.

7 Heat damaged diodes. Use pliers as heat sink when unsoldering or soldering. Wrong connections will cause damage to diodes.

8 Detach the battery leads when charging the battery in the car.

Maintenance:

Apart from checking the belt tension (see **Chapter 4, Section 4:1**) no routine maintenance of the alternator or the voltage regulator is required. Bearings are lubricated for life.

Testing an alternator:

Connect the voltage regulator leads so that blue and red go to D+, black goes to DF and brown goes to D−. The location of the regulator is shown at 8 in **FIG 12:3**.

For a quick test with the alternator installed, run the engine at 2500 ± 150rev/min with lamps and accessories switched on to give a load of 28 to 30amp. The voltage between terminals B+ and D− must be between 13.4 and 14.6 volts.

Removing an alternator:

Do this as described earlier for the Bosch alternator.

Checking the brush gear:

Remove the brush holder (two bolts, see **FIG 12:11**). Use an ohmmeter and probes to check for continuity, the insulated brush with the DF terminal and the earthed brush with the holder. Resistance should be nil. Resistance should be infinitely high when the probes are touching the brushes only.

Checking the rotor:

Test for shorting to D− by connecting one ohmmeter probe to D− and the other to one of the slip rings. Resistance should be infinite.

Test the rotor coil for continuity by connecting one ohmmeter probe to each slip ring. The circuit resistance should be 4.5 to 6.5ohm. Renew the rotor is faulty.

FIG 12:10   Circuit diagram of Motorola alternator, regulator and battery

Key to Fig 12:10   1 Battery   2 Regulator   3 Slip rings   4 Brushes   5 Rotor   6 Stator   7 Isolation diode   8 Generator control lamp   9 Ignition/starter switch   10 To accessories   11 To starter   12 Diodes

FIG 12:11 Removing brush holder on Motorola alternator

Testing the isolation diode:

First test the heat sink for earthing by connecting one ohmmeter probe to D+ 61 and the other D− on the alternator and then in reverse. Resistance should be infinite in one direction and less than 50 ohm in the other. If readings differ from these, check the heat sink insulation behind the housing.

Test the diode by connecting one ohmmeter probe to terminal B+ and the other D+ 61 and then reversing them. Resistance should be infinite in one direction and less than 50 ohm in the other.

Testing the rectifier diodes:

Positive diodes are marked red and negative diodes black. Test negative diodes by connecting an ohmmeter across the diode terminal and D−. Reverse the connections and note the result, which should be the same as that described for the isolation diode. For positive diodes connect the ohmmeter to D+ 61 and the diode and then reverse the connections to get the same results as for the isolation diode.

Testing the stator coil:

This is done by connecting one ohmmeter probe to one end of a coil and the other to the stator frame. Resistance must be infinite. Check all coil ends and renew the stator if any test shows a lower resistance.

Dismantling the alternator:

1 Remove the brush assembly (see **FIG 12:11**). Remove the isolation diode assembly 1 in **FIG 12:9** (two outer nuts).

2 Remove the through bolts and separate the front housing 5 and rotor 10 from the stator and rear housing 4.

3 The rotor may be pressed out of the front housing and the ballbearing pulled off the rear end. To remove the bearing in the front cover, remove the bearing cover (three screws) and press out the bearing.

4 Release the diode assembly 6 and 7 from the rear housing and withdraw together with the stator 8. Mark the negative and positive diode leads if the diodes are to be removed. It would be best to leave servicing

the diodes to a service station, but the method is as follows:

5 Hold each lead with a pair of pliers on the diode side so that heat cannot travel into the diode, and quickly unsolder the connections.

Reassembling:

1 If the stator leads were unsoldered from diodes, pull them through the clips so that they lie correctly and will not need bending after soldering. Make sure connections are correct, noting that positive diodes are marked red and negative diodes black.

2 Hold diode leads with pliers which will act as a heat sink. **Use a hot iron and solder the leads as quickly as possible.**

3 Fit the stator and diode assemblies into the housing after placing an insulating washer and sleeve on each fixing stud of the positive diode assembly.

4 After fitting the stator and diode assemblies, put insulating washers on the two positive diode studs and secure both assemblies with nuts. Make sure the stator leads are properly arranged.

5 Press the rotor into front bearing in housing. Press the other ballbearing into place up to the stop on the rear end of the rotor shaft.

6 Make sure that the bore in the rear housing is clear and that the 'O' ring is in good condition. Join the two housings together and tighten the six bolts evenly and diagonally.

7 Secure the isolation diode assembly in position and attach the brush assembly. Install the alternator as described earlier for the Bosch alternator.

12:6 The alternator regulator

The voltage regulator is mounted as shown at 8 in **FIG 12:3**. It is a single unit controlling the field circuit of the alternator and there is no current regulator or cut-out. As there is no provision for servicing, it is important to consult a service station if the regulator gives trouble. A defective unit should be replaced by one of the same type.

Great care must be taken to ensure that the connections to the regulator are correctly fitted. The blue and red leads go to D+, the black lead to DF and the brown lead to D−.

Symptoms of regulator trouble may be no charge, or too low or too high an output from the alternator.

12:7 Headlights

The headlamp rims are secured by a screw at the lowest point indicated at **c** in **FIG 12:12**. Whatever the type of light unit fitted, avoid touching the reflecting surface or the light unit when working on a headlight or renewing a light unit.

Alignment:

Professional facilities are required for a complete and accurate alignment of the main and dipped beams but if a temporarily acceptable setting has to be carried out by an owner, the procedure is as follows:

Refer to **FIG 12:13**. Select a piece of level ground and mount a board as shown, distance 'd' being about 5m

(16.5ft). The tyres must be properly inflated and the car bounced to normalise the suspension. The board must be central on the car axis.

Mark the height of the headlamp centres at '**b**'. Mark a line '**c**' on the board at 1 per cent of the distance '**d**'. If 5m (16.5ft), '**c**' will be 50mm (2in). Mark the width between the headlamp centres (valve '**a**') on line '**c**' centrally about the axis. Make a cross at the intersection.

Cover one headlamp while setting the other. First adjust horizontally to bring the point of the angle between the dark and light areas onto the cross on the board. Make horizontal adjustments by turning screw '**a**' in **FIG 12:12**.

Adjust vertically by turning screw '**b**' until the horizontal plane of the dark and bright areas lies on the line marked at '**c**' (see **FIG 12:13**). After setting vertically, check the horizontal setting again.

12:8 Safety belt warning system

From the beginning of 1972 onwards, all vehicles exported to the USA are equipped with a safety belt warning system. The fitment is obligatory to conform with the federal laws on safety.

The system comprises, two inertia reel safety belts with automatic locking retractions; a control lamp with the inscription 'Fasten Seat Belt'; a built-in passenger seat contact switch; a new parking brake switch and a modified warning buzzer. The modified buzzer is a three-pole type which can be used, if necessary, to replace the existing two-pole type.

A switch is built into each safety belt buckle, it remains closed when the belts are not worn and provides an earth contact for terminal 'G' in the control lamp. The handbrake switch provides an earth connection to terminal 50a when the handbrake lever is fully released. The buzzer terminal 86 is energised when the ignition is switched on. To avoid activating the system when there is no passenger in the front seat a two-pole connector is located under the seat which breaks the independent earth contact when the seat is unoccupied.

The control lamp lights up and a simultaneous warning from the buzzer will operate when:

1 The ignition is switched on.
2 The drive (and passenger) have not put on their seat belts.
3 The parking brake is not fully released.

From 1974 models, the circuits were modified and each seat had a contact in conjunction with a logic relay and integrated buzzer, but the system was completely modified in 1975 with a timer relay and built in buzzer, the passenger seat being divorced from the warning system.

European models from 1977 are equipped with a seat belt indicator lamp mounted in the centre of the instrument panel with the parking brake and brake failure warning lamps. It lights for 8sec after the ignition is switched on whether seat belts are fastened or not.

12:9 Flasher unit

This is located under the luggage compartment mat adjacent to the steering column. It is a push fit in a three-pronged connector. There is an indicator lamp to show when a flasher bulb has failed, a magnetic switch breaking the earth connection to the lamp. The flasher unit cannot be repaired and it must be renewed in the event of failure.

FIG 12:12 To set headlamp beam vertically, turn screw **a** to right to lower and to left to raise it. Turn screw **b** for horizontal setting, turning to right sets beam to left, turning to left sets beam to right. Screw **c** secures rim

12:10 Windscreen wiper and washer

No procedures are prescribed for the repair or overhaul of the windscreen-wiper motor or the washer pump. In the event of either of these units becoming unserviceable it should be removed and a new or an exchange replacement unit fitted.

Removing the wiper motor and linkage:

Pull the luggage compartment mat forward and remove the front ventilating case after releasing the clip and air duct. These are located just below the grille in front of the wiper blades. Pull off the five cables from the wiper motor. Remove the wiper arms and the rubber grommets, unscrew the large nuts to release the spindles and withdraw the motor and linkage downwards. The linkage joints are service-free.

FIG 12:13 Headlamp beam setting

Key to Fig 12:13   a, b, c and d See text

FIG 12:14   Components of combination switches fitted to steering column

Key to Fig 12:14   1 Screw   2 Serrated lockwasher   3 Contact ring   4 Nut   5 Lockwasher   6 Screw   7 Round head countersunk screw   8 Upper housing assembly   9 Combination switch   10 Spring   11 Spring   12 Screw   13 Clamp   14 Steering post extension   15 Wiper and washer switch   16 Allen bolt   17 Lower housing assembly   18 Lever knob

When refitting the assembly, make sure the wire connections are correctly made. Check that the linkage moves freely. Fit the wiper blades so that they wipe a symmetrical arc.

Windscreen washer:

To remove the pump, detach the wiring cables and suction and pressure hoses. Loosen the retaining straps and lift out the pump. Note, that in the case of later models, access for the removal of the washer reservoir requires removal of the lefthand front wheel.

12:11   Horns

No procedures are prescribed for the adjustment or repair of the horns and a defective unit should be removed and a new or an exchange replacement fitted.

Horns operate through a relay. The location of this relay is shown in **FIGS 12:1** and **12:2**. If the horns do not operate, check that the relevant fuse is intact, that the horn button is serviceable and that the relay is also serviceable before suspecting the horns themselves.

12:12   Instruments

Withdraw an instrument by prying against the back of its protruding ring. The leads, etc. may then be disconnected.

Speedometer, mechanical:

The speedometer is mechanically driven by a flexible cable from the transmission. If the speedometer becomes inoperative, check that the drive cable is intact and correctly coupled at both ends before suspecting the instrument itself. On California equipped cars with EGR the cable is coupled to the elapsed mileage odometer switch (see **Chapter 4**). An unserviceable speedometer should be passed to a specialist for repair.

Speedometer, electronic:

The sensor can be checked by removing the tunnel cover in front of the emergency seats and disconnecting the flat male plugs at the connector.

Connect a test buzzer to the wires leading to the rear.

Jack up the righthand rear wheel. The buzzer should sound eight times for each two revolutions of the wheel, or with a limited slip differential eight times for each revolution, if not change the sensor.

Turn on the ignition and touch the wires together quickly that lead to the front, there should be a deflection of the speedometer needle, if not and the connections to the speedometer are correctly fitted change the speedometer.

Tachometer:

The tachometer is electronically operated and is wired into the ignition system. If the tachometer becomes inoperative, check the wiring continuity before having the instrument itself tested.

Level, pressure and temperature gauges:

These are electrically operated from fuel level, oil pressure and oil temperature transmitters. If a gauge becomes inoperative, check the relevant fuse. If this is intact, check the wiring continuity. If this is in order, have the transmitter checked or carry out a cross-check by substituting a transmitter which is known to be serviceable. If the gauge still does not record, remove it and fit a replacement.

Warning lights:

If, when the ignition is switched on but before the engine is started, a warning light fails to light up, check the bulb. If the bulb has not failed, check the wiring continuity, the fuse, the relevant switch (if applicable) or other reason for the warning light being inoperative.

12:13 Steering column switches

The steering wheel must be removed as described in **Chapter 10, Section 10:3** before the combination switch assembly can be dismounted. With the steering wheel removed, refer to **FIG 12:14**, identify and separate all the wiring connections. Remove the horn contact ring 3. Remove the nuts and pull the upper housing assembly 8 upwards, pushing the leads and connectors through the holes provided. Remove combination switch 9 (three screws).

Faulty switch units are best renewed as an assembly, but a broken flasher return spring may be renewed separately. Check all electrical contacts for firm seating and cleanliness. Refit the parts in the reverse of the dismantling order, making sure the connections are correctly made.

12:14 Fault diagnosis

(a) Battery discharged

1 Terminals loose or dirty
2 Battery internally faulty

3 Shortcircuits in system
4 Alternator not charging
5 Regulator defective

(b) Insufficient charging current

1 Check 1, 4 and 5 in (a)
2 Driving belt slipping

(c) Battery will not hold charge

1 Low level of electrolyte
2 Battery plates sulphated
3 Electrolyte leakage from cracked case or top seal
4 Plate separators ineffective

(d) Battery overcharged

1 Check 5 in (a)
2 Poor connections between regulator and alternator

(e) Alternator output low or nil

1 Check 3 and 5 in (a) and 2 in (b)
2 Faulty brushes, rotor coil or isolation diode

(f) Noisy alternator

1 Worn belt, loose pulley
2 Defective bearings

(g) Control lamp not lighting with ignition on

1 Defective bulb or broken connection

(h) Control lamp stays on with ignition switched off

1 Defective diodes in alternator (disconnect battery at once)

(i) Starter motor lacks power or will not operate

1 Battery discharged, loose connections
2 Solenoid switch contacts worn or dirty
3 Brushes worn or sticking, springs weak or broken
4 Commutator, armature or field coils defective
5 Engine abnormally stiff

(j) Starter motor runs but does not turn engine

1 Pinion or flywheel gear defective

(k) Starter pinion stays in mesh

1 Bent armature shaft, dirty or defective pinion
2 Solenoid switch faulty

(l) Lamps inoperative or erratic

1 Battery low, bulbs burned out
2 Switch faulty, poor earthing, loose connections, broken wires

NOTES

CHAPTER 13

THE BODYWORK

13:1 Bodywork finish

Large-scale repairs to body panels are best left to expert panel beaters. Even small dents can be tricky, as too much hammering will stretch the metal and make things worse instead of better. Filling minor dents and scratches is probably the best method of restoring the surface. Use a modern filling compound and work to the manufacturer's instructions. The touching-up of paintwork is well within the ability of most owners, particularly as self-spraying cans of the correct colours are now readily available. Use an air-drying enamel rather than a cellulose lacquer.

Before spraying, remove all traces of wax polish with white spirit. More drastic treatment will be required if silicone polish has been applied. Use a primer surfacer or a paste stopper or a filler according to the amount of filling required. When dry, rub down with 400 grade (or equivalent) 'Wet or Dry' paper until the surface is smooth and flush with the surrounding area. Spend time on getting a good finish as this will control the final effect. Apply the retouching paint and, when dry, use a cutting compound to remove the dry spray. Finish off with a liquid polish.

13:2 Engine and luggage compartment lids

Two operators are required to dismount and refit either of these lids. The procedures are similar for both lids.

Removal:

Open the lid and scribe round the hinge brackets on the underside of the lid so that, on refitment, the minimum of adjustment will be needed. While the lid is being held firmly, uncouple the prop from the lid and remove the bolts which retain each hinge bracket to the lid. Lift off the lid.

Fitment:

Fitment of a lid is the reverse of the removal sequence. Before finally tightening the bolts which secure the hinge brackets to the lid, position the lid to the scribed marks made before removal. When finally fitted, the gap between the lid and the body aperture should be equal and even all round. This gap should be 3.5 to 5.0mm (0.14 to 0.20in). The height of a lid in relation to the body may be adjusted by fitting (or removing) washers between the lid and

FIG 13:1 Removing the hand pull (earlier models)

the hinge brackets and, if necessary, adjusting the vertical position of the lock striker.

Reconnect the prop to the lid noting that, if it was removed for any reason, it should be fitted with the piston end of the prop attached to the lid.

13:3 Doors, locks, fittings and glass

Malfunctioning of the locks and window winding mechanisms can only be corrected by dismantling a door as far as may be necessary to gain access to the broken spring, pin, rod, clip or lever. Full dismantling will be necessary to renew the door glass. Unless accident damage has occurred, it will not normally be necessary to dismount a door from its hinges. To cover the model and modification standard variants, supplement the following procedure descriptions by making appropriate notes and sketches. If new units (locks, glass, winding mechanism) are required, ensure that they are identical with those being replaced. If they are not identical, new associated parts may have to be obtained in addition.

FIG 13:2 Two types of door lock

Dismantling and dismounting a door (earlier models):

1 Unscrew the decorative strip and the internal door lock knob. Remove the padded cover and unscrew the window winder.

2 Remove the rubber surround from the folding storage box, detach the box from its retaining spring and unscrew the box. Dismount the armrest after removing the retaining bolts and detaching the lock operating lever from its linkage.

3 Loosen the plastic sheet (note where adhesive was used) and, from inside as shown in FIG 13:1, remove the door pull rear retaining screw. Remove the front screw and unscrew the pocket at the bottom.

4 Separate the door panel from the frame, unscrew the spring plate, pull off the window aperture seal and the plastic sheet and lift off the chrome strip. Unscrew all the threaded connections for the window frame or, in the case of Targa models, the window guide rails and pull the frame up and out.

5 In the case of coupé models, push the glass forwards until the sliding block can be freed from the lift rail and remove the glass. Unscrew the window lift regulator. In the case of Targa models, first detach the window lift screws and then remove the window.

6 Unscrew the outside door handle. Remove the lock retaining screws and withdraw the door lock complete with the inside locking mechanism and the remote control device. FIG 13:2 shows two lock variants.

7 Unscrew the external mirror. Detach the door stay at the hinge pillar. Using tool P290, drive out the hinge pins and lift off the door.

Dismantling and dismounting a door (later models):

1 Dismount the storage compartment after removing the screws from below, from each end and from below the cover. Unscrew the door lock button, the screws from both ends and remove the door ledge cover.

2 Remove the storage compartment after detaching at the rear. Detach the connecting rod at the handle (see FIG 13:3 and 13:4), unscrew the fasteners from the top and bottom of the hand grip. Remove the window winding crank.

3 Remove the supporting brackets, unhook the door panel, remove the control lever from the door inner panel and disconnect the spring.

4 Further operations are as described earlier for the dismantling and dismounting of a door from earlier models. When removing the door stop roll pin, use tool P290 with tool P290a.

Door refitment and reassembly:

Follow the reverse of the dismantling and removal sequence. If new glass is being fitted, ensure that it is the same size and thickness as that originally fitted. Attach the rubber pad to the base with adhesive. Torque tighten window regulator 6mm screws to 1.2kgm (8.7lb ft) and window frame 6mm screws to 0.9kgm (6.5lb ft). 8mm screws should be torque tightened to 2.2kgm (16lb ft).

On Targa models, wind up the window glass fully, adjust the position of the stop angle (see FIG 13:5)

FIG 13:3   Removing the hand pull (later models)

FIG 13:4   Remote control mechanism (later models)

FIG 13:5   Window glass adjustment (Targa models)

and then tighten firmly. Check the condition of the window frame corner pieces to ensure that they will make good joints with the folding roof.

Use sealing compound where shown arrowed in **FIG 13:6**. Ensure that the door pocket and armrest holes align with those in the inner panel.

13:4 Sliding and folding roofs

Manual operation of sliding roof:

If the electric motor drive fails, the roof can be operated by means of an emergency manual crank which is fitted as follows:

Open the zip. Detach the plastic cap from the gear and remove the screw with the screwdriver end of the manual crank as shown in **FIG 13:7**. Remove and **retain the spacing washers**. Screw the manual crank into the gear by means of the knurled nut. The teeth on the crank must locate in the groove in the gear before the knurled nut is tightened. The sliding roof can now be operated by the crank.

Sliding roof motor drive removal and fitment:

If the drive does not operate, confirm that the battery is not flat, that the fuse is intact and that all connections are tight and that there is no discontinuity in the wiring. If these are in order, remove the motor drive as follows:

Open the zip and disconnect the wiring from the motor. Remove the screws which retain the gear (see **FIG 13:8**). Unbolt the motor and its bracket from the roof frame and separate the motor from the bracket.

FIG 13:6   Apply sealing compound where arrowed

FIG 13:7   Fitting the manual winding crank

FIG 13:8   Removing the sliding roof motor drive

FIG 13:9   Fitting a backlight glass

Renew the motor complete with the gear and flexible drive and, following the reverse of the removal sequence, refit the drive assembly. No procedures are prescribed for the repair or overhaul of the sliding roof motor.

Sliding roof guides and guide rails:

Renewal of the guides, rails and cable requires removal of the complete sliding roof. This work is best carried out by a Porsche agent. On completion, check that the height of the sliding roof has been satisfactorily adjusted.

Folding roof dismantling and reassembling:

1 Unlock and dismount the roof. Collapse the braces and fold the roof.
2 Place the roof on soft pads to preclude damage to the outer material and to reinforce the braces. Pry out the plastic stopper from the front hinge pin which retains the upholstery pads.
3 Remove the screws from the side covers. Remove the covers and cover strips. Remove the circlips from the outer hinge pins. Press out the pins. Separate the centre hinge in the same manner. Renew worn hinge pins.
4 Pry out the roof lock grip mouldings. Carefully remove the glued on upholstery pads from the forward frame and at the same time, remove the plastic rivet from the frame. Remove the lock moulding screws and remove the locks.
5 Check the front locating studs for signs of wear. Remove the circlips from the rear hinge pins. Press out the pins and separate the rear frame sections. Check all hinge joints. If necessary, remove burrs from the edges and lubricate lightly.
6 Remove the screws from the aluminium rear cover. Remove the covers and unfasten the roof covering from the pins in the lefthand and righthand frames. The brackets can now be adjusted or, if necessary, renewed.

Reassembly is the reverse of the dismantling sequence. Since modifications have introduced differences between earlier and later type roofs, check that any new parts obtained are suitable for the model being worked on.

Folding roof front to frame:

To dismantle this unit, proceed as follows:
Remove the four countersunk screws from the roof side frame. Renew any damaged weatherstrip by removing the screws in the rear part of the frame and separating the glued on ends of the weatherstrip. If the water drain strip is damaged, remove the retaining screws and discard the strip.

Reassembly is the reverse of the dismantling sequence. Use waterproof adhesive to fix the ends of the weatherstrip. With the roof installed and locked, adjust the weatherstrip so that it seals against the door windows and fasten in place. If adjustment is required, unlock the roof before adjusting as necessary (adjustment, front, 42.5mm [1.67in]; rear, 43.5mm [1.71in]).

13:5 Windscreen and backlight glass

The procedure for renewing a windscreen or a backlight glass is similar except, where applicable, for the

FIG 13:10 Air conditioning installation features

Key to Fig 13:10   1 Compressor and clutch   2 Rear condenser   3 Hose   4 Front condenser   5 Condenser cooling fan
6 Receiver   7 Expansion valve and evaporator core   8 Three-speed switch, temperature control and conditioned air outlet
9 Hose

threading and connection of heater cables. If the wind-screen is being dealt with, remove the wiper blade arms and position a protective covering over the luggage compartment lid and over the dashboard. **A new mould-ing will be required.**

Removing the original glass:

1 In the case of a windscreen, push a thin blade or knife carefully between the glass and the interior mirror base plate until it can be dismounted from the glass. Clean off all traces of adhesive from the plate.

2 In the case of a **Targa** backlight, remove the folding roof before proceeding to unscrew the box clamps and rear bulkhead lining. Remove the upper rear panel section and seat decorative strips. Detach the inner treadle panel and remove upwards. Detach the sealing frame at the front along the roll bar. Remove the screws on the chrome treadle panel. Unscrew the chrome panel. Unscrew the chrome panel below the wings and remove upwards. Pull off the seal upwards. In the case of **other models**, take out the rear bulkhead lining.

3 On all models, cut round the moulding on the outside of the glass. Remove the trim strips. Disconnect the electrical heater connections (if applicable) and dismount the glass.

4 If the glass was shattered, remove sections until the remains and the moulding can be pulled away from the aperture.

5 If the glass is heated, retain the moulding so that it may be used as a pattern for the position of the slots and/or holes in the new moulding through which the heater cables will be threaded.

6 Thoroughly clean the body aperture and remove old moulding, sealer glass particles, etc. It is important that the aperture should be thoroughly clean as any remnants left behind may induce breakage of the new glass.

7 Check the body aperture for bumps and irregularities

and, if there are any, file them away as they too may induce breakage of the new glass. If accident damage could have distorted the aperture profile, have the contour checked with the relevant gauge by a Porsche agent. It will not be prudent to attempt to fit a new glass to a distorted aperture frame.

Fitting new glass:

1 Moisten the edge of the glass with soapy water or with turpentine. Position the moulding with its joint at the top centre and fit it round the glass. Using the old moulding as a pattern, make apertures for the heater cables (if applicable).

2 Thread the cables into position and connect up. Thread a strong cord all round the moulding recess which will be fitted over the body aperture. The cord ends should overlap by about 40cm (16in) at the top in the case of a windscreen or at the bottom in the case of a backlight.

3 Lubricate the trim groove with soapy water or with turpentine, fit the trim frame. Make sure that there is a gap of about 1cm (0.4in) between the ends before pushing on the connecting clip.

4 Fit the assembly to the body aperture. With one operator supporting the glass and maintaining hand pressure from outside the vehicle (see **FIG 13:9**), a second operator pulls the cord along the edge of the aperture so that the moulding lip is forced over the projecting edge. The first operator assists by lightly striking the glass with the palm of the hand at the point where the cord is being pulled.

5 Check, where applicable, that the heated glass is operating correctly. If this is in order, proceed to seal the glass to the moulding and to the body aperture. Use a pressure gun fitted with a copper nozzle (which will not scratch the glass) and, round the outside, inject sealing compound between the glass and the moulding and between the moulding and the body flange.

FIG 13:11   Air conditioning system wiring diagram

Key to Fig 13:11   1 Fusebox (10 terminal)   2 Fusebox (2 terminal)   3 Standard relay   4 Fan motor (front condenser)
5 Working contact relay   6 Three-terminal coupling   7 Two-terminal coupling   8 Blower motor (evaporator)   9 Thermostat
10 Blower switch   11 Temperature switch   12 Electro-magnetic clutch   13 Connector   14 Earth connection (to body)

6 Remove excess sealer with a rag and white spirit. Do not use thinners as this will damage the paintwork. The remaining operations are the reverse of those carried out before removing the original glass.

13:6 Bumpers

A damaged front or rear standard type bumper may be removed by an owner for possible repair or for replacement by a new unit. In the case, however, of energy-absorbing type units which incorporate deformation tubes or hydraulic absorption struts, it is advisable to entrust the work to a Porsche agent. The following procedures refer to standard types of bumpers.

Refitting a front bumper:

Straighten the surface below the front edge of the lid to get an even gap between the bumper and the lid. Fit the bumper without the rubber strip and check the distance to the flasher housing and adjust if necessary. Fit the flasher lens.

Adjust the bumper brackets so that there will be considerable tension during reassembly. Bend the rear bracket forward for this purpose.

Secure the bumper braces so that there will be as much preload tension on the bumpers as possible. Cement the sealing rubber to the body and install the bumper.

Refitting a rear bumper:

Fit the bumper side pieces and straighten the attaching tabs. Fit the bumper centre piece, insert the bumper horns and adjust to equal height. File the gap between the bumper and horn if necessary.

Cement the sealing rubber strip and cut off the edges. Fit the bumper parts and horns and cover the holes with plastic caps.

13:7 Front wings

A damaged front wing may be removed for repair or replacement by a new wing but, unless an owner has experience of this type of work (see **Section 13:1**) or can be assisted by someone who has, the work is best entrusted to a specialist. Note the following points.

Before fitting the lefthand wing, install the fuel filler cover if applicable. Apply body sealer strip to the mounting flange of the wing and then fit the snap nuts. Fit the wing, and screw in the bolts finger tight. While guiding the wing into place make sure the cable conduit for the filler cover release is correctly positioned. Do not, at this stage, install the sealing strip as it may be necessary to apply body solder in places. As a result, the gap between the wing and the door may be wider at the top edge by 1mm (0.04in).

Tighten the second bolt in from the rear end first and lightly tighten one at the front. Do the rearmost top bolt followed by the lowest one by the door sill, then tighten the remaining bolts on the vertical flange starting at the top. Finally, work along the top flange, starting at the rear.

When satisfied with the fit, drill two 4mm (0.16in) holes through the attaching flanges at front and rear locations, insert steel rivets in the holes and weld the heads to the body panel. These will act as dowels so that when the wing is removed for painting and then refitted it can be restored to its correct position and be properly aligned.

13:8 Air conditioning

The installation features of the Behr air conditioning system are shown in **FIG 13:10** and its wiring diagram is shown in **FIG 13:11**. The compressor is belt driven from the engine. For control purposes an electro-magnetic clutch is positioned between the compressor and its drive pulley. Hot compressed refrigerant vapour passes under pressure to the condensers in which the vapour is cooled and liquefied. The refrigerant then passes to the receiver which acts as a storage tank. Refrigerant passes through the expansion valve to the evaporator core. Cold, low pressure refrigerant is drawn through the core by the suction of the compressor. Warm air, passing over the evaporator core, is cooled by the refrigerant vapour while the vapour, heated by the air, passes again to the compressor. The cooled air is circulated to the interior of the vehicle.

This description and the installation feature illustration is given for information purposes only. **It is dangerous for an unqualified person to attempt to disconnect any part of the refrigeration circuit.** Units may be dismounted from their locations without the assistance of a qualified refrigeration engineer **provided that pipe connections are not disturbed.** An owner must enlist specialist assistance if it is necessary to discharge, evacuate or recharge the system. If such assistance is not available, arrange for a Porsche agent to carry out the work.

The three-speed switch turns the system on or off and also controls the volume of conditioned air. The temperature switch provides thermostatic control of the temperature of the conditioned air. If the system does not operate, check that the compressor drive belt is intact and correctly tensioned. If it is in order, check that the fuses (see **FIG 13:11**) are intact and that the relays (see **Chapter 12**, **FIGS 12:1** or **12:2** and also **FIG 13:11**) are operative. If these are in order, check that the switches are serviceable and that there is no wiring discontinuity. If all these appear to be in order but the system is still inoperative, consult a Porsche agent.

NOTES

APPENDIX

TECHNICAL DATA

HINTS ON MAINTENANCE AND OVERHAUL

GLOSSARY OF TERMS

INDEX

Inches	Decimals	Millimetres	Inches to Millimetres (Inches)	Inches to Millimetres (mm)	Millimetres to Inches (mm)	Millimetres to Inches (Inches)
1/64	.015625	.3969	.001	.0254	.01	.00039
1/32	.03125	.7937	.002	.0508	.02	.00079
3/64	.046875	1.1906	.003	.0762	.03	.00118
1/16	.0625	1.5875	.004	.1016	.04	.00157
5/64	.078125	1.9844	.005	.1270	.05	.00197
3/32	.09375	2.3812	.006	.1524	.06	.00236
7/64	.109375	2.7781	.007	.1778	.07	.00276
1/8	.125	3.1750	.008	.2032	.08	.00315
9/64	.140625	3.5719	.009	.2286	.09	.00354
5/32	.15625	3.9687	.01	.254	.1	.00394
11/64	.171875	4.3656	.02	.508	.2	.00787
3/16	.1875	4.7625	.03	.762	.3	.01181
13/64	.203125	5·1594	.04	1.016	.4	.01575
7/32	.21875	5.5562	.05	1.270	.5	.01969
15/64	.234375	5.9531	.06	1.524	.6	.02362
1/4	.25	6.3500	.07	1.778	.7	.02756
17/64	.265625	6.7469	.08	2.032	.8	.03150
9/32	.28125	7.1437	.09	2.286	.9	.03543
19/64	.296875	7.5406	.1	2.54	1	.03937
5/16	.3125	7.9375	.2	5.08	2	.07874
21/64	.328125	8.3344	.3	7.62	3	.11811
11/32	.34375	8.7312	.4	10.16	4	.15748
23/64	.359375	9.1281	.5	12.70	5	.19685
3/8	.375	9.5250	.6	15.24	6	.23622
25/64	.390625	9.9219	.7	17.78	7	.27559
13/32	.40625	10.3187	.8	20.32	8	.31496
27/64	.421875	10.7156	.9	22.86	9	.35433
7/16	.4375	11.1125	1	25.4	10	.39370
29/64	.453125	11.5094	2	50.8	11	.43307
15/32	.46875	11.9062	3	76.2	12	.47244
31/64	.484375	12.3031	4	101.6	13	.51181
1/2	.5	12.7000	5	127.0	14	.55118
33/64	.515625	13.0969	6	152.4	15	.59055
17/32	.53125	13.4937	7	177.8	16	.62992
35/64	.546875	13.8906	8	203.2	17	.66929
9/16	.5625	14.2875	9	228.6	18	.70866
37/64	.578125	14.6844	10	254.0	19	.74803
19/32	.59375	15.0812	11	279.4	20	.78740
39/64	.609375	15.4781	12	304.8	21	.82677
5/8	.625	15.8750	13	330.2	22	.86614
41/64	.640625	16.2719	14	355.6	23	.90551
21/32	.65625	16.6687	15	381.0	24	.94488
43/64	.671875	17.0656	16	406.4	25	.98425
11/16	.6875	17.4625	17	431.8	26	1.02362
45/64	.703125	17.8594	18	457.2	27	1.06299
23/32	.71875	18.2562	19	482.6	28	1.10236
47/64	.734375	18.6531	20	508.0	29	1.14173
3/4	.75	19.0500	21	533.4	30	1.18110
49/64	.765625	19.4469	22	558.8	31	1.22047
25/32	.78125	19.8437	23	584.2	32	1.25984
51/64	.796875	20.2406	24	609.6	33	1.29921
13/16	.8125	20.6375	25	635.0	34	1.33858
53/64	.828125	21.0344	26	660.4	35	1.37795
27/32	.84375	21.4312	27	685.8	36	1.41732
55/64	.859375	21.8281	28	711.2	37	1.4567
7/8	.875	22.2250	29	736.6	38	1.4961
57/64	.890625	22.6219	30	762.0	39	1.5354
29/32	.90625	23.0187	31	787.4	40	1.5748
59/64	.921875	23.4156	32	812.8	41	1.6142
15/16	.9375	23.8125	33	838.2	42	1.6535
61/64	.953125	24.2094	34	863.6	43	1.6929
31/32	.96875	24.6062	35	889.0	44	1.7323
63/64	.984375	25.0031	36	914.4	45	1.7717

UNITS	Pints to Litres	Gallons to Litres	Litres to Pints	Litres to Gallons	Miles to Kilometres	Kilometres to Miles	Lbs. per sq. In. to Kg. per sq. Cm.	Kg. per sq. Cm. to Lbs. per sq. In.
1	.57	4.55	1.76	.22	1.61	.62	.07	14.22
2	1.14	9.09	3.52	.44	3.22	1.24	.14	28.50
3	1.70	13.64	5.28	.66	4.83	1.86	.21	42.67
4	2.27	18.18	7.04	.88	6.44	2.49	.28	56.89
5	2.84	22.73	8.80	1.10	8.05	3.11	.35	71.12
6	3.41	27.28	10.56	1.32	9.66	3.73	.42	85.34
7	3.98	31.82	12.32	1.54	11.27	4.35	.49	99.56
8	4.55	36.37	14.08	1.76	12.88	4.97	.56	113.79
9		40.91	15.84	1.98	14.48	5.59	.63	128.00
10		45.46	17.60	2.20	16.09	6.21	.70	142.23
20				4.40	32.19	12.43	1.41	284.47
30				6.60	48.28	18.64	2.11	426.70
40				8.80	64.37	24.85		
50					80.47	31.07		
60					96.56	37.28		
70					112.65	43.50		
80					128.75	49.71		
90					144.84	55.92		
100					160.93	62.14		

UNITS	Lb ft to kgm	Kgm to lb ft	UNITS	Lb ft to kgm	Kgm to lb ft
1	.138	7.233	7	.967	50.631
2	.276	14.466	8	1.106	57.864
3	.414	21.699	9	1.244	65.097
4	.553	28.932	10	1.382	72.330
5	.691	36.165	20	2.765	144.660
6	.829	43.398	30	4.147	216.990

TECHNICAL DATA

Unless otherwise stated, dimensions are in mm but, where relevant, non-metric equivalents are given in brackets

ENGINE

Capacity:

Nominal, litres	2.2	2.4	2.7	3.0
Actual, cc	2195	2341	2687	2994

Bore and stroke .. .. .. 84 × 66   84 × 70.4   90 × 70.4   95 × 70.4

Compression ratio .. .. (TC) 8.6   (T/TV) 7.5   8.0   8.5
                       (EC) 9.1   (E) 8.0   (S) 8.5
                       (SC) 9.8   (S) 8.5

Crankshaft:

Main journal diameters:
- Nos 1 to 7 .. .. 56.990 to 56.971
- No 8 .. .. 30.993 to 30.980
- Undersizes .. .. −0.25, −0.50 and −0.75

Running clearance:
- Nos 1 to 7 .. .. 0.030 to 0.088
- No 8 .. .. 0.048 to 0.104

End float .. .. 0.10 to 0.02

Crankpin diameters:
- 2.2 litre .. .. As main journals
- 2.4, 2.7 and 3.0 litre .. .. 51.990 to 51.971
- Undersizes .. .. −0.25, −0.50 and −0.75
- Running clearance .. .. As main journals 1 to 7

Interference fits:
- Timing and distributor gears .. .. .. 0.002 to 0.038
- Flywheel .. .. Zero to 0.049

Connecting rods:

- Big-end running clearance .. .. .. As main journals 1 to 7
- Gudgeon pin running clearance .. .. .. 0.020 to 0.039
- Wear limit 0.050

Pistons:

- Clearance in cylinder bores .. .. .. See tabulation in **Section 1:10**
- Measurement position .. .. .. See tabulation in **Section 1:10**
- Wear limit on diameter 0.10 (0.004in)
- Weight variation per set .. .. 6 to 8gr (0.21 to 0.28oz)

Piston diameter:

2.2 litre:	**911TC**	**911EC**	**911SC**
Make	*Schmidt* *Mahle*	*Mahle*	*Mahle*
Standard sizes:			
0	83.96 83.97	83.96	83.95
1	83.97 83.98	83.97	83.96
2	83.98 83.99	83.98	83.97
Oversizes:			
0.KD1	84.21 84.22	84.21	84.20
1.KD1	84.22 84.23	84.22	84.21
2.KD1	84.23 84.24	84.23	84.22
Tolerances	± 0.007 ± 0.005	± 0.005	± 0.005
2.4 and 2.7 litre:	**911T**	**911E**	**911S**
Standard sizes:			
0	83.97	83.97	83.95
1	83.98	83.98	83.96
2	83.99	83.99	83.97

Oversizes:

0.KD1	..	..	..	..	..	84.22	84.22	84.20
1.KD1	..	..	..	..	..	84.23	84.23	84.21
2.KD1	..	..	..	..	..	84.24	84.24	84.22

Carrera 2.7 litre .. .. .. As 2.7 litre 911S

Carrera 3.0 litre:

Early:

0 ..	..	..	..	..	..	94.943 to 94.957
1 ..	..	..	..	..	..	94.953 to 94.967
2 ..	..	..	..	..	..	94.963 to 94.977

From engine no 666 0446 or 666 9091:

0 ..	..	..	..	..	..	94.963 to 94.977
1 ..	..	..	..	..	..	94.970 to 94.984
2 ..	..	..	..	..	..	94.977 to 94.991
3 ..	..	..	..	..	..	94.984 to 94.998

Cylinders:

Cylinder/piston clearances		..	..	..	See tabulation in **Section 1:10**
Wear limit on diameter	..	..	..	..	0.10 (0.004in)
Maximum ovality	..	..	..	..	0.04 (0.0016in)
Height tolerance ..	..	..	..	..	See **Section 1:10**

Camshafts:

Bearing diameters	..	..	..	..	46.926 to 46.942
Running clearance	..	..	..	..	0.025 to 0.066
Wear limit	..	..	..	..	0.100
End float ..	..	..	..	..	0.15 to 0.20
Sprocket clearance on shaft		..	..	..	Zero to 0.034

Camshaft housing:

Bores for camshaft	..	..	..	..	46.967 to 46.992
Bores for rocker shafts	..	..	..	..	18.000 to 18.018
Rocker shaft diameter	..	..	..	..	17.992 to 18.00
Clearance	..	..	..	..	0.016 to 0.035
Wear limit	..	..	..	..	0.080
End float ..	..	..	..	..	0.100 to 0.350
Wear limit	..	..	..	..	0.500

Clearances (timing case):

Carrier shaft/tensioner housing		..	..	..	0.016 to 0.045
Carrier shaft/sprocket housing..		..	..	..	0.016 to 0.045
Sprocket carrier/sprocket shaft		..	..	..	Zero to 0.029
Sprocket to shaft	..	..	..	..	0.032 to 0.061
Shaft to chain guide rail	..	..	..	..	0.105 to 0.129
Shaft to chain housing	..	..	..	..	−0.014 to −0.037
Sprocket alignment	..	..	..	..	Maximum deviation 0.25

Intermediate shaft:

Bearing 1 diameter	..	..	..	..	29.767 to 29.780
Bearing 2 diameter	..	..	..	..	23.967 to 23.980
Running clearance	..	..	..	..	0.020 to 0.054
Wear limit	..	..	..	..	0.100
End float ..	..	..	..	..	0.080 to 0.150
Sprocket mounting diameter	..	..	..	36.020 to 36.037
Interference fit	..	..	..	..	0.010 to 0.037

Crankcase .. .. See **Section 1:11**

Oil spray jets (if fitted) .. .. .. Open at 42 to 56lb/sq in

Valves:

Head diameter, inlet	..	..	..	..	46.00 ± 0.10, 3 litre 49.00
exhaust	..	..	..	..	40.00 ± 0.10, 3 litre 41.50
Stem diameter, inlet	..	..	..	..	8.97 − 0.012
exhaust	..	..	..	..	8.95 − 0.012

Length, inlet					114.00 ± 0.10			
exhaust					113.50 ± 0.10			
Seat angle					45°			

Valve springs .. .. 2 per valve
  Installed lengths .. .. See tabulation in **Section 1:8**
  Loaded length .. .. 42.0 to 42.5 under 20kg load

Valve clearance:
  Inlet and exhaust (cold) 0.10 (0.004in)

Valve guides:
  Interference fit in head .. .. 0.03 to 0.06
  Ream bore diameter to .. .. 9.000 + 0.015

Valve seats:
  Interference fit in head .. .. 0.14 to 0.18
  Seat width, inlet valve .. .. 1.25 ± 0.10
  exhaust valve .. .. .. 1.55 ± 0.10

Valve timing (degrees):

	IO/BTC	*IC/ABC*	*EO/BBC*	*EC/BTC*
2.2 litre engines:				
911TC	15	29	41	5
911EC	20	34	40	6
911SC	38	50	40	20
2.4 litre engines:				
911TV and T	16	30	42	4
911E	18	36	38	8
911S	38	50	40	20
2.7 litre engines:				
1973 Carrera	0	32	30	10
1974 Carrera	38	50	40	20
911	1 (ATC)	35	29	7
911S	6 (ATC)	50	24	2
3.0 litre engines	1	53	43	3

***Inlet valve lift:**
  1969 models:
    911T .. .. 2.4 to 2.8 (0.094 to 0.110in)
    911E .. .. 3.0 to 3.3 (0.118 to 0.130)
    911S .. .. 5.0 to 5.4 (0.197 to 0.213)
  1972 models:
    911E .. .. 2.7 to 3.1 (0.106 to 0.122in)
  1974 models:
    911 .. .. 0.7 to 0.9 (0.028 to 0.035in)
    911 (model 75) .. .. 0.5 to 0.7 (0.020 to 0.028in)
    911S .. .. 0.4 to 0.54 (0.016 to 0.021in)
    Carrera.. .. .. 5.0 to 5.4 (0.197 to 0.213in)
  1975 models:
    911S and Carrera (USA) .. .. .. 0.4 to 0.54 (0.016 to 0.021in)
  1976 models:
    911, 911S (USA) .. .. 0.4 to 0.54 (0.016 to 0.021in)
    Carrera 3.0 litre .. .. 0.90 to 1.10 (0.035 to 0.043in)

* Measured at overlap TC with 0.1 (0.004in) valve clearance

Flywheel:
  Bore for crankshaft .. .. 65.00 to 65.03
  Clearance in bore .. .. Up to 0.049
  Lateral runout at clutch mounting .. .. 0.040 max.
  Lateral runout at clutch face .. .. .. 0.040 max.
  Pilot bearing running clearance .. .. .. 0.075 to 0.229

Lubrication .. .. Dry sump
  Engine oil .. .. SAE 30
  Oil pressure (relief valve opens) .. .. .. 78lb/sq in
  Thermostats open at .. .. 83°C (182°F)

FUEL SYSTEM

Carburetter models
Solex-Zenith 40TIN: . . . . Two three-choke downdraught

	1970	1972
Venturi	K 27.5	K 28.5
Main jet	Gg 110	Gg 120
Air correction jet	a 195	a 190
	a 170	—
Emulsion tube diameter	4.3	4.3
Idle air jet	g 47.5p	g 47.5
Idle air bleed	u 155	u 160
	u 165	—
Float needle valve	P 1.5	P 1.5
Float weight	15.7gr	15.7gr
Fuel jet	50	50
Air correction jet (submersion)	100	100
CO in exhaust at idling	—	3.5 ± 0.5%

Fuel supply pump:
    911T . . . . Bosch 058096 0009
    911E and S . . . . Bosch 058097 0001
  Idling speed . . . . 850 to 950rev/min
Fuel injection pump (FIP) models . . . . Bosch injection pump
  2.4 litre, 911T . . . . Pump type, 0408 126015
           911E 0408 126014
           911S 0408 126013
  Idling speed, manual transmission . . . . 850 to 950rev/min
           Sportomatic . . . . 900 to 1000rev/min
Continuous injection system (CIS) . . . . Bosch, K-Jetronic
  Idling speed, manual transmission up to 1977
          models . . . . 850 to 950rev/min
      Sportomatic up to 1977 models . . 900 to 1000rev/min
      From 1977 models:
        Europe . . . . 850 to 950rev/min
        USA (except California) . . . . 900 to 1000rev/min
        California, high altitude States . . 950 to 1050rev/min

IGNITION

Type:
  Earlier models . . . . Coil ignition
  Later models . . . . Capacitive discharge

Distributor:

	Marelli	Bosch
Type	S 112BX	JFDRG
2.2 litre, 911T	—	0231159008
911E	—	0231159006
911S	—	0231159007
Type	—	JFUDR6
2.4 litre, 911TV	50.10.974.1	0231169003
911T (USA)	50.10.974.1	0231169003
911E	50.10.974.2	0231169004
911S	50.10.974.3	0231169005
2.7 litre	61015155	0231169011
Breaker points gap	0.4 (0.016in)	0.35 (0.014in)

Speed limiter cut-off speed:
  2.2 and 2.4 litre:
    911T . . . . 6500 ± 100rev/min
    911E . . . . 7100 ± 100rev/min
    911S . . . . 7300 ± 100rev/min

2.7 litre	.. ..	6500 ± 200rev/min
2.7 litre Carrera	.. ..	7300rev/min
3.0 litre Carrera	.. ..	6800 ± 200rev/min

Basic ignition timing:

2.2 litre:

911T	.. ..	35° BTC at 6000rev/min
911E, 911S	.. ..	30° BTC at 6000rev/min
2.4, 2.7 and 3.0 litre	.. ..	5° ATC at 900rev/min
Carrera	.. ..	TC at 900rev/min

1977 North America:

911S (not California)	.. ..	TC ± 2° at 950 ± 50rev/min*
911S (California)	.. ..	15° ATC ± 2° at 1000 ± 50 rev/min*

Oil temperature 80°C and vacuum hose connected

Sparking plugs:

2.2 litre:

911T	.. ..	Bosch W230/T30 or W250/P21
		Beru 240/14/3 or 250/14/3P
911E, 911S	.. ..	Bosch W265/P21
		Beru 265/14/3P

2.4 litre:

911TV	.. ..	Bosch W230/T30
		Beru 225/14/3
911T (USA)	.. ..	Bosch W235/P21
911E, 911S	.. ..	Bosch W265/P21
		Beru 265/14/3P

2.7 litre:

Pre-1976	.. ..	Bosch W265/P21 or W260/T2
		Beru 265/14/3P or 260/14/3
1976 (not USA)	.. .. ..	Bosch W225/T30
		Beru 225/14/3A
USA	.. ..	Bosch W235/P21
		Beru 235/14/3P
3.0 litre	.. ..	Bosch W260/T2
		Beru 260/14/3

Plug gaps:

Plugs numbered in 260 series	.. .. ..	0.7 (0.028in)
Other types	.. ..	0.55 (0.022in)
Firing order	.. ..	1, 6, 2, 4, 3, 5

CLUTCH

Type	.. ..	Single dry plate, diaphragm spring

Driven plate:

Thickness (uncompressed)	.. ..	10.1 − 0.4 (0.397 − 0.015in)
Maximum runout	.. .. ..	0.60 (0.023in)
Pedal free play	.. .. ..	20 to 25 (0.80 to 1.00in)

TRANSMISSION

Manual transmission:

Forward ratios:

	1st	2nd	3rd	4th	5th
911	3.091	1.631	1.040	0.759	
911	3.091	1.778	1.217	0.926	0.759
915	3.182	1.778	1.125	0.821	—
915	3.182	1.834	1.261	0.962	0.759
915/16	3.182	1.600	1.040	0.724	—
915/06, 08	3.182	1.833	1.261	0.926	0.724
915/18	3.182	1.600	1.040	0.759	—
915/45, 49, 65, 66	3.182	1.600	1.080	0.821	—
915/40, 44, 60, 61	3.182	1.833	1.261	1.000	0.821

Reverse ratio:
    911   ..   ..   3.147
    915 series 3.325
Final drive ratio:
    911S and 1975 USA models 3.875
    Other models 4.428

Sportomatic transmission:

Forward ratios:	1st	2nd	3rd	4th
905, 925, 925/01	2.400	1.550	1.125	0.857
925/02	2.400	1.550	1.125	0.821
925/10	2.125	1.318	0.926	—
925/09, 12, 13	2.400	1.429	0.926	—

Reverse ratio 2.534
Final drive ratio:
    905, 925, 925/01, 02   ..   ..   3.857
    925/09, 10, 12, 13   ..   ..   ..   3.375

Torque converter stall speed (rev/min):
1974 and earlier:

Transmission type	905, 925	925/01	925/02	925/10
911TV	2600*	—	—	—
911E, 911S	2600*	3000*	1950	—
911	—	—	2050	—
911, 911T (USA)	2600*	—	—	1900

1975 models:
    911   2000
    911S, 911 (USA)   1900
    911 (California)   1850
    1976, 1977 all models   1900
These speeds ± 100rev/min; all others ± 200rev/min

Backlash:
Pinion to ring gear   ..   ..   Adjust to 0.12 to 0.18
Gearbox mating gears:
    New   ..   ..   0.06 to 0.12
    Wear limit 0.22

End play:
1st speed gear   ..   ..   0.3 to 0.4
Wear limit 0.5
Other gears   ..   ..   0.2 to 0.3
Wear limit 0.4

Lubrication:
Gearbox and standard differential   ..   ..   SAE 90 Hypoid
Gearbox and limited slip differential   ..   ..   Shell S 1747A or equivalent
Torque converter   ..   ..   Pressure engine oil

STEERING

Type   ..   ..   Rack and pinion
Ratio   ..   ..   1 :17.78
Wheel turns lock to lock   ..   ..   ..   3.1 approx.
Turning circle   ..   ..   10.7m (35ft) approx.

SUSPENSION

Front   ..   ..   MacPherson type struts with
                                                transverse arms
    Springing..   ..   ..   Torsion bars or self-levelling
                                                  hydropneumatic dampers

Dampers:
    Torsion bar springing ..   ..   Hydraulic, telescopic
    Self-levelling ..   ..   Hydropneumatic
    Anti-roll bar ..   ..   Fitted to 2.2 and 2.4 litre S models
            and to 2.7 and 3.0 litre models.
            Optional on other models

Rear ..   ..   Independent, triangulated control arms

    Springing..   ..   ..   Transverse torsion bars
    Dampers ..   ..   Hydraulic, telescopic
    Anti-roll bar ..   ..   Fitted to 2.2 and 2.4 litre S models, to 2.7 and 3.0 litre and to Carrera models. Other models optional

Geometry	Front	Rear
Toe-in, 2.2 litre	0°	0° ± 10' per wheel
2.4, 2.7 and 3.0 litre ..	0°	0° + 20' per wheel
Caster	6° ± 15'	—
Pivot inclination	10° 55'	—
Camber, 2.2 litre	0° ± 20'	− 50' ± 20'
2.4, 2.7 and 3.0 litre ..	0° ± 10'	− 1° ± 10'
USA models 1975 on ..	—	0° ± 10'

Tyre pressures (cold):	Front	Rear
2.2 litre	26lb/sq in*	29lb/sq in*
2.4, 2.7 and 3.0 litre	29lb/sq in	35lb/sq in

Increase by 6lb/sq in for speeds in excess of 125 miles/hr

BRAKES

Type:
    Foot ..   ..   Dual circuit hydraulic
    Handbrake ..   ..   Mechanical on rear (drum) hubs
Discs ..   ..   Ventilated
    Diameter, front 282.5
          rear   290
    Thickness, new ..   ..   19.8 to 20.0
          wear limit 18.0 (0.71in)
Pad lining thickness:
    Wear limit 2.0 (0.08in)
Pedal free play 1.0 (0.04in)
Brake fluid ..   ..   ATE Blue or equivalent
Brake servo:
    Type T52, 7in

ELECTRICAL EQUIPMENT

Batteries ..   ..   12-volt, negative earth
Starter ..   ..   Bosch
    2.2 litre ..   ..   0.8 HP
    2.4 litre ..   ..   1.5 HP
    911TV Sportomatic ..   ..   ..   0.8 HP
    2.7 and 3.0 litre ..   ..   ..   1.5 HP
    Commutator diameter ..   ..   ..   33.5 (1.319in) min.
    Brush wear limit ..   See **Section 12:4**
Alternator ..   ..   Bosch or Motorola
    Rectifier and capacity ..   ..   Integral diodes, 770 W
    Brush wear limit ..   14.0 (0.55in)
Fuses and relays ..   ..   See **Section 12:3**

CAPACITIES

*Fuel tank:	Litres	Imperial	USA
2.2 litre	62	13.6 galls	16.4 galls
Optional on E and S models	90	19.7 galls	23.8 galls
2.4 litre (1972)	62	13.6 galls	16.4 galls
E 1973 models	85	18.7 galls	22.5 galls
2.7 litre (1973)	85	18.7 galls	22.5 galls
1974 and later models	80	17.6 galls	21.0 galls

Inclusive of approx. 10% reserve

Oil tank:			
Up to 1973 T, E	9	15.8 pints	19 pints
S	10	17.5 pints	21.1 pints
1974 models T, E	11	19.2 pints	23.2 pints
S and 1977 models**	13	22.9 pints	27.5 pints
Sportomatic models:			
Extra to refill converter***	2.5	4.4 pints	5.2 pints

** *With additional oil cooler*
*** *Not required for normal oil change*

Transmission:			
Gearbox and differential:			
2.2 litre	2.5	4.4 pints	5.2 pints
2.4, 2.7 and 3.0 litre	3.0	5.2 pints	6.3 pints

Brakes:			
Master reservoirs	0.2	0.35 pints	0.42 pints

Windscreen washer:	1970-73	1974 on
Capacity, litres	2.0	8.5

DIMENSIONS

Wheelbase/track:	Front track	Rear track	Wheelbase
2.2 litre, T	1362	1343	2268
E and S	1374*	1355*	2268
2.4 and 2.7 litre, T and TV	1360	1342	2271
E and S	1372	1354	2271
2.7 litre Carrera 1973	1372	1368	2271
2.7 litre Carrera 1974	1372	1394**	2271
2.7 litre Carrera 1976	1321	1397	2271
1977 models	1369	1354	2271

* *10mm less with alloy wheels*
** *With spacers on each rear wheel*

Overall:	Length	Width	Height
2.2 litre	4163	1610	1320
2.4 litre:			
1972 USA	4163	1610	1320
Other countries	4147	1610	1320
1973 USA	4277	1610	1320
Other countries, TV	4127	1610	1320
S	4147	1610	1320
2.7 litre:			
1973 Carrera	4147	1652	1320
1975 Carrera	4291	1652	1320
Other models	4291	1610	1320
3.0 litre	4291	1652	1320

Ground clearance:		
Depending on model and loading	120 to 180	

Key to Figs 14:1 and 14:2
Numbers on right relate to those on diagram base line to locate items

Code	Description	Numbers
E	Windshield wiper switch	39
E¹	Headlight switch	6, 8, 9, 11, 15, 20
E²	Turn signal switch	28
E³	Emergency flasher switch	24, 25, 28, 31, 34
E⁴	Dimmer switch	6, 39
E⁵	Headlight flasher switch	4
E¹⁹	Parking light switch	13
E²⁰	Instrument panel illumination potentiometer	20
E²⁶	Switch for glove compartment light	41
F	Stoplight switch	50
F²	Left door switch	45
F³	Right door switch	46
F⁴	Back-up light switch	48
F⁵	Switch for luggage compartment light	42
H	Horn switch	39
H²	Horns	36, 37, 38
J¹	Hazard/turn signal flasher	33, 34, 35
J⁴	Horn relay	36, 37
K¹	High beam indicator light	2
K⁴	Parking lights indicator light	1
K⁵	Turn signal indicator light	27, 29
K⁶	Hazard flasher indicator light	24
L¹	Left headlight	3, 7
L²	Right headlight	4, 8
L⁶	Speedometer illumination light	22
L⁷	Fuel gauge illumination light	22
L⁸	Clock illumination light	22
L¹⁵	Ashtray illumination light	20
L¹⁶	Heater control assembly illumination light	18
L²⁴	Oil temperature indicator illumination light	22
L²⁶	Tachometer illumination light	22
L²⁷	Oil pressure indicator illumination light	22
M¹	Left parking light	11
M²	Right stop/rear light	17, 50
M³	Right parking light	15
M⁴	Left stop/rear light	13, 51
M⁵	Left front turn signal	25
M⁶	Left rear turn signal	26
M⁷	Right front turn signal	31
M⁸	Right rear turn signal	30
M¹⁶	Left back-up light	48
M¹⁷	Right back-up light	49
S²	Fuses	9, 15, 11
to	on the	8, 7, 4
S¹¹	fuse box	3, 31, 25, 48
S¹⁷		34
S¹⁸		40
T¹	Cable connector, single:	14
a	Near regulator panel	
b	Behind sealed beam unit, left	11, 25
c	Behind sealed beam unit, right	15, 31
d	Behind fuse box	37
e	On luggage compartment floor	22, 42, 44, 45, 46
f	Behind instrument panel	6, 22, 24, 28
h	Near left rear lights	24
T⁶	Cable connector, sixfold:	
a	In the engine compartment, rear left	9, 13, 24, 26, 48, 51
b	In the engine compartment, rear right	10, 17, 30, 49, 50
d	Below instrument panel	4, 6, 26, 30, 39
e	Below instrument panel	25, 31, 32, 34
g	Below instrument panel	8, 9, 11, 15, 22
h	Below instrument panel	41
T¹⁴	Cable connector, fourteenfold, on regulator panel, front	22
W	Interior panel light	48
W³	Luggage compartment light	45, 46, 47
W⁶	Glove compartment light	42
X	Number plate light	41
Y	Clock	9, 10
		40

Wiring colour code   B Blue   E Green   G Grey   L Black   M Mauve   O Brown   R Red   W White   Y Yellow

When wires have two colour code letters, the first denotes the main colour, the second the stripe. Numbers in wires (eg 2.5, 0.5) indicate cross-sectional area of wire in sq mm

FIG 14:1 Current flow diagram—part 1

FIG 14:2 Current flow diagram—part 2

FIG 14:3 Current flow diagram—part 3

FIG 14:4 Current flow diagram—part 4

Key to Figs 14:3 and 14:4

Numbers on right relate to those on diagram base line to locate items

Code	Item	Numbers
A	Battery	105
B	Starter	102, 103
C	Generator	88, 89, 92
C^2	Voltage regulator	88, 89, 90
C^{12}	Capacitor for ignition unit	116
D	Ignition/starter switch	73, 74, 75, 76, 77
E	Windshield wiper switch	69–77
E^9	Fresh air blower switch	60
E^{15}	Rear window defogger switch	55, 56
E^{16}	Heater blower switch	99
E^{43}	Outside mirror control switch	64, 65
F	Oil pressure switch	86
F^6	Brake warning switch	79
F^9	Parking brake switch	79
F^{26}	Thermo-switch for cold start valve	100
G	Fuel sender unit	82
G^1	Fuel gauge	83
G^5	Tachometer	85
G^6	Fuel pump	96
G^8	Oil temperature sender unit	84
G^9	Oil temperature indicator	84
G^{10}	Oil pressure sender unit	87
G^{11}	Oil pressure indicator	85
G^{12}	Oil level sender unit	80
G^{13}	Oil level gauge	80
G^{19}	Air meter contact	95
G^{21}	Speedometer	67
G^{22}	Speedometer sensor	67
J^9	Rear window defogger relay	56, 57
J^{14}	Relay for heater blower	98, 99
J^{16}	Relay for fuel pump	95, 96
J^{31}	Relay for intermittent wiper operation	72–76
J^{34}	Relay for seat belt warning system	77, 78

Code	Item	Numbers
K^2	Generator charge indicator light	84
K^3	Oil pressure indicator light	85
K^7	Parking brake/brake warning indicator light	61
K^8	Blower indicator light	61
K^{10}	Rear window defogger indicator light	55
K^{16}	Low fuel warning light	81
K^{19}	Seat belt warning light	79
N	Ignition transformer	106
N^9	Warm-up regulator	93
N^{15}	HT ignition unit	106, 107
N^{17}	Cold start valve	101
N^{21}	Supplementary air valve	94
N^{35}	Magnetic clutch for mirror control	66
N^{43}	Thermo-valve for cold starting device	94
O	Distributor	107–113
P	Spark plug connector	108–113
Q	Spark plug	108–113
S^{12}	Fuses on the fuse box	55, 68
S^{16}	Fuses on the	63, 61, 96
S^{22}	Fuses on the rear fuse box	114
T^1	Cable connector, single (regulator panel)	99
a	Near regulator panel	57
d	Behind fuse box	56, 57, 58, 95, 99, 116
e	On luggage compartment floor	77, 93, 72, 76, 77, 115
f	Behind instrument panel	58, 75, 76, 79
g	Below shift lever housing	114

Code	Item	Numbers
T^2	Cable connector, double:	
a	Below regulator panel	113, 114
b	In engine compartment, left	91, 98
i	In tunnel, rear	67
k	Below regulator panel	95, 96
T^4	Cable connector, quadruple in outside mirror housing	63, 64
T^6	Cable connector, sixfold:	
b	In engine compartment, right	80
c	Below instrument panel	69, 70, 71, 72, 77
f	Below instrument panel	70, 71, 72, 77, 104, 105
h	Below instrument panel	60, 61
T^{14}	Cable connector, fourteenfold on regulator panel	84, 86, 87, 92, 93, 98, 102, 114, 115
U^1	Cigar lighter	62
V	Windshield wiper motor	69, 70, 71, 72
V^2	Blower motor	60
V^4	Heater blower	98
V^5	Washer pump	77
V^{17}	Outside mirror control motor	64
Z^1	Rear window defogger	57
Z^4	Outside mirror defogger	63

Wiring colour code   B Blue   E Green   G Grey   L Black   M Mauve   O Brown   R Red   W White   Y Yellow

When wires have two colour code letters, the first denotes the main colour, the second the stripe. Numbers in wires (eg 2.5, 0.5) indicate cross-sectional area of wire in sq mm

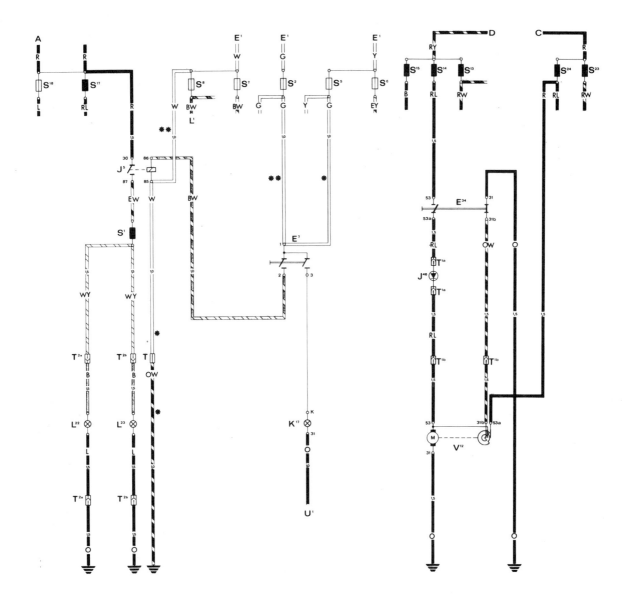

FIG 14:5 Additional current flow diagrams. Fog lights, left; rear window wiper, right

Key to Fig 14:5 Fog lights: A To battery E^1 To headlight switch E^7 Fog light switch J^5 Fog light relay K^{17} Fog light indicator light L^1 To left headlight L^{22} Left fog light L^{23} Right fog light S^1, S^2, S^5, S^6, S^8, S^{17}, S^{18} Fuses in the fuse box   T Cable connector T^2 Cable connector double: a In luggage compartment, left   b In luggage compartment, right   *USA   **Europe

Rear window wiper: C To generator   D To ignition/starter switch E^{34} Rear wiper switch J^{46} Diode for rear wiper S^{13}, S^{14}, S^{15} Fuses in the fuse box S^{23}, S^{24} Fuses in the rear fuse box T^1 Cable connector, single: a Behind instrument panel   b In engine compartment, left V^{12} Rear wiper motor

Wiring colour code   **B** Blue   **E** Green   **G** Grey   **L** Black   **M** Mauve   **O** Brown   **R** Red   **W** White   **Y** Yellow

When wires have two colour code letters, the first denotes the main colour, the second the stripe. Numbers in wires (eg 2.5, 0.5) indicate cross-sectional area of wire in sq mm

FIG 14:6 Additional current flow diagrams. Electrically operated windows, left; headlight washers, right

Key to Fig 14:6 Electric windows: A To battery D To ignition/starter switch E³⁹ Power window switch, driver side, for passenger side E⁴⁰ Power window switch, driver side E⁴¹ Power window switch, passenger side J⁵¹ Power window relay S¹², S¹⁶, S¹⁷, S¹⁸ Fuses in the fuse box T¹ Cable connector, single, behind fuse box T⁶ Cable connector, sixfold: a In door well, left b In door well, right V¹⁴ Power window motor, left V¹⁵ Power window motor, right Headlight washers: A To battery D To ignition/starter switch E¹ Headlight switch E⁴ Dimmer switch E³⁷ Headlight washer switch J²⁵ To headlight relay (from model 76 to fuse S⁶) J³⁹ Headlight washer relay S¹⁷ To fuse S¹⁷ S², S¹⁸, S¹⁹ Fuses in the fuse box T¹f Cable connector, single, behind instrument panel T² Cable connector, double, near battery T⁶ Cable connector, sixfold: d Below instrument panel g Below instrument panel V¹¹ Headlight washer pump

Wiring colour code   **B** Blue   **E** Green   **G** Grey   **L** Black   **M** Mauve   **O** Brown   **R** Red   **W** White   **Y** Yellow

When wires have two colour code letters, the first denotes the main colour, the second the stripe. Numbers in wires (eg 2.5, 0.5) indicate cross-sectional area of wire in sq mm

HINTS ON MAINTENANCE AND OVERHAUL

There are few things more rewarding than the restoration of a vehicle's original peak of efficiency and smooth performance.

The following notes are intended to help the owner to reach that state of perfection. Providing that he possesses the basic manual skills he should have no difficulty in performing most of the operations detailed in this manual. It must be stressed, however, that where recommended in the manual, highly-skilled operations ought to be entrusted to experts, who have the necessary equipment, to carry out the work satisfactorily.

Quality of workmanship:

The hazardous driving conditions on the roads to-day demand that vehicles should be as nearly perfect, mechanically, as possible. It is therefore most important that amateur work be carried out with care, bearing in mind the often inadequate working conditions, and also the inferior tools which may have to be used. It is easy to counsel perfection in all things, and we recognise that it may be setting an impossibly high standard. We do, however, suggest that every care should be taken to ensure that a vehicle is as safe to take on the road as it is humanly possible to make it.

Safe working conditions:

Even though a vehicle may be stationary, it is still potentially dangerous if certain sensible precautions are not taken when working on it while it is supported on jacks or blocks. It is indeed preferable not to use jacks alone, but to supplement them with carefully placed blocks, so that there will be plenty of support if the car rolls off the jacks during a strenuous manoeuvre. Axle stands are an excellent way of providing a rigid base which is not readily disturbed. Piles of bricks are a dangerous substitute. Be careful not to get under heavy loads on lifting tackle, the load could fall. It is preferable not to work alone when lifting an engine, or when working underneath a vehicle which is supported well off the ground. To be trapped, particularly under the vehicle, may have unpleasant results if help is not quickly forthcoming. Make some provision, however humble, to deal with fires. Always disconnect a battery if there is a likelihood of electrical shorts. These may start a fire if there is leaking fuel about. This applies particularly to leads which can carry a heavy current, like those in the starter circuit. While on the subject of electricity, we must also stress the danger of using equipment which is run off the mains and which has no earth or has faulty wiring or connections. So many workshops have damp floors, and electrical shocks are of such a nature that it is sometimes impossible to let go of a live lead or piece of equipment due to the muscular spasms which take place.

Work demanding special care:

This involves the servicing of braking, steering and suspension systems. On the road, failure of the braking system may be disastrous. Make quite sure that there can be no possibility of failure through the bursting of rusty brake pipes or rotten hoses, nor to a sudden loss of pressure due to defective seals or valves.

Problems:

The chief problems which may face an operator are:
1 External dirt.
2 Difficulty in undoing tight fixings.
3 Dismantling unfamiliar mechanisms.
4 Deciding in what respect parts are defective.
5 Confusion about the correct order for reassembly.
6 Adjusting running clearance.
7 Road testing.
8 Final tuning.

Practical suggestions to solve the problems:

1 Preliminary cleaning of large parts—engines, transmissions, steering, suspensions, etc.—should be carried out before removal from the car. Where road dirt and mud alone are present, wash clean with a high-pressure water jet, brushing to remove stubborn adhesions, and allow to drain and dry. Where oil or grease is also present, wash down with a proprietary compound (Gunk, Teepol etc,) applying with a stiff brush—an old paint brush is suitable—into all crevices. Cover the distributor and ignition coils with a polythene bag and then apply a strong water jet to clear the loosened deposits. Allow to drain and dry. The assemblies will then be sufficiently clean to remove and transfer to the bench for the next stage.

On the bench, further cleaning can be carried out, first wiping the parts as free as possible from grease with old newspaper. Avoid using rag or cotton waste which can leave clogging fibres behind. Any remaining grease can be removed with a brush dipped in paraffin. If necessary, traces of paraffin can be removed by carbon tetrachloride. Avoid using paraffin or petrol in large quantities for cleaning in enclosed areas, such as garages, on account of the high fire risk.

When all exteriors have been cleaned, and not before, dismantling can be commenced. This ensures that dirt will not enter into interiors and orifices revealed by dismantling. In the next phases, where components have to be cleaned, use carbon tetrachloride in preference to petrol and keep the containers covered except when in use. After the components have been cleaned, plug small holes with tapered hard wood plugs cut to size and blank off larger orifices with greaseproof paper and masking tape. Do not use soft wood plugs or matchsticks as they may break.

2 It is not advisable to hammer on the end of a screw thread, but if it must be done, first screw on a nut to protect the thread, and use a lead hammer. This applies particularly to the removal of tapered cotters. Nuts and bolts seem to 'grow' together, especially in exhaust systems. If penetrating oil does not work, try the judicious application of heat, but be careful of starting a fire. Asbestos sheet or cloth is useful to isolate heat.

Tight bushes or pieces of tail-pipe rusted into a silencer can be removed by splitting them with an open-ended hacksaw. Tight screws can sometimes be started by a tap from a hammer on the end of a suitable screwdriver. Many tight fittings will yield to the judicious use of a hammer, but it must be a soft-faced hammer if damage is to be avoided, use a heavy block on the opposite side to absorb shock. Any parts of the steering system which have been damaged should be renewed, as attempts to repair them may lead to cracking and subsequent failure, and steering ball joints should be disconnected using a recommended tool to prevent damage.

3 It often happens that an owner is baffled when trying to dismantle an unfamiliar piece of equipment. So many modern devices are pressed together or assembled by spinning-over flanges, that they must be sawn apart. The intention is that the whole assembly must be renewed. However, parts which appear to be in one piece to the naked eye, may reveal close-fitting joint lines when inspected with a magnifying glass, and, this may provide the necessary clue to dismantling. Lefthanded screw threads are used where rotational forces would tend to unscrew a righthanded screw thread.

Be very careful when dismantling mechanisms which may come apart suddenly. Work in an enclosed space where the parts will be contained, and drape a piece of cloth over the device if springs are likely to fly in all directions. Mark everything which might be reassembled in the wrong position, scratched symbols may be used on unstressed parts, or a sequence of tiny dots from a centre punch can be useful. Stressed parts should never be scratched or centre-popped as this may lead to cracking under working conditions. Store parts which look alike in the correct order for reassembly. Never rely upon memory to assist in the assembly of complicated mechanisms, especially when they will be dismantled for a long time, but make notes, and drawings to supplement the diagrams in the manual, and put labels on detached wires. Rust stains may indicate unlubricated wear. This can sometimes be seen round the outside edge of a bearing cup in a universal joint. Look for bright rubbing marks on parts which normally should not make heavy contact. These might prove that something is bent or running out of truth. For example, there might be bright marks on one side of a piston, at the top near the ring grooves, and others at the bottom of the skirt on the other side. This could well be the clue to a bent connecting rod. Suspected cracks can be proved by heating the component in a light oil to approximately 100°C, removing, drying off, and dusting with french chalk, if a crack is present the oil retained in the crack will stain the french chalk.

4 In determining wear, and the degree, against the permissible limits set in the manual, accurate measurement can only be achieved by the use of a micrometer. In many cases, the wear is given to the fourth place of decimals; that is in ten-thousandths of an inch. This can be read by the vernier scale on the barrel of a good micrometer. Bore diameters are more difficult to determine. If, however, the matching shaft is accurately measured, the degree of play in the bore can be felt as a guide to its suitability. In other cases, the shank of a twist drill of known diameter is a handy check.

Many methods have been devised for determining the clearance between bearing surfaces. To-day the best and simplest is by the use of Plastigage, obtainable from most garages. A thin plastic thread is laid between the two surfaces and the bearing is tightened, flattening

the thread. On removal, the width of the thread is compared with a scale supplied with the thread and the clearance is read off directly. Sometimes joint faces leak persistently, even after gasket renewal. The fault will then be traceable to distortion, dirt or burrs. Studs which are screwed into soft metal frequently raise burrs at the point of entry. A quick cure for this is to chamfer the edge of the hole in the part which fits over the stud.

5 **Always check a replacement part with the original one before it is fitted.**

If parts are not marked, and the order for reassembly is not known, a little detective work will help. Look for marks which are due to wear to see if they can be mated. Joint faces may not be identical due to manufacturing errors, and parts which overlap may be stained, giving a clue to the correct position. Most fixings leave identifying marks especially if they were painted over on assembly. It is then easier to decide whether a nut, for instance, has a plain, a spring, or a shakeproof washer under it. All running surfaces become 'bedded' together after long spells of work and tiny imperfections on one part will be found to have left corresponding marks on the other. This is particularly true of shafts and bearings and even a score on a cylinder wall will show on the piston.

6 Checking end float or rocker clearances by feeler gauge may not always give accurate results because of wear. For instance, the rocker tip which bears on a valve stem may be deeply pitted, in which case the feeler will simply be bridging a depression. Thrust washers may also wear depressions in opposing faces to make accurate measurement difficult. End float is then easier to check by using a dial gauge. It is common practice to adjust end play in bearing assemblies, like front hubs with taper rollers, by doing up the axle nut until the hub becomes stiff to turn and then backing it off a little. Do not use this method with ballbearing hubs as the assembly is often preloaded by tightening the axle nut to its fullest extent. If the splitpin hole will not line up, file the base of the nut a little.

Steering assemblies often wear in the straight-ahead position. If any part is adjusted, make sure that it remains free when moved from lock to lock. Do not be surprised if an assembly like a steering gearbox, which is known to be carefully adjusted outside the car, becomes stiff when it is bolted in place. This will be due to distortion of the case by the pull of the mounting bolts, particularly if the mounting points are not all touching together. This problem may be met in other equipment and is cured by careful attention to the alignment of mounting points.

When a spanner is stamped with a size and A/F it means that the dimension is the width between the jaws and has no connection with ANF, which is the designation for the American National Fine thread. Coarse threads like Whitworth are rarely used on cars to-day except for studs which screw into soft aluminium or cast iron. For this reason it might be found that the top end of a cylinder head stud has a fine thread and the lower end a coarse thread to screw into the cylinder block. If the car has mainly UNF threads then it is likely that any coarse threads will be UNC, which are not the same as Whitworth. Small sizes have the same number of threads in Whitworth and UNC, but in the $\frac{1}{2}$ inch size for example, there are twelve threads to the inch in the former and thirteen in the latter.

7 After a major overhaul, particularly if a great deal of work has been done on the braking, steering and suspension systems, it is advisable to approach the problem of testing with care. If the braking system has been overhauled, apply heavy pressure to the brake pedal and get a second operator to check every possible source of leakage. The brakes may work extremely well, but a leak could cause complete failure after a few miles.

Do not fit the hub caps until every wheel nut has been checked for tightness, and make sure the tyre pressures are correct. Check the levels of coolant, lubricants and hydraulic fluids. Being satisfied that all is well, take the car on the road and test the brakes at once. Check the steering and the action of the handbrake. Do all this at moderate speeds on quiet roads, and make sure there

is no other vehicle behind you when you try a rapid stop.

Finally, remember that many parts settle down after a time, so check for tightness of all fixings after the car has been on the road for a hundred miles or so.

8 It is useless to tune an engine which has not reached its normal running temperature. In the same way, the tune of an engine which is stiff after a rebore will be different when the engine is again running free. Remember too, that rocker clearances on pushrod operated valve gear will change when the cylinder head nuts are tightened after an initial period of running with a new head gasket.

Trouble may not always be due to what seems the obvious cause. Ignition, carburation and mechanical condition are interdependent and spitting back through the carburetter, which might be attributed to a weak mixture, can be caused by a sticking inlet valve.

For one final hint on tuning, never adjust more than one thing at a time or it will be impossible to tell which adjustment produced the desired result.

NOTES

GLOSSARY OF TERMS

Allen key — Cranked wrench of hexagonal section for use with socket head screws.

Alternator — Electrical generator producing alternating current. Rectified to direct current for battery charging.

Ambient temperature — Surrounding atmospheric temperature.

Annulus — Used in engineering to indicate the outer ring gear of an epicyclic gear train.

Armature — The shaft carrying the windings, which rotates in the magnetic field of a generator or starter motor. That part of a solenoid or relay which is activated by the magnetic field.

Axial — In line with, or pertaining to, an axis.

Backlash — Play in meshing gears.

Balance lever — A bar where force applied at the centre is equally divided between connections at the ends.

Banjo axle — Axle casing with large diameter housing for the crownwheel and differential.

Bendix pinion — A self-engaging and self-disengaging drive on a starter motor shaft.

Bevel pinion — A conical shaped gearwheel, designed to mesh with a similar gear with an axis usually at 90 deg. to its own.

bhp — Brake horse power, measured on a dynamometer.

bmep — Brake mean effective pressure. Average pressure on a piston during the working stroke.

Brake cylinder — Cylinder with hydraulically operated piston(s) acting on brake shoes or pad(s).

Brake regulator — Control valve fitted in hydraulic braking system which limits brake pressure to rear brakes during heavy braking to prevent rear wheel locking.

Camber — Angle at which a wheel is tilted from the vertical.

Capacitor — Modern term for an electrical condenser. Part of distributor assembly, connected across contact breaker points, acts as an interference suppressor.

Castellated — Top face of a nut, slotted across the flats, to take a locking splitpin.

Castor — Angle at which the kingpin or swivel pin is tilted when viewed from the side.

cc — Cubic centimetres. Engine capacity is arrived at by multiplying the area of the bore in sq cm by the stroke in cm by the number of cylinders.

Clevis — U-shaped forked connector used with a clevis pin, usually at handbrake connections.

Collet — A type of collar, usually split and located in a groove in a shaft, and held in place by a retainer. The arrangement used to retain the spring(s) on a valve stem in most cases.

Commutator — Rotating segmented current distributor between armature windings and brushes in generator or motor.

Compression ratio — The ratio, or quantitative relation, of the total volume (piston at bottom of stroke) to the unswept volume (piston at top of stroke) in an engine cylinder.

Condenser — See 'Capacitor'.

Core plug — Plug for blanking off a manufacturing hole in a casting.

Crownwheel — Large bevel gear in rear axle, driven by a bevel pinion attached to the propeller shaft. Sometimes called a 'ring gear'.

'C'-spanner — Like a 'C' with a handle. For use on screwed collars without flats, but with slots or holes.

Damper — Modern term for shock absorber, used in vehicle suspension systems to damp out spring oscillations.

Depression — The lowering of atmospheric pressure as in the inlet manifold and carburetter.

Dowel — Close tolerance pin, peg, tube, or bolt, which accurately locates mating parts.

Drag link — Rod connecting steering box drop arm (pitman arm) to nearest front wheel steering arm in certain types of steering systems.

Dry liner — Thinwall tube pressed into cylinder bore.

Dry sump — Lubrication system where all oil is scavenged from the sump, and returned to a separate tank.

Dynamo — See 'Generator'.

Electrode — Terminal part of an electrical component, such as the points or 'Electrodes' of a sparking plug.

Electrolyte — In lead-acid car batteries a solution of sulphuric acid and distilled water.

End float — The axial movement between associated parts, end play.

EP — Extreme pressure. In lubricants, special grades for heavily loaded bearing surfaces, such as gear teeth in a gearbox, or crownwheel and pinion in a rear axle.

Fade	Of brakes. Reduced efficiency due to overheating.	**Journals**	Those parts of a shaft that are in contact with the bearings.
Field coils	Windings on the polepieces of motors and generators.	**Kingpin**	The main vertical pin which carries the front wheel spindle, and permits steering movement. May be called 'steering pin' or 'swivel pin'.
Fillets	Narrow finishing strips usually applied to interior bodywork.		
First motion shaft	Input shaft from clutch to gearbox.	**Layshaft**	The shaft which carries the laygear in the gearbox. The laygear is driven by the first motion shaft and drives the third motion shaft according to the gear selected. Sometimes called the 'countershaft' or 'second motion shaft'.
Fullflow filter	Filters in which all the oil is pumped to the engine. If the element becomes clogged, a bypass valve operates to pass unfiltered oil to the engine.		
FWD	Front wheel drive.	**lb ft**	A measure of twist or torque. A pull of 10 lb at a radius of 1 ft is a torque of 10 lb ft.
Gear pump	Two meshing gears in a close fitting casing. Oil is carried from the inlet round the outside of both gears in the spaces between the gear teeth and casing to the outlet, the meshing gear teeth prevent oil passing back to the inlet, and the oil is forced through the outlet port.		
		lb/sq in	Pounds per square inch.
		Little-end	The small, or piston end of a connecting rod. Sometimes called the 'small-end'.
		LT	Low Tension. The current output from the battery.
Generator	Modern term for 'Dynamo'. When rotated produces electrical current.	**Mandrel**	Accurately manufactured bar or rod used for test or centring purposes.
Grommet	A ring of protective or sealing material. Can be used to protect pipes or leads passing through bulkheads.	**Manifold**	A pipe, duct, or chamber, with several branches.
Grubscrew	Fully threaded headless screw with screwdriver slot. Used for locking, or alignment purposes.	**Needle rollers**	Bearing rollers with a length many times their diameter.
Gudgeon pin	Shaft which connects a piston to its connecting rod. Sometimes called 'wrist pin', or 'piston pin'.	**Oil bath**	Reservoir which lubricates parts by immersion. In air filters, a separate oil supply for wetting a wire mesh element to hold the dust.
Halfshaft	One of a pair transmitting drive from the differential.		
Helical	In spiral form. The teeth of helical gears are cut at a spiral angle to the side faces of the gearwheel.	**Oil wetted**	In air filters, a wire mesh element lightly oiled to trap and hold airborne dust.
		Overlap	Period during which inlet and exhaust valves are open together.
Hot pot	Hot area that assists vapourisation of fuel on its way to cylinders. Often provided by close contact between inlet and exhaust manifolds.	**Panhard rod**	Bar connected between fixed point on chassis and another on axle to control sideways movement.
HT	High Tension. Applied to electrical current produced by the ignition coil for the sparking plugs.	**Pawl**	Pivoted catch which engages in the teeth of a ratchet to permit movement in one direction only.
		Peg spanner	Tool with pegs, or pins, to engage in holes or slots in the part to be turned.
Hydrometer	A device for checking specific gravity of liquids. Used to check specific gravity of electrolyte.	**Pendant pedals**	Pedals with levers that are pivoted at the top end.
Hypoid bevel gears	A form of bevel gear used in the rear axle drive gears. The bevel pinion meshes below the centre line of the crownwheel, giving a lower propeller shaft line.	**Phillips screwdriver**	A cross-point screwdriver for use with the cross-slotted heads of Phillips screws.
		Pinion	A small gear, usually in relation to another gear.
Idler	A device for passing on movement. A free running gear between driving and driven gears. A lever transmitting track rod movement to a side rod in steering gear.	**Piston-type damper**	Shock absorber in which damping is controlled by a piston working in a closed oil-filled cylinder.
		Preloading	Preset static pressure on ball or roller bearings not due to working loads.
Impeller	A centrifugal pumping element. Used in water pumps to stimulate flow.	**Radial**	Radiating from a centre, like the spokes of a wheel.

Radius rod	Pivoted arm confining movement of a part to an arc of fixed radius.
Ratchet	Toothed wheel or rack which can move in one direction only, movement in the other being prevented by a pawl.
Ring gear	A gear tooth ring attached to outer periphery of flywheel. Starter pinion engages with it during starting.
Runout	Amount by which rotating part is out of true.
Semi-floating axle	Outer end of rear axle halfshaft is carried on bearing inside axle casing. Wheel hub is secured to end of shaft.
Servo	A hydraulic or pneumatic system for assisting, or, augmenting a physical effort. See 'Vacuum Servo'.
Setscrew	One which is threaded for the full length of the shank.
Shackle	A coupling link, used in the form of two parallel pins connected by side plates to secure the end of the master suspension spring and absorb the effects of deflection.
Shell bearing	Thinwalled steel shell lined with anti-friction metal. Usually semi-circular and used in pairs for main and big-end bearings.
Shock absorber	See 'Damper'.
Silentbloc	Rubber bush bonded to inner and outer metal sleeves.
Socket-head screw	Screw with hexagonal socket for an Allen key.
Solenoid	A coil of wire creating a magnetic field when electric current passes through it. Used with a soft iron core to operate contacts or a mechanical device.
Spur gear	A gear with teeth cut axially across the periphery.
Stub axle	Short axle fixed at one end only.
Tachometer	An instrument for accurate measurement of rotating speed. Usually indicates in revolutions per minute.
TDC	Top Dead Centre. The highest point reached by a piston in a cylinder, with the crank and connecting rod in line.
Thermostat	Automatic device for regulating temperature. Used in vehicle coolant systems to open a valve which restricts circulation at low temperature.
Third motion shaft	Output shaft of gearbox.
Threequarter floating axle	Outer end of rear axle halfshaft flanged and bolted to wheel hub, which runs on bearing mounted on outside of axle casing. Vehicle weight is not carried by the axle shaft.
Thrust bearing or washer	Used to reduce friction in rotating parts subject to axial loads.
Torque	Turning or twisting effort. See 'lb ft'.
Track rod	The bar(s) across the vehicle which connect the steering arms and maintain the front wheels in their correct alignment.
UJ	Universal joint. A coupling between shafts which permits angular movement.
UNF	Unified National Fine screw thread.
Vacuum servo	Device used in brake system, using difference between atmospheric pressure and inlet manifold depression to operate a piston which acts to augment brake pressure as required. See 'Servo'.
Venturi	A restriction or 'choke' in a tube, as in a carburetter, used to increase velocity to obtain a reduction in pressure.
Vernier	A sliding scale for obtaining fractional readings of the graduations of an adjacent scale.
Welch plug	A domed thin metal disc which is partially flattened to lock in a recess. Used to plug core holes in castings.
Wet liner	Removable cylinder barrel, sealed against coolant leakage, where the coolant is in direct contact with the outer surface.
Wet sump	A reservoir attached to the crankcase to hold the lubricating oil.

NOTES

INDEX

NOTES

NOTES

NOTES